U0771146

全球法人识别编码实施情况
专题同行评估报告

金融稳定理事会　著

全国金融标准化技术委员会　译

中国金融出版社

责任编辑：肖　炜　董梦雅
责任校对：张志文
责任印制：张也男

图书在版编目（CIP）数据

全球法人识别编码实施情况专题同行评估报告／金融稳定理事会著．全国
金融标准化技术委员会译．—北京：中国金融出版社，2020.5
ISBN 978 – 7 – 5220 – 0440 – 2

Ⅰ.①全… Ⅱ.①金… ②金… Ⅲ.①法人—识别—编码—标准化—技术
评估—研究报告—世界 Ⅳ.①F271.5 – 65

中国版本图书馆 CIP 数据核字（2020）第 011621 号

全球法人识别编码实施情况专题同行评估报告
Quanqiu Faren Shibie Bianma Shishi Qingkuang Zhuanti Tonghang Pinggu Baogao

出版
发行　中国金融出版社

社址　北京市丰台区益泽路 2 号
市场开发部　（010）66024766，63805472，63439533（传真）
网 上 书 店　http://www.chinafph.com
　　　　　　（010）66024766，63372837（传真）
读者服务部　（010）66070833，62568380
邮编　100071
经销　新华书店
印刷　北京侨友印刷有限公司
尺寸　169 毫米 × 239 毫米
印张　15.25
字数　165 千
版次　2020 年 5 月第 1 版
印次　2020 年 5 月第 1 次印刷
定价　50.00 元
ISBN 978 – 7 – 5220 – 0440 – 2
如出现印装错误本社负责调换　联系电话(010)63263947

金融稳定理事会（Financial Stability Board，FSB）在国际层面协调各国家/地区金融当局和国际标准制定组织的工作，以推动和促进有效的监管、监督和其他金融部门政策的执行。《金融稳定理事会章程》（FSB Charter，以下简称 FSB 章程）规定了 FSB 的职责，其中包括政策制定和相关活动。根据 FSB 章程的规定，这些活动以及活动过程中作出的任何决定均不具有强制性，也不产生任何法律权利或义务。

编委会名单

主　　编　李　伟

副主编　许再越　杨富玉　李曙光

委　　员　曲维民　贾树辉　杨　倩　吴晓光

翻　　译　冯　蕾　沈薇薇　易霓虹　赵芳旭

　　　　　周培浩　韩婷婷　郭克盈　黄宇栋

　　　　　刘彼洋

序　言

自 2012 年国际上提出构建全球法人识别编码（Legal Entity Identifier, LEI）以来，在二十国集团（G20）和金融稳定理事会（FSB）的支持和推动下，全球 LEI 建设朝着预设目标不断推进。截至目前，LEI 已覆盖全球 160 余万法人，在衍生品市场、银行监管、证券监管、保险监管、信用评级、资产管理、资产证券化、证券融资交易、机构处置、支付服务、信用登记等领域应用广泛，在维护金融稳定、支持金融监管部门防范系统性金融风险、提高金融机构经营效率、优化全球营商环境等方面发挥积极作用。

推进 LEI 在中国的应用实施是履行中国作为 G20 成员责任的重要体现，是推进落实中国"一带一路"倡议、支持金融业双向开放的重要举措。人民银行作为全球 LEI 体系监管委员会成员，高度重视 LEI 工作，积极统筹金融管理部门做好我国 LEI 应用实施顶层设计、优化实施路径、拓宽应用领域，加快构建与国际接轨的 LEI 应用实施环境和发展格局。

2019 年 5 月，金融稳定理事会发布《全球法人识别编码实施

情况专题同行评估报告》，对全球 LEI 应用实施情况和挑战进行了系统全面的总结和分析，并提出若干实施建议。为使广大业内工作者和社会各界全面了解全球 LEI 实施进展，启发我国 LEI 相关工作思路，现将该报告翻译出版，为大家提供有益参考。

全国金融标准化技术委员会秘书处

► 前　言　　　　　　　　　　FOREWORD

　　根据《金融稳定理事会章程》和《金融稳定理事会关于
加强遵守国际标准的框架》，① FSB 各成员所在的司法管辖区
（以下简称 FSB 司法管辖区）承诺定期接受同行评估。为履行
这一职责，FSB 建立了对其成员司法管辖区定期开展国家
（地区）实施情况专题同行评估的机制。

　　专题评估聚焦于 FSB 成员对国际金融标准和政策的执行
情况和成效，相关标准由国际标准制定组织（Standard – Setting Bodies，SSB）所制定，相关政策由 FSB 内部围绕某些对
全球金融稳定至关重要的领域所商定。同时，专题评估还可
对尚无国际标准或政策但对全球金融稳定至关重要的其他领
域进行分析。评估的目的是鼓励跨国、跨部门间标准及政策
实施的一致性，在可能的情况下评价标准和政策的成效，找
出所评估领域的差距和不足，并为 FSB 成员后续行动提出建
议（包括制定新标准）。

---

　　① 参见 http://www.fsb.org/2010/01/r_100109a/。

本报告描述了对全球法人识别编码（Legal Entity Identifier，LEI）实施情况的评估结果，包括 FSB 标准实施常务委员会（SCSI）的讨论要点。这是 FSB 以 2017 年 4 月版《FSB 同行评估手册》[①] 中提出的同行评估目标和指导方针为基础开展的第十五次专题评估。

SCSI 讨论的报告草案由 Amir Zaidi（来自美国商品期货交易委员会）担任主席的团队编写，团队成员包括 Khaled H. Alshammary（来自沙特阿拉伯货币管理局）、Vinicius Brandi（来自巴西中央银行）、Olaf Kurpiers（来自德国联邦金融监管局）、Franck Lasry（来自法国金融市场管理局）、Kirill Markov（来自俄罗斯央行）、Tim Pinkowski（来自国际证监会组织总秘书处）、Beju Shah（来自英格兰银行）、Wolfgang Sommerfeld（来自欧洲中央银行）、Antonio Tiberio（来自意大利银行）和 Robert Michael Willis（来自美国证券交易委员会）。Stephane Mahieu、Gianmatteo Piazza（于 2018 年 6 月之前加入）、Michael Januska（于 2018 年 7 月之后加入）和 Costas Stephanou（来自 FSB 秘书处）为团队提供支持，并为编写同行评估报告作出了贡献。

---

① 参见 http：//www.fsb.org/2017/04/handbook - for - fsb - peer - reviews - 2/。

关键术语解释 EXPLANATION

受益所有人：指对某一法人具有重要的控制、管理和指导责任的单一个体。

中央对手方：指介于一个或多个金融市场交易合约的对手方之间的机构，成为买方的卖方、卖方的买方，从而确保公开合约的履行。

子机构：指在公司集团中被另一个机构所有或控制的机构。

对手方：指金融合约或金融交易中的另一方，比如贷款合约中的借方或者买卖交易中的买方。

有效 LEI：指机构通过与全球 LEI 基金会认可的 LEI 发码机构（LOU）签订合同的方式维护的已发行 LEI。因此，机构数据（如机构名称、地址、母公司机构）的变更应由机构及时报告，第三方对数据提出的质疑应由 LOU 和机构解决，机构至少每年一次重新确认数据准确性，并由 LOU 进行验证。

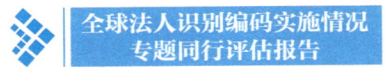
有效 LEI 不包括重复、失效、收回、废止或合并的 LEI。[①]

数字认证：指对以数字形式向系统呈现的用户身份建立信任的过程。

电子发票处理：指电子发票文件在供应商和买方之间的交换过程。电子发票（E–invioce）是以结构化数据格式发放、传输和接收的发票，允许自动、电子化处理。

总名义余额：指在报告日当天订立但尚未结算的全部衍生品合约的名义总额。

了解你的客户（KYC）：指验证客户身份的过程。

失效 LEI：指未按时进行续期的 LEI。

全球法人识别编码（LEI）：它是一串由20位字母、数字组成的用于唯一识别参与金融交易的法人的编码。

第二层级数据：指由法人提供的母公司信息。第二层级数据回答了"谁拥有谁"的问题。具体来说，法人在申请 LEI 时需提供"直接会计并表母公司"和"最终会计并表母公司"的信息。

本地系统（LOU）：指经过全球 LEI 基金会认可的负责向法人发放 LEI 的组织。它提供 LEI 注册、续期和其他服务，是与 LEI 注册人的主要沟通渠道。本地系统可在已授权的司法管辖区中发放 LEI。

选择性使用（Optional）：无论法人是否持有 LEI，对于在

---

① 有效 LEI 的状态包括"已发放"（issued）或"等待迁移"（pending transfer）。如果 LEI 的注册状态显示为"等待入档"（pending archival）且该编码没有被其他 LOU 以"已发放"的状态公开，则该编码也被认为是有效编码，但这种情况较为罕见。

报送信息时是否将 LEI 作为交易信息的一部分进行报送不做强制性要求。

母公司：指拥有或以其他方式控制公司集团内其他机构的机构。在全球 LEI 体系中，机构 X 的"最终会计并表母公司"是根据适用于该母公司的会计并表准则编制的包含机构 X 的合并财务报表的最高级别法人。

支付报文：指为实现金融机构间的资金转移，在借记账户和贷记账户之间进行的指令沟通，比如通过环球同业银行金融电讯协会（SWIFT）提供的报文服务。

再保险：指保险商为防范其所发行保单的部分或全部风险的一种机制。一般来讲，再保险人为了获取报酬同意向分出保险商（或直接保险商）赔偿后者所发行保单可能产生的部分或全部损失。

续期：指法人每年确认其 LEI 参考数据（如机构名称、地址、母公司等信息）的准确性，并由 LOU 对照权威来源核实该数据的真实性。一般来讲，LOU 会收取一定费用。

报送机构：指报告交易信息的机构，比如向交易报告库报送信息。

持有则使用（Requested）：指如果法人持有 LEI，则必须提供 LEI，但没有 LEI 的法人并不强制其申请 LEI。

必须持有（Required）：指法人必须持有 LEI 才能开展交易。

（金融机构）处置：指处置当局对符合处置条件的银行行使处置权力的过程（无论是否有私人部门参与），特别是《金

融机构有效处置机制核心要素》第 3 条所列示的权力,^① 从而达到第 2.3 条所提出的处置目标。

附属机构：指被另一家实体控制的实体。

供应链：指供应商网络，公司从中购买产品和服务以生产和交付最终产品。

贸易融资：指国际贸易流通融资。

唯一产品识别码（UPI）：指在唯一识别当局要求报送至交易报告库的场外衍生品产品的编码。

唯一交易识别码（UTI）：指在唯一识别当局要求报送至交易报告库的场外衍生品交易的编码。

---

① 参见 http：//www. fsb. org/2014/10/key - attributes - of - effective - resolution - regimes - for - financial - institutions - 2/。

 缩略语^①　　　　　**ABBREVIATION**

ADIMA	个别跨国公司及其附属组织的分析数据库（OECD）
AML/CFT	反洗钱和反恐怖主义融资
AnaCredit	分析信用数据集
AVID	Avox 国际商业机构识别编码
BCBS	巴塞尔银行监管委员会
BIC	银行标识码
BIS	国际清算银行
BMARS	债券市场准入备案（中国）
CCP	中央对手方
CDS	信用违约互换
CGFS	全球金融体系委员会
CIBM	中国银行间债券市场
CLO	担保债务凭证
CPIS	协调证券投资调查（IMF）
CPMI	支付和市场基础设施委员会
CRILC	大额信贷中央信息库（印度）
CSDB	中央证券数据库（ECB）
EMIR	欧洲市场基础设施监管条例
EU	欧盟
FATS	外国分支机构统计数据，也称跨国公司活动（AMNE）统计数据

---

① 本报告提及的国家当局的缩略语参见附录 1。

FDI	外商直接投资
FSB	金融稳定理事会
GLEIF	全球法人识别编码基金会
GLEIS	全球法人识别编码体系
G – SIB	全球系统重要性银行
G – SII	全球系统重要性保险公司
IAIS	国际保险监管者协会
IASB	国际会计准则理事会
IBAN	国际银行账号
IFC	国际银行统计欧文费舍尔委员会（BIS）
IMF	国际货币基金组织
IOSCO	国际证监会组织
ISIN	国际证券识别编码
ISO	国际标准化组织
KYC	了解你的客户
LEI	法人识别编码
LEI ROC	全球法人识别编码体系监管委员会
LOU	本地运营单元
MIC	市场识别编码
MiFID Ⅱ	金融工具市场指令Ⅱ（欧盟）
MiFIR	金融工具市场法规（欧盟）
MNE	跨国公司
OECD	经济合作与发展组织
OTC	场外交易（衍生品）
PLI	隐私法识别编码（美国）
QIS	定量影响研究（BCBS）
Repos	回购协议
RIAD	机构和附属机构登记数据库
RSSD ID	研究及统计监管贴现ID（美国）
S – b – S	证券明细逐项登记
SCSI	标准实施常务委员会（FSB）
SWIFT	环球同业银行金融电讯协会
UCITS	可转让证券共同投资计划

UIC	最终投资国
UK	英国
UPI	唯一产品识别码
US	美国
UTI	唯一交易识别码
VAT	增值税
XBRL	可扩展商业报告语言

其他缩略语①

SSB	Standard – Setting Body	标准制定机构
OCC	Office of Comptroller of Currency	美国货币监理署
FCA	Financial Conduct Authority	英国金融行为监管局
EBA	European Banking Authority	欧洲银行管理局
CNJP	Cadastro Nacional da Pessoa Juridica	法人国家登记号（巴西）
CIB	Corporate and Investment Bank	企业及投资银行（法国）
ACPR	Autorité de Contrôle Prudentiel et de Résolution	法国审慎监管局
SIREN	Système d' Identification du Répertoire des ENtreprises	企业名称识别系统（法国）
HKTR	Trade Repository in Hong Kong	中国香港交易数据库
REN	Répertoire des ENtreprises	企业名称（法国）
BHC	Bank Holding Company	银行控股公司
FAQ	Frequently Asked Questions	常见问题解答

---

① 其他缩略语为原文缩略语表中未列出、但在原文中出现的缩略语。

 **目　录**　　　　　　　　　**CONTENTS**

Table of Contents

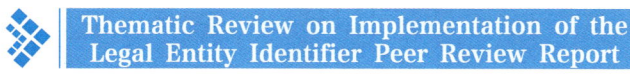

主要内容概述①

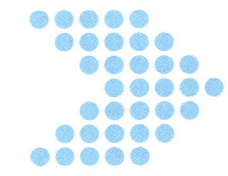

一、LEI 体系实施情况和背景

自 2012 年获得二十国集团（G20）认可以来，全球 LEI 体系（GLEIS）平稳运行，目前已覆盖200 多个国家共 140 多万个法人。LEI 在一些金融细分市场的覆盖率非常广泛，覆盖了 FSB 司法管辖区场外衍生品交易总名义余额近 100％，FSB 司法管辖区债务和股票未偿还额约 78％。在上述领域，LEI 已经基本接近实现 G20 所提出的"鼓励全球范围内使用 LEI 支持主管当局和市场参与者进行金融风险识别与管理"的目标。

大多数 FSB 司法管辖区已经在至少一个领域提出强制使用 LEI 的要求。LEI 应用最为成功的情况是监管机构强制要求将 LEI 纳入一项国际标准中（如报告场外衍生品，某些司法管辖区的监管机构要求报送机构和对手方使用 LEI 的情况），或者在某一区域内多个细分市场使用（如欧盟）LEI 的情况。

LEI 具有多方面监管用途且带来巨大益处。LEI 在全球实现了法人识别的标准化，有助于大型数据库的管理和分析。应用 LEI

---

① 本书中文翻译由全国金融标准化技术委员会提供，非金融稳定理事会（Financial Stability Board）官方翻译。

的好处包括：通过跟踪跨机构、跨产品和跨司法管辖区的市场滥用情况加强市场监管；协助监管机构和市场参与者对来自多个数据源（如S－b－S数据库）的机构微观数据进行整合和更灵活地检索，同时对对手方风险、关联关系（如通过识别共同的风险敞口或资金来源）和复杂的集团结构（最近增加了150000条第二层级母公司关系数据）进行分析。在某些司法管辖区，LEI还用于向信贷登记机构报送信息、支持银行处置等。

金融行业十分支持LEI的实施，同时列举了使用LEI所带来的巨大好处和潜在利益。一些金融机构和贸易协会呼吁当局强制使用LEI，并要求法人进行续期，以方便监管报告，并在提高效率的同时降低客户识别、交易处理和数据整合的成本。

尽管取得一些进展，但LEI应用距离G20提出的目标还有很长的路要走。目前LEI在证券和衍生品市场之外的使用率仍然较低，限制了其对监管支持的有效性，也限制了其获取正外部性和最大化整个市场网络效应的能力。建议应在国家和国际层面做出更多努力，促进LEI的使用，以解决现有障碍，让主管当局和市场参与者获得更多好处和利益。

不同国家和地区之间LEI的实施水平仍不平衡。LEI应用主要集中在加拿大、欧盟和美国，在所有具备条件的法人中，LEI的覆盖范围从2%~7%不等，在其他司法管辖区的覆盖率更低。部分FSB司法管辖区，特别是在亚洲和新兴经济体中，目前尚未在任何领域提出强制使用LEI的要求，或者仅要求法人在已拥有LEI的情况下才使用LEI。鲜有司法管辖区提出扩大LEI使用的新战略。迄今为止，SSB仅在所制定的某些领域政策中建议使用LEI。在反洗钱和反恐融资、风险数据整合、代理银行业务等大多数领域，尚未制定明确的 LEI 应用时间表，仍将使用 LEI 仅作为一个可选项。

目前 LEI 的覆盖率仍然过低，不足以鼓励新的行业或监管应用，尚未达到市场参与者自愿采用 LEI 从而推动 LEI 更广泛应用的临界点。更高的 LEI 覆盖率（包括非金融企业）将支持 LEI 在诸如反洗钱/反恐融资等监管服务中的应用，以及在了解你的客户（KYC）、资金转移尤其是跨境资金转移等市场活动中的应用。此外，尽管所有全球系统重要性银行（G - SIBs）的母公司拥有了LEI，但其附属机构和主要对手方通常却没有 LEI。例如，如果在G - SIBs 的集团中的机构 LEI 覆盖率没有达到一个更高水平，监管机构和市场参与者对这些机构关联关系和共同风险敞口的有效分析、LEI 在机构处置计划中的潜在作用都会受到限制。

进一步使用和实施 LEI 需解决的障碍。这些障碍包括以下几个方面：第一，当前的业务模式还不能将市场参与者使用 LEI 的现有好处和成本明确匹配起来；第二，第二层级（关系）数据覆盖率较低；第三，与其他识别编码（特别是工商注册编码）的关联性较低。通过改进业务模式，最大限度地降低机构 LEI 注册和维护成本与管理负担，如更多地依靠银行、工商注册机构等第三方来进行数据验证和续期，可能有助于解决其中的一些挑战。进一步研究实施案例、改进关系数据可用性和质量、将 LEI 映射到其他识别编码，这将拓展 LEI 的应用范围。

二、司法管辖区实施 LEI 的方法和战略

除一个司法管辖区外，其余 FSB 司法管辖区都不同程度实施了 LEI。几乎所有 FSB 司法管辖区都制定了涉及 LEI 的监管规则，

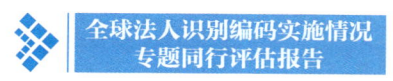
但是数量差异较大。FSB 成员发布的 101 项规则中，有 49 项强制要求所有或部分受规则约束的法人拥有 LEI。在其他情况下，当且仅当法人已拥有 LEI 时才报告 LEI，或 LEI 的报告是可选的。只有 12 个 FSB 司法管辖区对于某些用途的 LEI 提出了强制续期的要求。

LEI 的发展路径和当前分布情况表明，LEI 的应用是受监管要求驱动的，而不是受法人自愿或选择性使用驱动的。在没有出台强制使用和续期要求的国家和地区，LEI 的应用和维护率普遍较低。

极少数司法管辖区（通常是拥有大型金融市场的司法管辖区）在 OTC 衍生品市场和证券交易以外的领域应用了 LEI。一般来讲，LEI 优先被应用于识别金融交易参与各方。

多数司法管辖区表示已经制定了明确的 LEI 应用战略，但战略所涉及的范围不尽相同。① 在某些司法管辖区，应用战略主要是推动 LEI 的自愿使用。例如，提高市场参与者对 LEI 益处的认识，而其他司法管辖区要求制定具体的规则。在司法管辖区报告的已有实施战略中，国家层面和主管当局层面的战略数量持平，有 6 个 FSB 司法管辖区表示目前没有制定 LEI 实施战略。暂时没有司法管辖区计划将 LEI 应用至全部符合条件的法人。

三、LEI 的覆盖情况

虽然 LEI 的绝对覆盖率较低，但在 FSB 司法管辖区之间情况差异很大，在涉及 OTC 衍生品和证券交易的机构、受监管的金融

---

① 这里将"战略"定义为结构化方法或行动计划，通常包括一系列支持 LEI 使用的措施，如相关政府当局之间的协调、与其他利益相关方的沟通、法律和法规的制定。

中介、大型非金融公司中的覆盖率远高于其他领域。LEI 在大型金融和非金融集团的母公司中的覆盖率也很高，但并未完全覆盖它们的附属机构。

FSB 司法管辖区的中央银行除了三家以外都已持有 LEI，所有司法管辖区都报告至少有一个其他公共部门机构拥有 LEI，通常是主要的公共债务发行部门。

四、LEI 体系实施的成果和益处

目前，LEI 主要用于监管当局和其他公共部门的工作，比如监测金融风险、数据报告的敞口归集、统计分析、了解跨国公司的组织结构、市场结构和交易网络、推动市场监控和合规评估。

应用 LEI 的好处包括改善数据分析、节约成本。大部分 FSB 司法管辖区表示 LEI 的应用有助于改善数据质量和数据分析，只有 LEI 使用最为广泛的 FSB 司法管辖区（欧盟成员国和美国）才提到因实施 LEI 而使成本降低。

LEI 的其他好处包括提供了对境内外法人进行统一识别的方法，可推动司法管辖区之间、政府当局之间的数据融合。

一些商业市场利益相关方强调，在"了解你的客户"（KYC）和反洗钱业务中使用 LEI 具有益处。

五、采用和实施 LEI 的障碍

目前关系数据的可用性仍然低于当局的期望，根据最近收集的基于会计并表的母公司信息，由于 56% 的最终母公司没有 LEI（位于 FSB 司法管辖区的子机构中有 46% 没有 LEI），导致 LEI 使用受到限制。这在一定程度上是因为不参与某些类型产品交易的

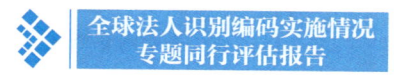
母公司不属于金融监管机构的管辖范围，可能需要通过立法来解决，例如墨西哥的解决措施。其他问题还包括全球 LEI 体系目前无法收集保密信息，而且会计并表规则并不总能满足关系数据的所有需求。

经济负担和效益的明显不对称似乎是各个司法管辖区面临的共同问题。私营部门机构普遍认为，从 LEI 体系中获益最大的相关方对 LEI 体系作出的经济贡献较小（如金融监管部门、承担报告义务的大型金融机构等），反而那些需要支付 LEI 注册费和续期费、规模较小的机构无法清晰地看到 LEI 对自身运营带来的效益，特别是考虑到当前工商注册成本很低，而拥有 LEI 未能带来诸如数字认证、数字身份识别等领域的流程优化，效益不明显的问题更加凸显。

其他识别编码的存在，尤其是无成本或低成本的国家识别编码以及这些识别编码的配套系统被多个司法管辖区视为 LEI 实施的障碍，因为其减少了强制使用 LEI 的动力，这一点在企业跨境交易有限的市场尤为明显。

六、推进 LEI 应用的前进方向

各司法管辖区和市场参与者所确定的未来有潜力的 LEI 应用场景包括数字认证、KYC、支付报文、贸易/供应链融资提效、电子发票处理和金融机构处置等。

七、工作建议

FSB 将继续致力于在全球范围内更广泛地使用 LEI，以实现 G20 的目标。根据上述研究结果，为达到这个目标，我们向 FSB

成员司法管辖区、FSB 自身、相关 SSB 和国际组织，以及全球 LEI 体系监管委员会 LEI ROC 和全球 LEI 基金会（GLEIF）提出以下四项建议。

（一）FSB 司法管辖区应开展以下工作：

1. 根据 CPMI－IOSCO 指南采取后续行动，该指南力促当局提出监管要求，在向 OTC 衍生品交易报告库报送数据时使用 LEI 来识别法人。

2. 考虑在报告或披露框架中提出 LEI 使用和续期的要求，以识别主要金融集团中的所有机构、更广泛的金融市场参与者和基础设施以及它们的对手方和相关机构（包括直接和最终母公司），尤其对跨境交易更应如此要求。

3. 探索进一步提升 LEI 使用率的方式，例如制定全国性的实施战略，以最大限度地发挥 LEI 的跨部门效益；通过社会公众活动宣传 LEI 的好处；通过案例推广，引导中央银行和其他公共部门机构，特别是公共债务发行人使用 LEI；在引入新的识别编码前多了解 LEI 的好处，同时优先考虑使用 LEI。

（二）FSB 应开展以下工作：

1. 探讨 LEI 在其工作任务中的潜在好处，在处置金融机构和金融创新问题方面的优势。

2. 为了有效支持实时分析风险敞口和相互依赖关系，与 SSB 和行业机构合作，促进所有集团机构和全球系统重要性金融机构的主要对手方以及中央对手方（CCP）清算成员及其最终母公司采用 LEI。

3. 通过与 SSB 和行业机构合作，在支付报文中增加 LEI 选项，帮助解决代理银行关系数量下降的问题。

（三）相关 SSB（BCBS、CPMI、IAIS、IOSCO）和国际组织（IMF、OECD、世界银行）应当评估和思考如何在其工作框架中纳入并加强 LEI 应用，为主管当局和市场参与者应用 LEI 提供便利。例如提出在法人数据披露中使用 LEI 的相关指引，促进 LEI 在证券交易和跨境支付中的应用。

（四）LEI ROC 和 GLEIF 应开展以下工作：

1. 考虑完善 LEI 业务模式，以降低机构获取和维护 LEI 的成本和管理负担。例如调整资金来源方式，平衡用户的成本与收益，探讨如何促进 LEI 注册维护与相关流程之间的相互补充和支持。

2. 完善数据质量管理流程，如鼓励更新 LEI 参考数据并监测更新流程，以提高 LEI 数据的可靠性，从而提高 LEI 对于市场参与者和监管机构的可用性。

3. 与行业和公共部门合作，总结现有实践应用情况的案例分析，支持开展具有新用途、前景看好的试点项目或研究项目，提高对 LEI 益处的认识，鼓励自愿采用 LEI。

4. 通过以下方式强化第二层级（关系）数据的覆盖范围和可用性：

（1）考虑以经济且可靠的方式增加可以提高 LEI 价值的关系数据，如有访问权限和适当控制的保密关系数据、受益所有人信息、对母公司其他方面的定义所涉及的关系数据。

（2）采取措施拓宽数据的覆盖面，如向大型跨国公司开展有针对性的 LEI 应用推广活动，为集团母公司的关系报告提供便利。

一、引言

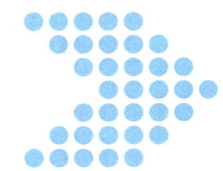

2008 年国际金融危机表明，迅速准确地识别跨境金融交易对手方存在很大难度。为解决这一问题，G20 于 2011 年提出支持建立 LEI 体系，并呼吁 FSB 牵头协调相关监管机构为构建全球 LEI 体系搭建合理的治理框架。在 2012 年 6 月举办的洛斯卡沃斯峰会上，G20 领导人通过了 FSB《关于金融市场全球法人识别编码的报告》，并鼓励"在全球范围内应用 LEI，以支持当局和市场参与者识别和管理金融风险"[①]。自那时起，FSB 一直支持 LEI 实施，并于 2014 年成立全球 LEI 基金会（GLEIF）作为 LEI 体系的运营部门，在 LEI ROC 的监督下联合 LOU 开展工作。

本专题评估旨在评估 FSB 成员（包括各国家的主管当局和国际机构）在响应 G20 呼吁方面所取得的进展。同行评估的目标有以下几个方面：

第一，评估 FSB 成员为实施 LEI 所采用的方法和战略，包括 FSB 司法管辖区为满足监管要求而开展的 LEI 应用情况；

第二，评估目前 LEI 应用的水平和比例是否足以支持 FSB 成员当前和未来潜在的需求，尤其是金融稳定方面的需求；

---

① 参见 http：//www.fsb.org/wp－content/uploads/g20_leaders_declaration_los_cabos_2012.pdf 和 http：//www.fsb.org/2012/06/fsb－report－global－legal－entity－identifier－for－financial－markets/。

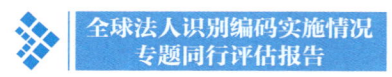

第三，分析 FSB 成员进一步推动 LEI 应用实施所面临的挑战，并酌情提出相关建议以应对共同挑战。

为了避免与 LEI ROC 和 GLEIF 的工作重复，同行评估不包含全球 LEI 体系的治理或技术职能，而是重点关注 FSB 成员中 LEI 的实施方法和在金融稳定方面的作用，以及进一步推进全球 LEI 应用的战略。

同行评估的主要信息来源是 FSB 成员提供的问卷调查反馈。此外，评估小组从 SSB 和国际金融机构收集了评估范围内各领域的资料（参见附录6）。在对利益相关方开展的延伸服务活动方面，2018 年 8 月，FSB 就评估所涉及的领域进行了公开征求意见。2018 年 12 月，工作组在英国伦敦与利益相关方举行了圆桌会议，就 LEI 的好处和用途以及全球 LEI 应用的相关战略和挑战交换了意见。附录5 概括了公开征求意见环节的书面反馈以及圆桌会议的主要观点。

本报告的结构如下：

• 第 1 节为引言部分；

• 第 2 节介绍 LEI 的背景情况，包括 LEI 治理和某些关键特性；

• 第 3 节介绍 FSB 成员在实施 LEI 时采用的方法和战略，包括监管和非监管工具以及覆盖领域；

• 第 4 节评估 LEI 在与金融稳定相关领域的覆盖情况，描述历年来 LEI 发码情况的演变，以及当前相关司法管辖区和跨部门的发码率；

• 第 5 节重点介绍 LEI 应用成果以及后续推进 LEI 应用所面临的挑战；

• 第 6 节提出应对 LEI 应用挑战的措施建议。

附录 1 总结了 FSB 司法管辖区金融当局的缩写清单。附录 2 描述了各司法管辖区使用的非 LEI 识别编码。附录 3 概述了各司法管辖区为实施 LEI 所采取的战略。附录 4a 和 4b 总结了 OTC 衍生品交易各方和证券发行机构 LEI 覆盖范围的详细信息，附录 4c 描述了法人不提供其直接和最终母公司信息的原因，附录 4d 梳理了全球金融市场协会（GFMA）与国际掉期和衍生品协会（ISDA）的 21 个成员样本客户群的 LEI 覆盖率。附录 5 概括了公开征求意见的反馈情况。附录 6 总结了 SSB 在政策制定、数据收集或研究项目上应用 LEI（目前和预期的）的情况以及 SSB 指出的 LEI 所具有的局限性。

二、背景

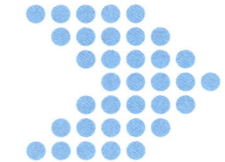

全球法人识别编码（LEI）是一串由 20 位字母、数字组成的用于唯一识别参与金融交易的法人的编码。LEI 与参考数据关联，这些参考数据描述了法人的基本信息，例如名称和地址及其所有权（直接和最终母公司）。LEI 是公共和私营部门共同努力推动的结果，编码结构和基本特征由国际标准化组织（ISO）制定的 ISO 17442 标准进行定义。[①]

2012 年，在 FSB 建议下，全球 LEI 体系治理架构分为三个层次：

● LEI 由 33 个本地系统负责发行，其中一些本地系统来自公共部门（如工商注册机构、国家统计部门）或私营部门［例如发行国际证券识别号码（ISIN）的编号机构、证券交易所］。任何组织都可以申请认证成为本地系统，一些本地系统在多个国家开展业务，而另一些则专注于本地业务。

● 这些本地系统由 GLEIF 进行评估认可。GLEIF 是 FSB 于 2014 年成立的一个非营利性组织，负责监督本地系统是否遵守 LEI 相关标准，负责为中央数据库收集 LEI 编码以及发布 LEI 数据。

---

① 参见 https：//www.iso.org/standard/59771.html。

● LEI 监管委员会（LEI ROC）是一个由全球 70 多个公共部门机构和 18 名观察员组成的组织，包括 FSB 和 34 个 FSB 成员机构，负责监督全球 LEI 体系运行，并制定政策标准。[①]

根据 FSB 的建议，LEI 是一个非专有系统，监管机构和公众可免费使用 LEI 和相关参考数据，本地系统之间具有竞争关系，LEI 可在本地系统之间可迁移。[②] LEI 的注册采用自主注册方式（Self – registration），编码注册者对其数据的准确性负责。

专栏1

自主注册 LEI

只有符合 LEI 申请资格的法人或其授权代表才可以申请 LEI。注册者允许第三方代为注册 LEI，注册者必须为此操作提供明确许可，才被认为符合自主注册的要求。该要求旨在降低同一法人申请多个 LEI 的风险，并确保机构对其数据的准确性负主要责任。在发布 LEI 和相关参考数据之前，本地系统还需要根据可靠来源（如工商注册机构等公共来源、私有法律文档）核实数据，并鼓励编码数据更新。

本地系统与机构之间的合同关系有助于注册者提供准确的最新信息，特别是各法人承诺提供真实、完整和可靠的信息，至少每年检查一次信息的准确性，并及时提交任何变更信息。除非该法人选择放弃使用 LEI，并在不将 LEI 迁移到其他本地系统的情况下终止合同，否则这些承诺在法人存续期

---

① 参见 https：//www. LEI ROC. org/。
② 参见 https：//www. gleif. org/en/lei – data/access – and – use – lei – data。

内一直有效。

全球 LEI 体系的资金来自机构注册和续期时支付的费用。基于成本回收原则，费用的一部分将用于资助 GLEIF（由本地系统支付给 GLEIF）。本地系统收取的 LEI 注册费用为 55～220 美元，续期费用为 35～125 美元。在几乎所有司法管辖区，用户都能以 65 美元（首次注册）和 50 美元（续期），甚至更低的价格获得 LEI。LEI 在中国相关费用为零，但仅限于中国的机构。与前几年相比，LEI 收费水平显著下降，许多司法管辖区的价格下降了一半以上。例如，2016 年 5 月，当时最大的三家发码机构的首次注册费用为 160～219 美元，续期费用为 103～159 美元，相关费用包括当地适用的增值税。鉴于 GLEIF 收取费用已从 2018 年的 17 美元下调至 11 美元，2019 年价格有望进一步下降。

三、LEI 实施的方法和战略

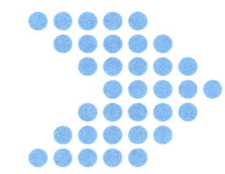

本节总结了 FSB 成员采取的推动 LEI 实施的方法，包括是否发布行业规则、是否采纳其他方法以及规则覆盖的主要领域，以及相关规则是国家层面综合战略的一部分还是某个监管当局自行制定的。由于欧盟成员国各自的法规基本都在欧盟层面制定，因此在本节中欧盟作为一个整体司法管辖区呈现，除非欧盟成员司法管辖区出现特殊情况才单独描述。①

（一）实施方法

几乎所有 FSB 司法管辖区均出台了关于 LEI 的监管规则，虽然规则数量差别很大（见图 1）。欧盟和美国各自采用了 20 多项规则，加拿大和澳大利亚也分别实施了 6 项和 4 项规则。其他 12 个司法管辖区②公布生效的规则最多不超过 3 项。迄今为止，印度尼西亚、南非尚未出台任何规则，但南非已经发布了一项规则草案。

这些规则对法人的要求有所不同。某些规则要求法人必须持

---

① 除了在欧盟层面发布的 LEI 规则外，英国还采用了其他 LEI 规则。

② 阿根廷、巴西、中国、中国香港、印度、日本、韩国、墨西哥、俄罗斯、沙特阿拉伯、新加坡和土耳其。

有 LEI（"必须持有"）。某些规则要求机构若已持有 LEI 则必须上报并使用 LEI（"持有则使用"）。 还有一些规则只提出了选择性使用 LEI 的要求（"选择性使用"）。

FSB 成员公布的 101 项 LEI 规则中，近一半要求部分或全部受规则约束的法人必须持有 LEI。在其他情况下，只有在可用或 LEI 报告是可选的情况下，才要求上告 LEI。阿根廷、澳大利亚、巴西、中国、日本和韩国在 LEI 实施规则中，专门有条款明确不强制要求法人持有 LEI，即"持有则使用"或"选择性使用"，如图 1 所示。

规则总数

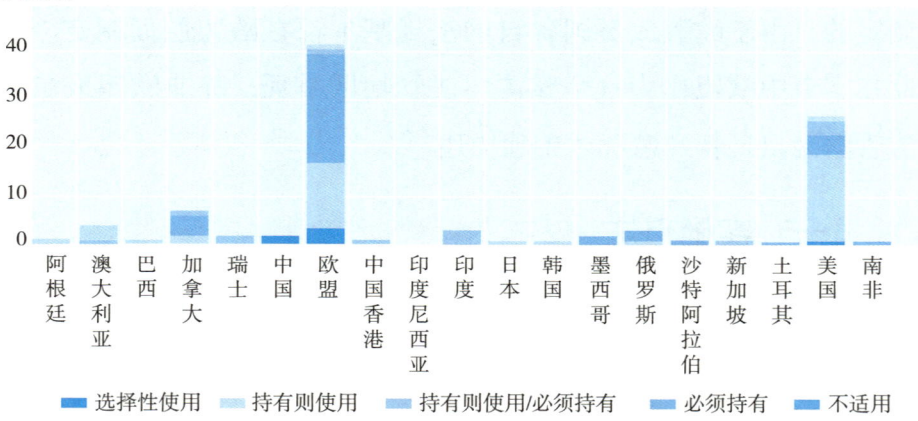

注："选择性使用"是指无论法人是否持有 LEI，都不必将 LEI 作为交易信息的一部分进行报送；"持有则使用"是指法人如持有 LEI 则必须使用 LEI；"必须持有"是指法人必须持有并使用 LEI；"持有则使用/必须持有"是指该规则包括"必须持有"和"持有则使用"两种要求。"不适用"是指该规则不适用于法人，但适用于监管机构信息公开披露或监管机构间的合作。

图 1　LEI 实施规则的数量

资料来源：LEI ROC 和 FSB 成员的调查。

---

① "持有则使用"类包括澳大利亚场外衍生品交易报告规则等案例，其中 LEI 被授权在三个全球标准编码优先级中排第一（其他选项包括 AVID 或 BIC），适用于作为报告场外衍生品交易参与方的非自然实体的标识。在实际操作中，澳大利亚指出，如果某家机构三个编码都没有，则必须申请 LEI；如果已经持有 AVID 或 BIC 码，则不会被强制要求申请 LEI。韩国也有类似情况。

图 1 和图 3 的数据表明，推动 LEI 实施的动力是提出强制性使用的监管要求，而不是自愿或选择性使用。在没有监管要求强制使用和续期的司法管辖区，LEI 应用和维护率明显更低（见第 4 节），这一结论与收集上来的问卷反馈结果是一致的（见附录 5）。

对某个部门提出"必须持有""持有则使用"还是"选择性使用"LEI 的要求所考虑的理由有所不同。有三个监管部门寻求负担最小化：美国证券交易委员会要求，某些情况下，仅在法人已拥有 LEI 时才要求报告人报告 LEI；澳大利亚证券投资委员会和日本允许国际商业机构识别编码（AVID）或银行识别编码（BIC）作为替代编码。墨西哥和英国则认为，强制性报告将是提高 LEI 覆盖率的必要手段。加拿大、中国香港、德国、意大利、瑞士和美国表示会对比分析"必须持有"和"持有则使用"两种方法的成本和效益。韩国提到，由于缺乏监管权力，难以对某些类型的法人提出强制申请 LEI 的要求，因此选择"持有则使用"的方式，但韩国打算要求金融投资企业法人、集体投资计划相关机构和各 CCP 必须持有 LEI。中国香港和新加坡采用分阶段或差异化方法，即仅要求某些类型的法人必须持有 LEI。在美国，选择"必须持有"还是"持有则使用"的依据由监管部门自行决定。①

LEI 的实施范围主要集中在金融业务交易参与方的识别，如 OTC 和交易所交易衍生品、投资活动、股权市场、回购市场、证券交易、证券融资交易等。这主要得益于国际上在这些领域所做

---

① CFTC 和 OFR 呼吁强制使用 LEI，以改善数据质量；SEC 在某些情况下要求必须使用 LEI 报送信息；FRB、OCC、FDIC 和其他联邦金融机构审查委员会（FFIEC）成员采用"持有则使用"的方式。美联储表示由于国内已有一个非常全面的编码——美联储研究统计监督贴现 ID，因此选择了"持有则使用"模式。FDIC 和 OCC 表示，由于美国有近 5000 家小型社区银行以及总资产不超过 1 亿美元的 2700 家信用社，在决定采用这种模式时考虑了报告方的监管负担。

的努力。国际 SSBs 很早就认识到 LEI 对于 OTC 衍生品数据整合的必要性，[①] 并在主要市场领域引入了 LEI 相关要求。[②] CPMI - IOSCO 在唯一交易识别码（UTIs）的技术指引[③]中，提出使用 LEI 来识别 UTI 的生成机构。欧盟要求场内交易和 OTC 衍生品的报告都要使用 LEI。

国际标准制定、国际标准在国家层面的实施、监管要求所覆盖的交易参与方 LEI 持码率相对较高，这三者之间的高度相关性表明监管要求是促进全球 LEI 应用的有效手段。

一些 FSB 司法管辖区就 LEI 的使用范围给出了补充理由。中国和印度尼西亚司法管辖区指出，应优先考虑在国际参与份额高、需要国际参与和系统重要性的市场中实施 LEI。美国金融研究办公室（OFR）指出，其战略是寻求采用 LEI 作为在美国从事金融市场交易的法人的主要标识符，应优先考虑那些积极参与金融交易并且可能产生金融稳定风险、加剧金融稳定风险形成或易被金融稳定风险所影响的机构。欧洲证券和市场管理局（ESMA）指出，在受主管当局直接监管的法人（受监管法人）中推广使用 LEI 更为容易。[④] 意大利认为渐进的做法更为可取，即首先在金融部门实

---

① FSB 于 2014 年 9 月发布的《OTC 衍生品交易数据聚合可行性研究》（http：//www.fsb.org/wp - content/uploads/r_140919.pdf）指出："对手方识别编码（LEI）对于聚合不同 TR 之间的准确头寸数据是十分必要的。待 LEI 应用成熟后，对某些任务来说具有法人关系信息的 LEI（用于整合目的）至少在第二阶段是需要的。"该报告得出结论："对任何数据整合选择而言，通过标准化和协调工作保持重要数据要素的完整性是非常重要的，特别包括在全球引入 LEI 以及创建唯一交易识别码（UTI）和唯一产品识别码（UPI）。"2015 年 9 月，CPMI 和 IOSCO 提议将 LEI 用于可报告衍生合约中支付主要债务人及付款人的身份标识，参见 http：//www.bis.org/cpmi/publ/d132.htm。

② 例如欧盟的 EMIR 和 MiFID Ⅱ。

③ 参见 http：//www.bis.org/cpmi/publ/d158.pdf。UPI 技术指引终稿于 2017 年 9 月发布。

④ 在没有直接监管的情况下，ESMA 建议阐述清楚受监管机构未能报告第三方 LEI 编码的后果，例如，明确告知受监管法人，在获得第三方 LEI 之前，不允许执行关于提交包含第三方 LEI 报告的义务。

施 LEI，然后再在其他部门实施 LEI。英国指出，应考虑采用全面的实施方法，因为一些规则可能会影响其他规则，并青睐于采用像意大利那样的渐进方法。美国指出，在新法规中实施 LEI 比在现有法规中更容易，因为现有法规已经规定使用其他识别编码。

只有澳大利亚、加拿大、欧盟、印度、墨西哥、俄罗斯、瑞士和美国对在 OTC 衍生品以外的领域出台了 LEI 实施规则（见表 1）。阿根廷、巴西和中国在衍生品方面尚未出台实施规则，但在其他领域已经使用了 LEI。许多司法管辖区正在或计划按照循序渐进的原则有步骤地实施 LEI。此外，尚没有司法管辖区计划用 LEI 完全取代现有机构识别编码，但美国 OFR 指出，LEI 的拓展使用展现了它在数据质量和成本方面的优势，可能会导致其他与 LEI 功能重复的编码逐步淘汰。

表 1　　　　　　　　　已公布的 LEI 实施规则覆盖的领域

FSB 司法管辖区	衍生品	证券法规	资产管理	信用评级机构	证券化	证券融资交易	银行监管	保险监管	机构处置	支付服务	信用登记	其他	合计
阿根廷	0	0	0	0	0	0	1	1	0	0	0	1	3
澳大利亚	2	1	0	0	0	0	1	0	0	0	0	0	4
巴西	0	0	0	0	0	0	0	0	0	0	0	1	1
加拿大	3	4	0	0	0	0	0	0	0	0	0	0	7
瑞士	1	1	0	0	0	0	0	0	0	0	0	0	2
中国	0	0	0	0	0	0	0	0	0	0	0	2	2
欧盟	1	23	2	2	1	1	4	3	1	1	1	2	42
中国香港	1	0	0	0	0	0	0	0	0	0	0	0	1
印度尼西亚	0	0	0	0	0	0	0	0	0	0	0	0	0
印度	1	1	0	0	0	0	1	0	0	0	1	1	5
日本	1	0	0	0	0	0	0	0	0	0	0	0	1
韩国	1	0	0	0	0	0	0	0	0	0	0	0	1

续表

FSB 司法管辖区	衍生品	证券法规	资产管理	信用评级机构	证券化	证券融资交易	银行监管	保险监管	机构处置	支付服务	信用登记	其他	合计
墨西哥	1	0	0	0	0	0	0	0	0	0	0	1	2
俄罗斯	1	1	0	0	0	1	0	0	0	0	0	1	4
沙特阿拉伯	0	0	0	0	0	0	1	1	0	0	0	1	3
新加坡	1	0	0	0	0	0	0	0	0	0	0	0	1
土耳其	1	0	0	0	0	0	0	0	0	0	0	0	1
美国	5	5	4	1	1	1	6	1	1	0	0	2	27
南非	1	0	0	0	0	0	0	0	0	0	0	0	1
合计	21	36	6	3	2	3	14	6	2	1	2	12	108

注：同一规则可覆盖不同领域，比如阿根廷的某条规则涉及三个领域，因此此表的统计数据与图 1 可能有出入。欧盟成员国各自的规则未在此列示。

还有部分司法管辖区已发布与金融监管无关的 LEI 使用规则，如美国关于能源市场、[①] 中国关于海关领域[②]的 LEI 使用规则。此外，在中国 LEI 也被用于动产质押融资领域。[③]

不同司法管辖区对强制续期 LEI 的要求有所不同。加拿大、欧盟成员国、印度、墨西哥、南非、瑞士和美国（FDIC、OFR 和 FRB）等 12 个司法管辖区要求某些用途的 LEI 强制续期。澳大利亚、中国香港、日本、新加坡、美国（CFTC 和 SEC）等一些司法管辖区或监管部门[④]有一些隐含要求，不直接要求机构每年续期 LEI 或在 LEI 失效时直接拒收机构报送的信息，但会要求或鼓励机

---

① 电力市场参与者报送相关机构信息时使用 LEI。
② LEI 作为产品通关时提供的企业编码之一。
③ 中国人民银行牵头推动 LEI 在中国的发放和使用，并表示正在制定 LEI 实施战略和行动计划，将覆盖几乎全部银行业机构和大部分非银行金融机构。
④ 美国 SEC 指出信息报送机构不得故意将不准确的 LEI 提交给综合审计追踪系统（Consolidated Audit Trail）。来源：关于综合审计追踪系统的国家市场系统计划的指令（No. 34 - 79318），2016 年 11 月 15 日，https://www.sec.gov/rules/sro/nms/2016/34 - 79318.pdf。

构保持信息更新。澳大利亚、中国、韩国、俄罗斯、沙特阿拉伯和美国（OFR）[①] 等司法管辖区或监管部门表示，正在考虑制定未来的续期实施要求。欧洲保险和职业养老金管理局（EIOPA）、ESMA 和意大利比例原则是一项重要的考虑因素。ESMA 将机构分为两类：一是具有报告义务的机构必须续期，主要包括 35 万金融和非金融衍生品合约的交易对手（报告方及另一方已失效的 LEI 在报告中的比例均低于 1%）、约 1 万家投资公司[②]和 40 家信用评级机构；二是报告方在报告中应标识的机构，包括 4.1 万家金融工具发行机构及数百万潜在客户。对于后者来讲，报送机构无须保证这些第三方机构的 LEI 已按时续期，但 ESMA 和欧盟国家主管当局表示，虽然法律上无法强制要求报送机构续期第三方机构的 LEI，但可在本地系统和申请机构的合同中增加关于 LEI 续期的条款。鉴于续期是全球 LEI 体系的一项基本原则，合同中一般都会包含相关内容。[③]

相应地，FSB 司法管辖区，包括欧盟内部，LEI 续期率存在很大差异（见表 2）。

表 2　　　　　　　　　　FSB 司法管辖区 LEI 续期率

FSB 司法管辖区	续期率（%）	FSB 司法管辖区	续期率（%）
印度	93	法国	69
日本	92	土耳其	66
瑞士	81	南非	58

① 截至本报告发布时，美国 OFR 已提出强制续期的要求，2019 年 2 月起实施。
② 许多投资公司作为衍生品合约的对手方包括在前述统计数据范围中。
③ 参见 ESMA 在全球金融市场协会在线研讨会上的说明：https：//www. esma. europa. eu/press - news/esma - news/webinar - new - update - use - lei - now - available. ESMA 网站关于 LEI 的简要说明：https：//www. esma. europa. eu/sites/default/files/library/esma70 - 145 - 238_lei_briefing_note. pdf.

续表

FSB 司法管辖区	续期率（%）	FSB 司法管辖区	续期率（%）
西班牙	78	墨西哥	57
荷兰	77	沙特阿拉伯	57
德国	76	中国	57
中国香港	74	加拿大	56
印度尼西亚	71	俄罗斯	53
澳大利亚	70	英国	52
意大利	70	美国	46
韩国	69	阿根廷	45
新加坡	69	巴西	41

资料来源：GLEIF，2019 年 1 月 3 日。续期率是指在特定司法管辖区拥有合法地址的、应续期且已经续期过的 LEI 的比例。

LEI ROC 于 2018 年 4 月发布了进展报告，总结了失效 LEI 所带来的数据质量问题，特别是同一机构可能被发放两个 LEI，如某机构名称变更未能及时记录；机构兼并导致对留存的 LEI 产生混淆；LEI 数据与其他数据库难以兼容，如同一机构地址不同；无法有效管理第三方机构对 LEI 数据提出的质疑，因为本地系统在没有获得机构同意的情况下无法自行更新数据。另一个问题是 LEI 失效后，没有对相关数据进行妥善处理，比如正在收集中的关系数据就容易出现此类问题。

（二）LEI 实施战略

有 20 个司法管辖区表示有实施 LEI 的明确战略（见附录 3）。但是某些司法管辖区的战略主要是推动法人自愿使用 LEI，而其他司法管辖区则采取更具体的措施作为其战略的要素。同样，一些欧盟成员国将欧盟视为发布法规和法律的管辖区，因此没有制定国家层面的战略，而其他欧盟成员国则将其 LEI 推广活动描述为其战略，例如针对非金融部门组织的公开会议。

国家层面①和监管部门层面②的战略几乎是平均分布的。目前阿根廷和俄罗斯没有制定明确的战略，但已实施一项或几项 LEI 规则。沙特阿拉伯表示已经制定了战略，但尚未制定任何规则。

有 4 个司法管辖区表示尚没有 LEI 战略，其中两个司法管辖区表示战略正在制定过程中。阿根廷表示，由于当地资本市场和场外衍生品市场的深度有限，而且国内相关实体受境外 LEI 规则的影响也会申请 LEI，因此战略制定不是当前的优先事项。印度尼西亚表示国内编码已能够满足需求。俄罗斯将制定鼓励市场参与者使用 LEI 的激励措施，实施与 ISO 17442 相同的国家标准，并纳入《关于金融市场发展关键优先事项实施的路线图（2019—2021年)》（草案），但是详细措施尚未出台。南非正在就 LEI 战略公开征求意见，需待征求意见结束后才可能开始实施。③

许多已有的战略提出了强制报告 LEI 的要求，其他一些战略主要是鼓励和支持机构自愿使用 LEI。

加拿大、欧盟、印度、墨西哥、瑞士、土耳其和美国通过法律法案或法规将 LEI 强制用于某些交易报告目的。特别是加拿大、法国、德国、印度、意大利、日本、墨西哥、新加坡、瑞士、英国和美国都强调实现以下几个工作目标：改进统计和监管报告的数据质量和数据分析、为金融实体和监管部门开展金融稳定风险

① 指巴西、加拿大、法国、中国香港、印度、意大利、沙特阿拉伯和瑞士。
② 指中国、欧盟、德国、日本、韩国、俄罗斯、新加坡、西班牙、英国、美国和土耳其。
③ 参见 https：//www. fsca. co. za/Regulatory%20Frameworks/Documents%20for%20Consultation/Discussion%20paper%20on%20the%20implementation%20of%20Legal%20Entity%20Identifiers%20–%202019%20November%202018. pdf。

评估提供便利、减轻金融机构的报告负担。中国香港应用 LEI 主要是为了金融部门的整体利益，顺应国际社会将 LEI 作为全球标准的趋势，响应 FSB 关于在 OTC 衍生品交易报告中应用 LEI 的建议。[①]

巴西、加拿大、中国香港、印度、意大利、日本、墨西哥、沙特阿拉伯、瑞士、美国和土耳其表示，相关国家主管部门在制定战略或起草相关法律法规过程中进行了密切合作。

其他司法管辖区指出，其战略旨在支持自愿申请 LEI，这主要是因为缺乏制定规则的权力，例如在欧盟，成员国制定战略和相应的规则不是在国家层面，而是在欧盟层面。

大多数司法管辖区正在利用研讨会、会议等方式提高对 LEI 的认识并推进其应用。大多数司法管辖区（除阿根廷、巴西、中国香港和土耳其外）都指出，公共部门与私营部门正在持续进行沟通。此外，各本地系统正在努力通过自身工作和网站等渠道增强公众意识并促进 LEI 应用。上述工作在没有本地系统的司法管辖区则无法开展。

在具有适用于全辖区战略的司法管辖区中，仅有加拿大、德国、中国香港、意大利和瑞士表示在制定战略的过程中进行了成本效益分析。即便在这些司法管辖区，成本效益分析也非单独针对 LEI，而是针对某项范围更广的监管措施。中国香港在制定战略时使用了非定量的成本效益分析。日本指出虽然一直努力推进 LEI 应用，但仍然很难让没有交易报告义务的机构认识到应用 LEI 的好处。而其他成本效益分析则是作为具体规则制定工作的一部分

---

① 参见 2018 年 2 月 FSB 关于中国香港的同行评估报告：http：//www. fsb. org/2018/02/peer - review - of - hong - kong/。

而进行的，例如在第 5 节欧盟和美国进行的分析。

　　LEI 实施战略通常涵盖 OTC 衍生品报告和其他向证券监管机构的报告。相比之下，在信贷登记、支付、反洗钱、反恐融资等领域用于身份识别的战略比较少（见图 2）。

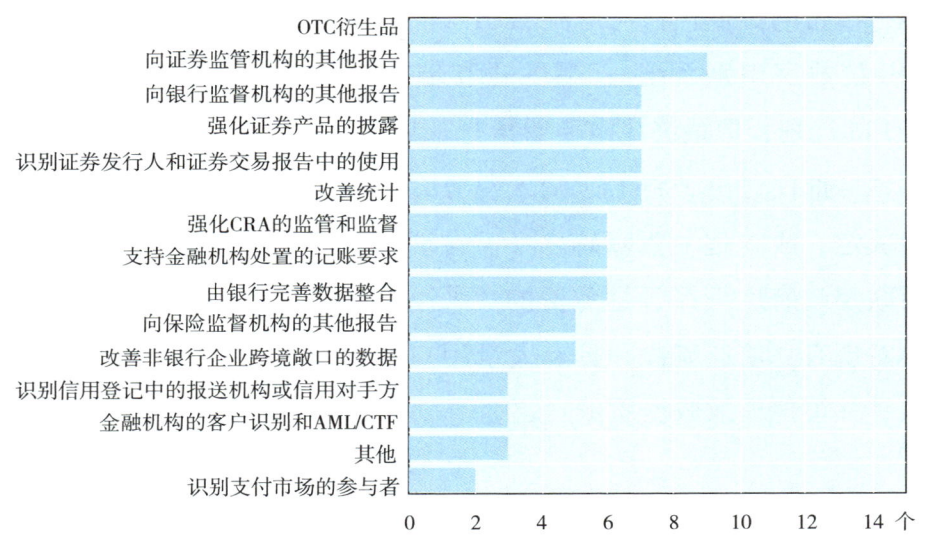

资料来源：同行评估问卷的反馈。

图 2　FSB 司法管辖区 LEI 战略覆盖领域（全覆盖或部分覆盖）

　　已经制定 LEI 战略的司法管辖区均没有调整战略的计划。作为战略举措的一部分，英国打算提高 LEI 及其在公共部门和私营部门应用的认知度，以支持 LEI 更广泛的应用。美国 CFTC 表示将修订掉期交易数据报送的相关规则，预计会调整与 LEI 相关的部分条款，并将在掉期交易对手方识别中继续强制要求使用 LEI。许多司法管辖区已开始评估其现有 LEI 战略的有效性，评估维度包括 LEI 发码量、覆盖范围或报告合规性，如法国、意大利、日本、墨西哥、瑞士和美国。然而，其他司法管辖区持观望态度，认为评估前期战略效果的时机尚不成熟，其中包括像沙特阿拉伯这样

刚刚制定战略的国家。

在少数司法管辖区，LEI 已经取代现有识别编码或与现有识别编码建立了联系（见附录2），但没有司法管辖区计划全面使用 LEI。德国计划在研究削减统计行政成本的过程中研究 LEI 的问题，沙特阿拉伯正在考虑将其引入能够兼容 LEI 的统一识别系统（10 位数字识别系统）。墨西哥和瑞士曾考虑实施一项普遍采用 LEI 的计划，但最终决定不予执行。在墨西哥，相关部门曾经与联邦税务部门讨论了将 LEI 纳入税务登记的可行性，但尚未作出最终决定，成本是主要障碍之一。在瑞士，唯一商业识别号码系统由联邦政府运行并且是免费的。采用 LEI 作为合法通用编码将需要对现有立法、流程和具有大量用户基础的基础设施进行重大改造，并可能导致数据质量问题。

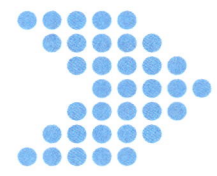

四、LEI 在金融稳定相关领域的 覆盖情况

（一）LEI 发码演变

LEI 发码演变反映了法规在促进 LEI 应用方面发挥的巨大作用（见图 3）。随着欧盟 EMIR 和 MiFID Ⅱ 的实施，LEI 发码量显著增加，这一增长在欧盟地区尤为明显。同样，LEI 的数量在欧盟和美国也是最多的，这两个地区都采用了多项与 LEI 相关的规则。

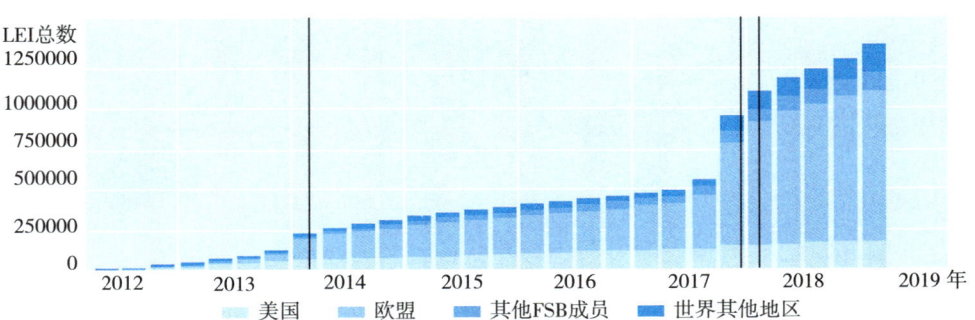

注：竖线表示 2014 年 1 月 EMIR 报告要求时、2017 年 11 月 EMIR 修订时和 2018 年 1 月 MiFID Ⅱ 实施时 LEI 的发放情况。

图 3　司法管辖区 LEI 累计发码量

资料来源：GLEIF。

（二）总体发码率

从编码数量和符合条件的法人覆盖率方面来看，LEI 的发码主要集中在加拿大、欧盟①和美国（见图 4）。LEI 编码已被发放给 220 多个地区的法人；然而，超过半数的司法管辖区 LEI 编码数量少于 100 个（见图 5）。

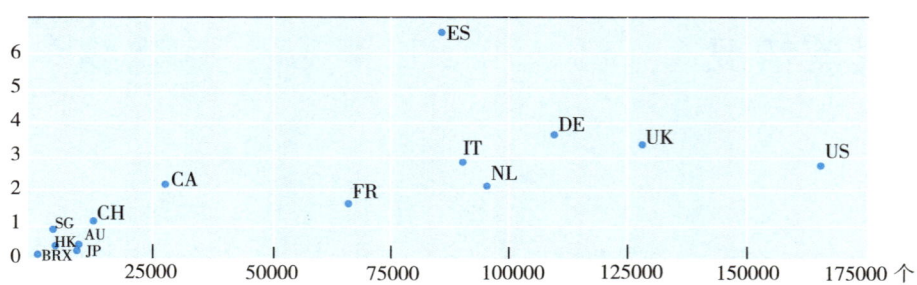

图 4　FSB 司法管辖区 LEI 的使用情况

资料来源：GLEIF 和同行评估问卷反馈，截至 2018 年 11 月。

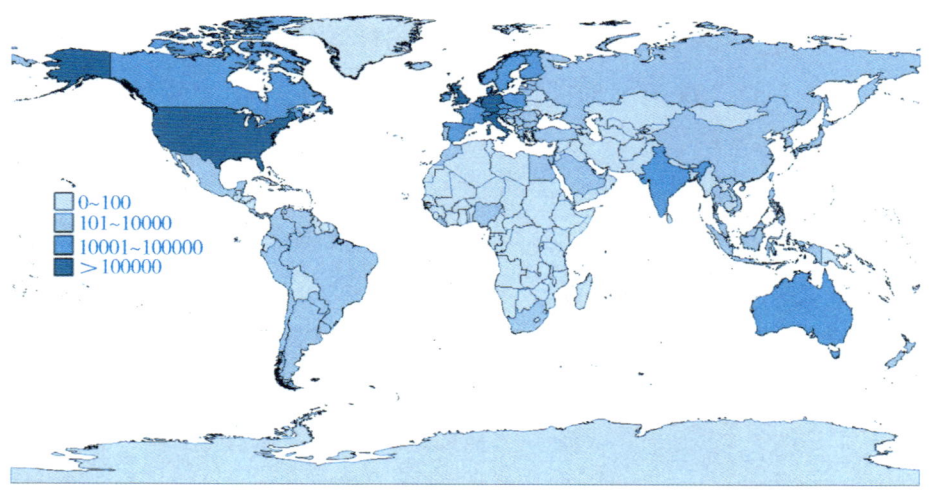

注：图中为各司法管辖区 LEI 的发放情况，截至 2019 年 3 月 31 日。

图 5　各司法管辖区发放 LEI 的数量

资料来源：https://www.gleif.org/en/lei-data/global-lei-index/lei-statistics。

LEI 的绝对覆盖率仍相对较低，并且在 FSB 司法管辖区间差

---

① 10%来自英国，8.7%来自德国，7.5%来自意大利，7.4%来自荷兰，7%来自西班牙，5.4%来自法国。

异很大。据估计，LEI 在加拿大、欧盟和美国所有符合条件的法人中的覆盖比例从 2%～7% 不等。[①] 第二类司法管辖区（澳大利亚、中国香港、日本、韩国、沙特阿拉伯、新加坡和瑞士）的覆盖率估计在 0.2%～2%；其余司法管辖区的覆盖率低于 0.1%（如巴西、印度尼西亚、墨西哥、俄罗斯和土耳其），或无从得知（如阿根廷、中国、印度和南非）。

（三）行业覆盖情况

LEI 在涉及场外衍生品、证券交易商以及金融中介机构中的覆盖率相对较高。如第 3 节所述，在金融稳定目标的驱使下，在这些行业强制使用 LEI 一直是立法的重点。

关于场外衍生品交易，许多 FSB 成员表示交易报告主体的 LEI 覆盖率接近 100%，但部分成员反应交易对手方的覆盖率有所下降（见表 3）。

表3　　　新 OTC 衍生品交易（按未清偿总额计算）中报告机构或
交易对手方 LEI 的覆盖率

覆盖率	报告机构	交易对手方
96%～100%	澳大利亚、加拿大、法国、德国、中国香港、印度、日本、墨西哥、荷兰、俄罗斯、新加坡、西班牙、英国、美国	加拿大、西班牙、欧盟、法国、德国、中国香港、印度、意大利、荷兰、俄罗斯、英国、美国
90%～95%	—	日本、新加坡
80%～89%	—	澳大利亚

---

① 符合条件的法人总数仅以公司来计算，即不包括在某些情况下可能符合 LEI 条件但在国家层面无法获取具体数量的个体商户。请注意，由于用于确定符合条件机构总量的数据来源和统计方法不同，计算精确的覆盖率不一定能得出完全可比的结果。

续表

覆盖率	报告机构	交易对手方
50%~79%	—	—
<50%	—	墨西哥
不可获得的	阿根廷、巴西、瑞士、中国、印度尼西亚、韩国、沙特阿拉伯、南非、土耳其	阿根廷、巴西、瑞士、中国、印度尼西亚、韩国、沙特阿拉伯、南非、土耳其

资料来源：司法管辖区对同行评估问卷的反馈，具体数字见附录4a。

此外，按照未清偿额计算，LEI 覆盖了大部分证券发行人。据欧洲中央银行（ECB）基于其中央证券数据库（CSDB）编制的一份详细报表显示，在全球范围内，按照未清偿额计算，超过70%的公开发行证券是由拥有 LEI 的机构发行的，FSB 司法管辖区为79%，世界其他地区为65%。据欧洲中央银行评估，证券发行人总体 LEI 覆盖率最低的（按未清偿额计）司法管辖区是巴西、中国、中国香港、印度、印度尼西亚、墨西哥和南非，覆盖率介于中国的36% 和南非的65% 之间，而其他司法管辖区覆盖率在70% 以上，包括九个司法管辖区超过90%（见表4 和附录4b）。

表4　FSB 司法管辖区内证券发行人的 LEI 覆盖率评估（基于未清偿额）

未清偿额	非金融机构	金融机构	政府	经济体[①]
90%~100%	瑞士、德国、西班牙、欧盟、法国、意大利、荷兰、英国、美国	澳大利亚、加拿大、瑞士、德国、西班牙、欧盟、法国、中国香港、意大利、荷兰、俄罗斯、沙特阿拉伯、新加坡、土耳其、英国	阿根廷、澳大利亚、巴西、加拿大、德国、西班牙、欧盟、法国、中国香港、印度尼西亚、日本、韩国、墨西哥、荷兰、俄罗斯、沙特阿拉伯、新加坡、土耳其、英国、美国、南非	阿根廷、瑞士、德国、西班牙、欧盟、法国、意大利、荷兰、英国

续表

未清偿额	非金融机构	金融机构	政府	经济体①
50%~89%	阿根廷、加拿大、印度、日本、韩国、墨西哥、俄罗斯、沙特阿拉伯、新加坡、土耳其	阿根廷、中国、印度尼西亚、印度、日本、韩国、墨西哥、美国、南非	瑞士	澳大利亚、巴西、加拿大、中国香港、印度尼西亚、印度、日本、韩国、墨西哥、俄罗斯、沙特阿拉伯、新加坡、土耳其、美国、南非
<50%	澳大利亚、巴西、中国、中国香港、印度尼西亚、南非	巴西	中国、印度	中国

注：LEI 覆盖率基于 ESCB 的 CSDB 数据计算。对非欧盟 FSB 成员司法管辖区来说，CSDB 中数据的深度和广度无法与欧盟国家相比，而且其证券及发行人可能存在一定的数据缺失。因此，对于非欧盟 FSB 司法管辖区的 LEI 覆盖率应视为近似估计。

①数据涵盖除货币市场基金和非货币市场投资基金以外的所有子行业。各司法管辖区的详细覆盖率见附录 4b。

LEI 更多应用于金融业法人，在其他行业的覆盖率差异较大。虽然很少有司法管辖区报告行业细分情况，但根据报告，金融业的覆盖率不低于 10%，在某个欧盟司法管辖区甚至达到了 80%。一些金融子行业的覆盖率更高：据 ECB 统计，91% 的欧盟信贷机构①和据 EIOPA 统计 88% 的欧盟保险公司②都有 LEI。在美国，在 OCC 监管的 1261 家国家银行和联邦储蓄协会中，只有 330 家有 LEI，占比为 26%。

---

① 参见 https：//www. ecb. europa. eu/stats/financial_corporations/list_of_financial_institutions/html/daily_listMID. en. html。

② 参见 https：//eiopa. europa. eu/publications/register – of – insurance – undertakings。

图 4 中的司法管辖区的 LEI 总体覆盖率少于 7％，是由于非金融业中的法人较多，并且现行法规对他们的约束力较小。按绝对值计算，不同司法管辖区内，拥有 LEI 的非金融法人和金融法人之间的比例从 1∶1 到 10∶1 不等。

同样，跨境金融法人用户的覆盖率似乎高于企业法人的平均水平，或因前者更有可能使用符合 LEI 要求的金融工具。例如，一家大型国际银行在同行评审圆桌会议上指出，LEI 覆盖了其 69％的欧洲客户、29％的美国客户和 4％的亚太地区客户。GFMA 和 ISDA 的一项调查也证实这并非个例。[1]

公共行业的 LEI 应用缓慢进步但仍未完善。21 个司法管辖区指出，它们的央行有 LEI（中国、中国香港和美国除外），同时所有司法管辖区都报告至少有一个除央行外的其他公共部门拥有 LEI。这通常包括政府债务的发行人，并且根据附录 4b 中的估算，除印度的 3％、中国的 42％和瑞士的 65％外，在所有 FSB 的司法管辖区，LEI 覆盖了超过 90％未清偿的政府一般性债务。[2]

（四）按机构规模及类别划分的覆盖率

企业规模是影响 LEI 覆盖率的另一个因素。根据意大利和西班牙反馈提供的对企业规模的分析，在金融和非金融行业中，大型机构的覆盖率分别为 40％和 77％。这一比例远远高于这些司法管辖区的中型企业，分别为 27％和 56％。

---

[1]　来自北美、亚太和日本的 21 家机构受访者表示，他们在欧洲和北美的企业客户平均 LEI 覆盖率超过 50％，亚洲超过 30％，其中一些机构覆盖率达到 100％（见附录 4d）。

[2]　ESMA 报告称，根据 ISIN 数量测算，在这三个没有 LEI 的司法管辖区中，中国和印度在欧盟交易的主权证券量最大。中国财政部于 2018 年 8 月获得了 LEI。

LEI 在大型银行、保险公司和非金融集团的母公司普遍应用，但这些公司的多数附属机构通常没有 LEI。从司法管辖区内前 20 个最大银行/接受存款机构的 LEI 覆盖率来看，有 15 个司法管辖区为 100%，7 个司法管辖区低于 100%，其余两个司法管辖区无法提供数据。综合所有司法管辖区数据来看，前 20 个最大银行/接受存款机构的 LEI 平均覆盖率为 94%。对于保险公司而言，有 10 个司法管辖区报告其前 20 个最大保险公司的 LEI 覆盖率为 100%，有 12 个司法管辖区报告其仅为部分覆盖。综合所有司法管辖区数据来看，前 20 个最大保险公司的 LEI 平均覆盖率为 75%。对于前 20 个最大的非金融集团总部所在的司法管辖区中，有 8 个司法管辖区表示 LEI 覆盖率为 100%，另外 12 个司法管辖区仅为部分覆盖，其余 4 个辖区无法提供数据。综合所有司法管辖区数据来看，所有司法管辖区的前 20 个最大非金融集团的 LEI 平均覆盖率为 78%。

表5　拥有 LEI 的 20 家最大银行、保险公司和非金融集团的母公司的占比情况

FSB 司法管辖区	银行/接受存款机构		保险公司		非金融集团	
	已有 LEI	占比（%）	已有 LEI	占比（%）	已有 LEI	占比（%）
阿根廷	—	—	—	—	—	—
澳大利亚	20	100	12	60	7	35
巴西	15	75	3	15	10	50
加拿大	17	85	19	95	18	90
中国	—	—	—	—	—	—
法国	20	100	20	100	20	100
德国	20	100	20	100	20	100
中国香港	20	100	19	95	20	100
印度	20	100	3	15	18	90
印度尼西亚	16	80	1	5	—	—

续表

FSB 司法管辖区	银行/接受存款机构		保险公司		非金融集团	
	已有 LEI	占比（％）	已有 LEI	占比（％）	已有 LEI	占比（％）
意大利	20	100	20	100	20	100
日本	20	100	20	100	20	100
韩国	16	80	20	100	14	70
墨西哥	20	100	8	40	17	85
荷兰	20	100	20	100	20	100
俄罗斯	18	90	12	60	8	40
沙特阿拉伯	20	100	20	100	3	15
新加坡	20	100	16	80	11	55
南非	12	60	15	75	11	55
西班牙	20	100	20	100	16	80
瑞士	20	100	19	95	19	95
土耳其	18	90	5	25	10	50
英国	20	100	20	100	20	100
美国	20	100	20	100	20	100
平均值	18.7	94	15.1	75	15.6	78

注：这些数字只显示了拥有 LEI 的母公司，而没有显示其子公司的情况。"—"表示没有可用的数据。蓝色阴影表示100%覆盖率。

全球系统重要性银行（G - SIB）和全球系统重要性保险机构（G - SII）的母公司的覆盖范围尤其广泛。2018 年确定的且总部设在 FSB 成员司法管辖区内的所有 G - SIBs 都有 LEI。2016 年确定的且总部位于 FSB 司法管辖区的 G - SIIs 仅有一家没有 LEI。

然而，LEI 的覆盖范围一般没有延伸到所有大型银行、保险公司和非金融集团的相关法人。在银行业，G - SIB 集团结构中的母公司有 LEI，但其附属机构却并非如此。为支持《保险资本标准》制定，参与国际保险监管者协会（IAIS）数据收集工作的保险集团中的所有法人中，LEI 覆盖率达到了 73％，但只有 1/3 的保险集团为旗下所有机构注册了 LEI。总部在欧盟的 G–SIIs 中，尽管其所有位于欧盟的附属机构（保险和再保险）都有 LEI，但它们在欧盟外的（保险和再保险）附属机构只有 70% 有 LEI。据报道，虽然欧盟大型企业借款人的 LEI 覆盖率接近 100%，但其他地区尤其是亚洲的 LEI 覆盖率要低得多。在一些针对非金融公司的项目中，例如 BIS 对公司贷款的分析以及 OECD 关于个别跨国公司及其附属公司（ADIMA）分析数据库的试点项目，LEI 的低覆盖率被视为 LEI 应用的障碍。

同样，有证据表明，较大的机构更可能拥有 LEI。除证券发行人的数据外，AnaCredit① 也显示，虽然仅 7% 的债务人有 LEI，但却占到所有未偿债务总额的 48%。在没有 LEI 的信贷金额中，有 18% 来自欧盟以外的机构，而这些机构仅占没有 LEI 的债务人的 0.2%，尽管这只是基于 9 个欧盟成员国的初步数据。这表明：第一，非欧盟债务国可能占相当大的比例，而 LEI 作为全球唯一识别编码，是汇总银行风险敞口的合适工具；第二，这些非欧盟的风险敞口可能主要来自大型机构，因此有必要通过国际合作来提高大型机构的 LEI 覆盖率。

---

① 提供欧元区个人银行贷款详细信息的数据集。

五、LEI 应用的成就及进一步应用的挑战

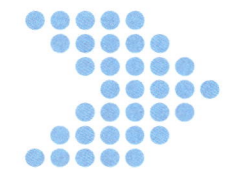

（一）监管应用

全球 LEI 体系监管委员会（ROC）于 2018 年 4 月 30 日发布的进展报告全面概述了 LEI 监管应用总体情况。①

LEI 的实施为监管部门提供了多种监管应用场景。

1. 监测金融风险。在监管报告中使用 LEI 可显著提升公共部门理解和识别横跨多个司法管辖区和复杂全球金融流程的风险累积的能力。例如，LEI 使得美国商品期货委员会（CFTC）可以识别向其申报的大多数掉期交易的对手方，并使其能够通过单一的、可兼容的且经过验证的识别编码来分析掉期交易活动和法人风险敞口。

2. 风险敞口的汇总/法人面向信贷登记机构的报告。LEI 有利于所有相关机构的数据整合。② 该信息可用于多种类型的分析，例

---

① 参见 LEI 体系监管委员会的进度报告，2018 年 4 月，https：//www. LEI ROC. org/publications/gls/roc_20180502 – 1. pdf。

② 关键交易对手的总体风险敞口往往涉及多个独立机构，在某些情况下，单个机构风险敞口与合并风险敞口之间存在非线性关系。若要简单地汇总这些相关机构的风险敞口，对风险敞口简单求和就可以做到。但对于更复杂的风险，例如受净额结算影响的衍生品头寸，机构级风险敞口的简单求和是行不通的。

如欧洲央行货币政策分析（见专栏 2）。[1]

另一个例子是在风险分析中信贷风险敞口汇总数据的应用。例如，ECB 指出监管机构需要识别和监测重要借款人集中风险。为此，监管机构将 LEI 编码作为识别交易对手方的唯一识别编码。这样就可以对单个交易对手方的风险敞口进行跨机构映射，从而了解每个交易对手方对银行业的整体风险。例如，这类分析可用于评估特定交易对手方的压力对该行业的影响，或在更高的层面上评估交易对手方对应的经济行业/国家对该行业的影响（蔓延风险）。这样做之所以可行，是因为与国内识别编码相比，LEI 是全球通用的，并且在所有数据报告中保持一致。[2]

澳大利亚在其 2019 年 1 月 1 日生效的大额风险敞口报告框架中使用了 LEI。该报告规范要求银行和其他存款机构报送每个风险敞口对应交易对手的 LEI。如果风险敞口对应一组关联交易对手时，则报告主要交易对手的 LEI，如果交易对手没有 LEI，则报送 N/A。目前，加拿大正在考虑在其新制定的大额风险敞口指南中使用 LEI 来识别交易对手方。

同样，印度储备银行（RBI）要求银行机构对于那些基金和非基金敞口总额高于任一银行特定上限的公司借款人强制使用 LEI。LEI 也将被录入大额信贷中央信息库（CRILC），以便于评估

---

[1] 这是基于 CornejoPérez 和 Huerga，中央证券数据库数据（CSDB）- 用于金融稳定目的的标准化微观数据（https：//www.bis.org/ifc/events/ws_micro_macro/perez_paper.pdf）。本文是国际金融公司 2016 年 5 月第 41 号公告（http：//www.bis.org/ifc/publ/ifcb41.htm）的一部分，内容涉及整合金融稳定的微观和宏观统计数据分析，该文描述了 2015 年 12 月 14 日至 15 日在波兰华沙召开的国际金融公司关于"整合微观和宏观统计数据进行金融稳定性分析的研讨会——经验、机遇和挑战"，的有关情况。

[2] 欧盟要求，若持有 LEI，则应当在欧洲央行（AnaCredit）信用登记处的数据库中用来识别银行的交易对手。参见 https：//www.ecb.europa.eu/explainers/tell-me-more/html/anacredit.en.html。

集团公司的借款总量，并监测机构/集团的财务状况。

专栏2

LEI 在欧洲央行中央证券数据库（CSDB）中的应用

自 2009 年运行以来，CSDB 作为一个 S－b－S 数据库，旨在保存所有单个证券完整、准确、一致和最新的信息。这些信息用于欧洲中央银行体系（ESCB）的统计用途，并且正越来越多地用于其他方面。这些信息包含与证券有关的参考数据，如未清偿证券总额、发行和到期日、证券类型、息票和股息信息、统计分类等；发行人，包含识别编码、名称、所在国、经济行业等；价格，包含市值、估值和违约价格；评级信息，包括证券、发行计划和所有评级机构，无论是否是证券发行人。CSDB 是一个多源系统，每天接收大约 250 万条价格信息和 40 万条参考信息记录。编制 S－b－S 数据库需要应用唯一识别编码，即国际证券识别编码（ISIN）和 LEI。

除了各种统计用途，CSDB 还支持多项涉及中央银行职能的分析和政策性工作，如货币政策、金融稳定分析、市场操作、风险管理、财政政策监测和经济研究。例如，CSDB 支持法人的再融资需求分析、存款公司的融资结构分析、融资成本分析以及金融工具信用评级的变化分析。

CSDB 这样的 S－b－S 数据库能提供预整合数据无法匹配的灵活性。微观数据可基于多种用途进行编制，也可基于每一种特定分析进行事后定制，或者不必向数据代报机构提出更多要求就能灵活地生成新的整合信息。CSDB 还能提供聚合数据未包含的属性以及对这些属性进行组合的可选方法。

目前，LEI 正被用来作为 CSDB 中的"分组识别编码"，以对同一发行机构下的证券进行分组。LEI 的应用极大地支持了 CSDB 与其他微观数据库的互联。由于过去没有一种可以横跨不同数据集和司法管辖区的通用机构识别编码，因此与其他数据集的互联通常很困难。LEI 作为唯一真正的全球法人识别编码，极大地促进了 CSDB 法人信息与其他 ECB 微观数据库以及其他微观数据源的链接。

3. 统计分析。通过对法人的准确识别，LEI 可以促进统计分析的广泛应用。例如，IMF 正在探索在其协调证券投资调查（CPIS）数据库中使用 LEI，以便按持有人和发行人所属的经济类别和行业向用户提供"从谁到谁"（From – whom – to – whom）的 CPIS 头寸。[①] 虽然 LEI 存在覆盖率不足的缺陷，但在 BIS 探讨如何通过大型公司贷款建立银企贷款关系的方法学论文中，已经得到应用。[②]

4. 了解公司结构。LEI 可对公司结构进行可靠识别。例如，OECD 的 ADIMA 在统计和供应链评估中利用了 LEI 和其他数据源，以更好地了解跨国公司（MNE）的公司结构和活动。[③] 俄罗斯央行使用 LEI 建立了俄罗斯控股公司的会计架构，并使用 LEI 监测俄罗斯银行向集团级法人发放的贷款。

———————————

① 见货币基金组织统计司论文，《关于用于消费物价指数报告的发行人和行业中央数据库项目》：下一步是什么？（2018 年 10 月，https：//www.imf.org/external/pubs/ft/bop/2018/pdf/18 - 08.pdf）。

② 瑟琳娜·加拉尔达，J. M. 跨国银企贷款关系：法人编码如何帮助？在国际金融公司公报中，危机后统计举措是否已经完成？第 49 卷 https：//www.bis.org/ifc/publ/ifcb49_13.pdf。

③ 见经合组织统计局关于使用大数据计量跨国公司的董事会文件：经合组织关于单个跨国公司及其附属公司的分析数据库（ADIMA）［2018 年 3 月，http：//www.oecd.org/officialdocuments/publicdis playdocumentpdf/？COTE = COM/STD/WPTGS/DAF/WGIIS（2018）1&DocLanguage = EN］。

5. 了解市场结构。LEI 可以明确识别交易网络和市场结构中 OTC 衍生品市场参与者的身份，从而有助于更好地了解市场结构。例如，新加坡金融管理局使用 LEI 和其他识别编码来识别 OTC 衍生品市场中的机构，从而构建交易网络，以便更好地了解这些市场的结构。

ESMA 称，在欧盟范围的 CCP 压力测试[①]中，使用 LEI 极大地提高了对 CCP 清算成员的识别度。例如，该压力测试通过共同清算成员评估 CCP 的相互关联程度。

ESMA 还在一篇分析企业通过可转让证券共同投资计划（UCITS）使用信用违约掉期情况的论文中，用 LEI 将衍生品报告中的信息与数据供应商提供的投资基金特征信息关联起来。[②] 该论文中，欧洲系统性风险委员会使用 LEI 进行了类似分析来举例说明：UCITS 之间不进行交易，而是主要依赖 13 家交易商进入 CDS 市场。[③]

6. 市场监督。LEI 有利于市场监督与合规评估。例如，MiFIR 强制要求使用 LEI 识别交易报告中的相关交易者。因为 LEI 提供了一致、可靠的方法实现唯一识别参与交易的法人，这增强了英国 FCA 对跨金融市场的市场滥用的监测能力。在此之前，识别一个机构需要使用多种识别编码，数据核对困难，因而难以监测到可能存在的市场滥用行为。唯一识别编码对于监测市场滥用行为

---

① 该测试旨在评估由 LEI 识别的 900 名清算成员以及他们的流动性提供者和托管人之间的相互关联性。参见 http：//firds. esma. europa. eu/webst/ESMA70 – 151 – 1154 EU – wide CCP Stress Test 2017 Report. pdf。

② 欧盟投资基金使用 CDS 的动因，载于《ESMA 趋势、风险和脆弱性报告》2018 年第 2 期，https：//www. esma. europa. eu/press – news/esma – news/what – drives – use – cds – eu – investment – funds。

③ 参见 V. 27 of https：//www. esma. europa. eu/sites/default/files/library/esma_50 – 165 – 632_report_on_ trends_risks_and_vulnerabilities_no. 2_2018. pdf#page =66。

的好处也适用于市场参与者，荷兰用 LEI 作为主键来关联不同的交易报告，以便获得某笔特殊交易的订单指令链的完整视图，并识别链条中所有的参与者。法国也在市场监管中使用了 LEI，并正在使用全新的 MiFIR 交易报告框架来迅速识别参与可疑行为的法人。法国金融市场管理局（AMF）创造了模式检测算法，用于检测法人是否多次尝试操作或曾经操作过特定金融工具的市场。监管部门指出，由于 LEI 在整个欧洲范围内的普遍使用，LEI 对监督工作确实带来了附加价值。

7. 为投资者提高透明度。LEI 可以为投资者提供更多证券化产品及其标的资产信息。例如在美国，一项由六家机构联合发布的规则要求，在向潜在投资者提供的信息中，应使用 LEI（如有）来识别通过公开市场贷款抵押债券（CLO）所持有或将持有的贷款或资产的债务人。LEI 也有助于信用评级的透明化，例如在欧盟，要求使用 LEI 识别以下对象：（1）信用评级机构；（2）已被信用评级的机构；（3）如果附属机构的母公司是被评级对象，则识别母公司；（4）在对结构性金融工具的信用评级中，识别发起人。使用 LEI 发布的机构信息，便于市场参与者去检索相应信息并用于自身分析。

LEI 也支持其他提升市场透明性的措施：ESMA 在某些情况下用 LEI 来计算金融工具的流动性，以确定金融工具的订单和/或交易是否符合实时透明度要求。[①] 例如，ESMA 使用 LEI 来识别单一名称信用违约互换（CDS）的标的参考实体，以及债券期货标的债券的发行人。

---

① 参见 https：//www. esma. europa. eu/policy – activities/mifid – ii – and – mifir/transparency – calculations。

8. 金融机构处置。为支持金融机构处置，欧盟监管部门要求金融集团中某些金融机构的特定金融合同记录中需包含 LEI，以方便主管当局和处置当局获取信息。① 类似地，美国要求某些被保险的存款机构持有 LEI，并要求使用 LEI 识别这些机构的合格金融合同的交易对手方。拥有一个跨法人、产品和地域的唯一识别编码，有助于更全面和快速地分析传染性风险，并有助于更及时地分析破产机构的资产质量，例如，为这些资产的第三方数据使用一个国际标准识别编码，就可避免手工比对不同的专有识别编码所造成的延迟。

（二）LEI 应用的好处

大部分司法管辖区指出，LEI 的使用改善了数据质量与分析质量，见表 6。

表 6 FSB 成员关于 LEI 对数据质量与分析质量的影响观点

观点	是	否	部分反馈，无反馈或尚未评估
在贵司法管辖区内，LEI 是否提高了金融监管报告、数据分析和其他监管活动的质量、效率与准确性？LEI 是否使新的金融监管项目成为可能？	加拿大、中国、欧盟②、西班牙、法国、德国、中国香港、意大利、日本、荷兰、新加坡、瑞士、英国、美国	澳大利亚、墨西哥	阿根廷、巴西、印度尼西亚、韩国、俄罗斯、沙特阿拉伯、南非、土耳其

司法管辖区列举的其他使用 LEI 的好处，包括提高法人识别

---

① 《银行追回和清算指令》第 2 (1) (100) 条对"金融合同"进行了定义，包括证券合同、商品合同、期货和远期合同、互换货币协议、短期银行间借款协议以及这些合同的主协议。

② 对于表 6–8，欧盟表示一个或多个欧盟机构，如欧洲央行、单一决议委员会、欧洲银行管理局和欧洲货币管理局。欧盟成员国单独列示（和计算）。

度、提高数据整合质量和改善母公司法人信息报送质量（见表 7）。

表 7   其他 LEI 好处

好处	报告 LEI 好处的司法管辖区数量（个）	报告 LEI 好处的司法管辖区占比（％）
支持识别国内外机构	20	80
支持数据整合	19	76
LEI 是一个非专有系统	17	68
LEI 的唯一性；有关继受机构的信息	16	64
LEI 提供直接和最终母公司信息	15	60
LEI 允许记录国际分支机构	14	56
支持多种语言与字符集	10	40
LEI 没有被特定的服务提供商锁定	10	40

据 20 个司法管辖区报告，LEI 最普遍的用途是有效识别国内和国外的法人。例如，中国和俄罗斯都强调 LEI 在识别国外法人方面效果显著，同时俄罗斯还指出，LEI 为映射俄罗斯法人的国外子公司提供了更好的方法。韩国也表示 LEI 降低了与国外法人的交易风险。意大利将 LEI 纳入报告模板，显著提高了对银行非本地交易对手方的识别能力。意大利在报告中还指出，使用 LEI 大大减少了数据整合和法人头寸计算的误差，进而显著提高了识别交易对手方的准确度和金融报告/数据整合的准确度（见专栏 3）。美国金融研究办公室（OFR）强调 LEI 的主要价值体现在跨境交易与跨类型交易中的使用，同时 LEI 对于监管非银行公司特别具有价值，正如 2008 年国际金融危机所表明的，非银行公司的金融监管数据历来存在重大缺口。

专栏 3

意大利 LEI 效益案例

在引入 LEI 之前，意大利中央信贷登记机构只能靠公司名称和公司注册国来唯一识别银行的非本地交易对手方。由于不同报告机构对同一交易对手方的描述可能各不相同，例如"ABC S. A."与"ABC Societe anonyme"可能被视为不同的机构，这种重复的情况很多，导致在计算银行系统相对于对手方的全球风险头寸时会出现低估的情况，因为其贷款总额已被分摊到重复机构。相反的情况，由于公司名称非常相似，两个不同的法人被"合并"为一个法人也可能发生，导致数据整合结果被错误高估。

在报告要求中引入 LEI 降低了机构重复或合并的风险。类似的，在 Anacredit 和 EMIR 报告中引入 LEI，可以更好地在欧洲层面上识别贷款合同与 OTC 衍生品交易的对手方。

19 个司法管辖区指出，LEI 有助于促进多个监管部门间的数据整合与协调。17 个司法管辖区表明，它们受益于 LEI 的非专有特性。16 个司法管辖区回应称，一家法人有唯一的 LEI 并在其整个生命周期内保持一致，包括其迁移到任何最终继受机构是有益的。

在此背景下，日本和英国指出 LEI 在便利企业履行 KYC 或 AML 规定的义务方面起到了关键作用。一些市场参与者也强调了 LEI 在 KYC 和 AML 相关流程中所带来的好处（见附录5），响应了 BCBS 关于客户尽职调查的指南，同时 FSB 和 CPMI 也建议在代理银行业务中使用 LEI。①

欧盟、法国、德国、意大利、荷兰和美国表示，LEI 的实施降低了金融监管报告、数据分析或其他监管活动的成本。美国指出，行业反馈表明 LEI 带来的效率能有效降低合规成本。意大利表示，在 AnaCredit 中，LEI 使对交易对手方的手工检查变得没有必要，从而降低了成本。法国指出，要求客户获取 LEI 能够降低投资公司为每个客户维护多个识别编码的成本。最后，德国的行业反馈表明，使用 LEI 可以减轻报送其他法人属性，例如工业部门的负担。

（三）应用实施中的障碍

FSB 司法管辖区也强调了进一步应用和实施 LEI 的各种障碍，并列于表8，其中最值得注意的部分摘要如下：

1. LEI 覆盖范围不足。10 个司法管辖区报告指出，LEI 覆盖范围不足是使用 LEI 所遇到的障碍之一，一些国家和地区（加拿大、欧盟、法国、印度、意大利）特别指出，国外交易对手方 LEI 缺失会导致报告制度中的一些问题。其他管辖区（欧盟、中国、新加坡）则分别将 LEI 在母公司、基金和国际分支机构的覆盖不足视为障碍。但是，也有一些管辖区（中国香港、日本、墨西哥、瑞士）认为 LEI 覆盖率并不是障碍，特别是在 MiFID Ⅱ（英国）实施之后。

---

① ISDA 和 GFMA 指出，"银行履行尽职调查是 KYC 流程的一部分，LOU 作为 LEI 发行流程的一部分发挥同样作用。作为客户入职和其他尽职调查程序的一部分，金融公司通常需要利用外部来源来核实关于客户的信息，即使它们拥有客户的 LEI。如果监管机构允许依赖 LOU 尽职调查，LEI 的效用将会大大提高，并有助于简化客户入职流程"。参见 https://www.isda.org/a/brvEE/ISDA_GFMA_FSB – Peer – Review_LEI – Implementation_3 – October – 2018_FINAL_Public.pdf。

2. 第二层级数据缺失。① 许多管辖区和监管部门②指出，由于法人的 LEI 覆盖范围不足或缺乏相关信息，第二层级（关系）数据不足以满足他们的需要。加拿大指出，目前只有一小部分法人提交直接和最终的母公司数据，而本地系统对这些信息的证实程度也低于第一层级数据。中国指出，基金关系数据的不完整以致数据质量无法得到保证。③ 德国则把缺乏 G – SIFI 信息作为问题提出，而中国香港指出只有 10% ~ 20% 相关法人提交了关系数据。意大利表示，母公司缺失 LEI 会影响数据的可靠性。墨西哥则把国际分支机构中 LEI 应用情况的不一致（分支机构是否有自己的 LEI）视为一个挑战，而 ESMA 强调，在它的一些报告架构中，法人本该提交母公司 LEI，却错误提交了分支机构的 LEI，这凸显了将两个 LEI 进行可靠关联的重要性。英国和美国指出，与会计并表不同，控制关系的信息将更加实用，但同时也承认收集此类信息的难度。美国目前尚未获取任何合资企业或拥有互兼董事公司的信息。EU – EIOPA 提出基于 Solvency II 的方案可能对它们更加实用。美国商品期货交易委员会（CFTC）指出，缺乏非公开信息限制了数据的应用。④ 加拿大期望第二层级数据将有助于理解相互关联性，而美国认为，完善母公司数据将很有用。

附录 4c 显示，综合所有 FSB 成员的法人，仅有 6.2% 提供了

---

① "第一层级"数据指与 LEI 参考数据一起提供的名片信息，"第二层级"数据包括回答"谁拥有谁"问题的关系数据，例如其直接和最终会计并表母公司。

② 澳大利亚、巴西、加拿大、中国、欧盟当局、德国、中国香港、意大利、墨西哥、沙特阿拉伯、西班牙和英国。

③ LEI 体系监管委员会于 2018 年 11 月发行《全球 LEI 体系下，基金关联二次咨询文件》。

④ 商品期货交易委员会认为，选择性退出（不报告第二层级数据）情况的激增成为提高第二层级数据整体质量的最大障碍，并认为，LEI 体系下，修订第二层级数据标准，以减少允许选择性退出的情况，将有助于提高第二层级数据的整体质量。

最终母公司信息，低于日本和整个欧盟以及欧盟的 FSB 成员（法国除外）的水平。11 名 FSB 成员①中，提供最终母公司信息的比例超过 14%，但这 11 个成员的 LEI 数量都较小（低于 6000 个），且在 LEI 管理方面监管要求往往较少，这可能是因为在这些国家或地区，拥有 LEI 的公司往往是大型集团的子公司。

法人不向 GLEIS（基于 GLEIF 数据——见附录 4c）报告母公司信息的理由因司法管辖区不同而有显著变化。自要求报告母公司信息以来，法人没有及时更新记录，成为美国和俄罗斯母公司信息缺失的首要原因，估计会对两国大约 1/3 的记录造成影响（占 FSB 成员国总数据的 12%）。② 在澳大利亚和巴西，缺乏母公司的许可是目前机构无法报送母公司信息的最重要原因，涉及约 1/3 的机构（尽管仅占全 FSB 所有成员总数据的 9%）。该问题在美国也很显著（影响 22% 的记录）。不到 1% 的 FSB 成员的机构提到了其他法律障碍，而且其在每个成员国的比例都低于 10%。③ 在没有对 LEI 进行监管的国家，或者近期才监管的国家（阿根廷、中国、印度尼西亚和南非存在 10% ~ 20% 的 LEI），母公司信息未报送的主要原因之一是母公司没有 LEI。其他原因是没有母公司符合 GLEIS 关于财务并表的定义，例如在印度（占 LEI 的 54%）和意大利（占 LEI 的 39%），高比例的法人由自然人控制；在荷兰（占拥有 LEI 的 78%）和西班牙（占 LEI 的 84%），控股母公司不

---

① 阿根廷、中国、中国香港、印度尼西亚、韩国、墨西哥、俄罗斯、沙特阿拉伯、新加坡和南非。

② 这些案件载于附录 4c，列在 "No parent reported and no exception given" 一栏下。

③ 其他情况是指在具有约束力的法律承诺中明确不披露信息，不披露的原因主要是考虑到披露将带来不利影响或者不利影响不能被排查，以及其他法律障碍。这些情况与未获同意的情况在附录 4c 中一并提出。

接受财务并表（一般是投资机构或政府机构的情况）的比例非常高；在日本和德国，最显著的因素是没有母公司按照会计准则来控制法人（例如，一个上市机构拥有多种类型的股东）。

3. LEI 成本。成员对 LEI 成本的反馈意见不一，13 个受访成员[①]表示成本是实施 LEI 的障碍，而 10 个成员[②]表示成本并非障碍。其中，8 个受访成员[③]指出，LEI 涉及的申请与续期费用可能会对小型法人形成障碍。一些受访成员指出，尤其是金融行业以外的法人，在分析成本效益[④]时，更关注现有流程和控制等方面（如注册上线、信用评估、KYC），但 LEI 在充分实施后所产生的新功能和新特性（如数字身份、商业智能合同等）以及相应带来的好处则没被考虑进去。而且，这些好处的兑现依赖于 LEI 更全面的应用，因此也形成了长期激励作用。

LEI 成本相比过去已大幅下降，但成本效益分析仍倾向于采用 LEI 历史成本。例如，EBA 对于 LEI 的建议中考虑了当前的平均注册成本，即 2014 年初确定的首次注册费用 129 欧元和年度维护费 74 欧元。[⑤] 在 2015 年发布实施 SBSR 法规时，SEC 也考虑了当时注册 LEI 的成本估计为 220 美元，另有每年 120 美元的维护费（可能是按美国市场估计，因此与欧盟的估值有所不同，欧盟的估值考虑了在欧洲专营的本地系统收费情况）。[⑥] 截至 2019 年初，在

① 澳大利亚、巴西、欧盟—欧洲一体化组织、德国、印度尼西亚、意大利、日本、荷兰、新加坡、西班牙、瑞士、英国和美国。

② 加拿大、中国、欧盟—ESMA、欧盟—工代机构、法国、中国香港、印度、韩国、墨西哥和沙特阿拉伯。

③ 澳大利亚、巴西、德国、印度尼西亚、意大利、日本、韩国和西班牙。

④ 参见 https：//lei. info/portal/resources/lei – benefits/。

⑤ 参见 https：//eba. europa. eu/documents/10180/561173/EBA – REC – 2014 – 01 + %28Recommendation + on + the + use + of + the + Legal + Entity + Identifier%29. pdf。

⑥ 参见 https：//www. sec. gov/rules/final/2015/34 – 74244. pdf。

大多数司法管辖区的一些本地系统仅收取少于 50 美元的维护费。考虑到随着 GLEIS 的稳步扩张，特别是正在考虑的监管要求将带来更高的 LEI 发放数量和续期数量，费用有可能进一步下调。因此，即使推广 LEI 这项工作并不容易，但仍值得继续开展。

在成本—效益分析中应避免重复计算成本。在上面的案例中，EBA 和 SEC 都考虑到许多法人受制于其他监管对 LEI 的强制要求申请了 LEI 或自行申请了 LEI，这些都降低了新规定带来的成本。

法人的管理负担也是一项相关成本。例如，在对美国掉期数据记录（Swap Data Recordkeeping）和报告要求（Reporting Requirements）[1] 的成本效益分析中，评估第一层级和第二层级参考数据报告需要两个小时。部分 LOU 争取缩短获取 LEI 的时间，例如，他们使用从工商注册机构自动提取的数据预先填充表单。[2] 监管部门确保国家工商注册数据易于检索，从而降低推广 LEI 的行政成本。

各司法管辖区还指出，成本投入和缺乏可见的效益，是让那些了解 LEI 的市场参与者主动应用 LEI 的最主要的阻碍因素（见下文对私营部门观点的讨论）。

4. 存在其他机构编码。一些司法管辖区（澳大利亚、巴西、加拿大、德国、中国香港、印度尼西亚、意大利、韩国、荷兰、新加坡、西班牙、瑞士、土耳其以及欧盟的 EBA）和一些私营部门的受访者表示，其他机构识别编码的存在对于 LEI 实施是一个障碍——尤其是那些无成本或低成本的国家级编码以及配套系统

---

① 参见 https：//www. govinfo. gov/content/pkg/FR－2012－01－13/pdf/2011－33199. pdf，p.41。

② 例如，https：//rapidlei. com/，一些 LOU 也是工商登记机构。

（见附录2）。这些编码的存在也降低了各管辖区推动强制使用 LEI 的积极性，[1] 特别是企业开展有限跨境业务的市场。有两个管辖区（德国和瑞典）指出，此类其他编码可能不会成为障碍，因为它们可以与 LEI 一起使用，并与其建立适当的关联；而另外一些司法管辖区（意大利、西班牙、法国）认为，只有当本地系统向 GLEIF 数据库正确地报告了登记机关的机构 ID（Registration Authority Entity ID）信息（强制性的），才有可能建立这些联系。目前，一部分 LOU 似乎并未遵守这一义务；如果 GLEIF 不能很快解决这个问题，那么这将成为 LEI 使用的一个严重障碍。在此背景下，一些利益相关方还指出，欧洲在"关于公司法中数字工具和程序的使用"的提议[2]中提出的发行公司及其分支机构的欧洲唯一编码，可能会在无意中与全球 LEI 倡议产生竞争，或转移对 LEI 的注意力。

表8 实施 LEI 的障碍

问题	障碍（%）	无障碍（%）	其他或空白（%）
LEI 覆盖率低是否是 LEI 应用的一个障碍？	55	17	28
母公司关系数据的可用性是否满足使用需要？	55	17	28
成本是否是实施 LEI 的障碍？	45	34	21
现有的其他识别编码的存在是否是实施或使用 LEI 的障碍？	41	41	17
是否有超过会计并表中母公司关系数据的需求？	28	38	34
是否有其他 LEI 实施的障碍？	28	34	38

---

① 例如，参见 2017 年 4 月巴西 FSB 同行评估报告（http：//www.fsb.org/2017/04/peer – review – of – brazil /）。

② 关于在公司法中使用数字工具和流程，请参见欧洲议会和理事会关于修改指令（EU）2017/1132 的提案（https：//eur – lex.europa.eu/legal – content/ EN/ TXT/？URI = COM%3A2018%3A239%3AFIN）。

续表

问题	障碍（%）	无障碍（%）	其他或空白（%）
是否有其他与关系数据的可用性有关的问题？	24	38	38
LEI 的数据质量是否对 LEI 应用构成障碍？	21	52	28
LEI 数据中是否有相关信息未被捕捉？	17	45	38
LEI 失效率是否对 LEI 应用构成障碍？	14	62	24

（四）私营部门关于实施 LEI 的用途、效益与障碍的意见（见附录5）

市场人士表示，LEI 在场外衍生品市场的广泛应用，以及在证券市场上的较好应用，是一项相当大的成就。大型金融机构认为 LEI 有利于它们自身的业务办理。LEI 使这些机构受益的主要机制是：通过 LEI 可以减少手工核对法人数据的成本，否则，名称的使用、不同语言和字符集的翻译或音译、或其他识别编码的多重性会使这项工作变得复杂。LEI 还有利于法人信息的获取。

具体而言，LEI 通过以下方式减少了法人身份识别与验证的相关成本：

● 减少对同一法人进行多次重复尽职调查的可能性。

● 更易于有关法人得到充分识别并确保拥有最新的合同文件，特别是在交易中包括 LEI 的情况下，更容易及时识别修改合同中需要更新的内容。

● 提供与国家工商注册机构的映射，使得获取工商注册数据更加容易。据行业协会估计，每位客户可节省近 30 分钟的时间。①

● 促进集团结构信息的管理。例如，花旗集团在 GLEIS 中登

---

① 参见 ISDA 和 GFMA 对 FSB 实施 LEI 专题同行评估的文献，https：//www.isda.org/a/brvEE/ISDA_GFMA_FSB－Peer－Review_LEI－Implementation_3－October－2018_final_public.pdf。

记了其按美国公认会计准则（GAAP）并表的直接和最终母公司以及集团结构中所有机构，总计约 700 个 LEI，并有规程保持数据更新，其客户、交易对手方和其他利益相关方均可受益。花旗集团还在中央客户主数据中收录了其他机构的层级信息，从而可以看到其他公司的会计并表公司的层次结构。

● 当监管政策变化只影响某些特定法人时，更容易确定是哪一个法人需要更新合同。行业协会列举了对非集中清算衍生品保证金要求的案例：即如果法律文件中使用了 LEI，金融机构就更容易确定哪些 ISDA 协议中哪些内容需要重新编制。

LEI 还能够通过以下方式帮助市场参与者管理风险：

● 通过使用全球一致且唯一的编码，有利于同一跨境交易对手方（或对手方集团）风险敞口的汇聚。

● 减少操作风险，例如在结算指令中使用 LEI，可避免对其指示的法人产生歧义。

● 监测适用于单个法人的限制和适用于某些法人交易的各种限制（如减少必须通过手动消除的错误警报）。

LEI 还支持直接处理，避免了客户延迟。如果将其应用于支付报文，LEI 还能支持对制裁清单的信息筛选。

由于 LEI 可以降低客户识别的成本，以及资本和债务证券中后台系统处理的成本，麦肯锡和 GLEIF 评估认为，如果全球采用

LEI 可以在投资银行业每年节省超过 1.5 亿美元。[①] 正如第 4 节所述，LEI 在这一领域的覆盖率已经很高，但是要完全获得这些收益，还需要所有交易对手方都使用 LEI，而不仅仅是规模较大的对手方。该研究还评估认为在银行签发信用证方面可节省高达 5 亿美元的成本。另一项研究评估了 GLEIS 的私有收益（在降低成本或增加收入方面的直接净利润）主要来自在基本运营流程中实施 LEI，该收益每年超过 10 亿美元。[②]

然而，市场参与者自愿采用 LEI 的一个主要障碍是在可见成本与可见收益之间缺乏对应关系。特别是一些同行评估的私营行业受访者认为，大型金融机构（如负有报告义务的机构）是最大的受益方，而所有法人因其必须缴纳 LEI 的注册与续期费用而增加了成本。以本地客户为主的小型法人从 LEI 中看到的收益较少，这是因为它们使用 LEI 进行的交易量较小，或者对全球唯一识别编码的需求较少。

市场参与者所报告的许多其他问题，与 FSB 司法管辖区所描述的类似。这些问题包括：覆盖率不足（如缺乏监管强制要求影响了覆盖率和续期率）；不同司法管辖区在时间和范围要求上存在差异；关系数据访问困难；失效 LEI 的比例高。

- 对 LEI 的认识正在增强，但主要是来自监管部门的强制推

---

① 参见麦肯锡和 GLEIF，《法人编码：交易对手唯一 ID 的价值》（2017 年 10 月），https：//www. gleif. org/en/lei – olutions/mckinsy – company – GLEIF – create – business Value – with – lei。该报告估计，将 LEI 引入资本市场和证券交易处理，可以将年度交易处理和上市成本降低 10%。这将导致整个资本市场运营成本降低 3.5%，仅全球投资银行业每年就可节省逾 1.5 亿美元。这并不包括实施 LEI 的成本，该成本可能包括一次性成本首次发行及在系统和流程中引入 LEI 和年度成本（LEI 维护费）。

② Ka Kei Chan 和 Alistair Milne，《全球法人识别系统：如何交付?》，《风险与财务管理》杂志，2019 年 3 月 7 日，https：//www. mdpi. com/1911 – 8074/12/1/39/htm。

动。因此，他们认为强制要求是提高 LEI 使用率的必要、首选的方法。

● 相关机构一致认为，不同司法管辖区在时间和范围要求上的差异可能会使 LEI 的应用更加复杂。LEI 的许多用途（如监管报告、审慎监管风险评估、金融机构处置和金融稳定工作，以及 AML/CFT 客户识别）不仅要求被监管的法人需要拥有 LEI，而且要求其国内外交易对手方也拥有 LEI。然而，交易对手方的主要监管部门可能并不要求他们拥有 LEI。事实上，并非所有监管部门都能够在其必要的管辖范围内强制要求法人使用 LEI，虽然在某些情况下，如果其他监管机构也要求使用 LEI，则可以在有限范围内强制要求使用 LEI。① 一些监管部门往往仅在法人已经拥有 LEI 或自愿的情况下才要求使用 LEI。正如前面讨论的，LEI 应用的受益和成本付出缺乏对应关系阻碍了参与者自愿采用 LEI，特别是当其认为大型金融机构（如负有报告义务的机构）是最大的受益方，而各法人因缴纳 LEI 注册和续期费用而增加了成本时。

关于 LEI 失效比例较高的问题，一些利益相关方担心有关参考数据的长期维护问题，并指出跨监管机构和司法管辖区对续期的指导和要求不统一，会导致跨监管机构和司法管辖区运营的法人面对不同的监管要求（见第 3 节）。来自公众的反馈建议包括：强制使用 LEI，对于在覆盖率低的领域需要监管机构与行业共同合作加强教育，在更大范围内使用 LEI（包括税收），将更多额外的

---

① 例如，在欧盟大量的区域级部门规则的实施取得了良好的覆盖率。欧盟是唯一强制所有金融工具发行商使用 LEI 的地区。截至 2018 年 10 月 17 日，非欧盟金融工具发行商覆盖率大约达到 60%（217000 个金融工具发行商已有 LEI，147000 个没有），如果把欧盟金融工具考虑进去，覆盖率要高得多，共有 900 万个金融工具发行商已使用 LEI。

数据元素增加到 GLEIS，减少成本和重复处理（特别是与其他编码共同使用时），解决 LEI 失效的问题以及 LEI 在新领域推广使用过程中，公共部门与私人机构之间要加强合作。

在下一节中，我们将讨论解决这些挑战的方法。

六、推动 LEI 实施的下一步计划

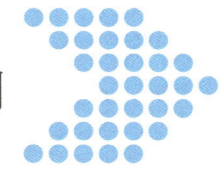

通过成员机构的反馈、LEI 数据分析以及与相关干系机构的讨论，我们发现主要有三个共同挑战需要解决：

●除证券和 OTC 衍生品市场以外，跨司法管辖区的 LEI 使用情况一直不均衡，并且使用率很低。

●LEI 覆盖率仍然太低，不足以鼓励监管领域的进一步应用，尚未达到市场参与者自愿采用 LEI 从而推动 LEI 更广泛应用的临界点。

●进一步使用和实施 LEI 的其他障碍，包括 LEI 业务模式、内容和流程。

对于第一个挑战，我们认为，并非所有司法管辖区或市场参与者都有相同的需求。因为就算 LEI 覆盖全球，能够减少对多种编码的维护需求，某些司法管辖区/市场在使用 LEI 时也并不能从中获益，因为它们已经花大力气建设了国内识别编码。因此，应把工作重点放在那些将从 LEI 更广泛应用中获益最大的领域和市场，会更加有益。

SSB 可支持确定从 LEI 统筹实施中受益最大的领域，并提出适当的时间表。在身份识别方面，OTC 衍生品已经开始应用了，尽管一些监管机构还没有强制要求在报给交易报告库的数据中使用 LEI 来识别所有法人。① 例如，在时间表方面，2017 年 12 月 FSB 建议成员在 2020 年底前实施唯一交易识别码（UTI，该编码中将嵌入 LEI）。② 除了要求 LEI 作为即将发布的 UTI 的一个组成部分外，CPMI – IOSCO《关键数据要素技术指南》还建议在向 OTC 衍生品交易报告库报送数据时，使用 LEI 作为法人的识别编码。

● FSB 司法管辖区应跟进 CPMI – IOSCO 指南，该指南大力鼓励监管部门提出要求，在向 OTC 衍生品交易报告库报送的数据中应使用 LEI 作为法人的识别编码（建议 1a）。

然而，虽然 SSB 在其特定领域的政策制定中包含了 LEI，但在大多数情况下（AML/CFT、风险数据整合和代理银行业务），LEI 是选择性使用的，SSB 并未提出 LEI 应用的时间表。例如，根据 CPMI 和 FSB 关于代理银行业务的建议，③ 跨境电汇是监管部门和行业大力支持用 LEI 识别发起人和收款人的一个领域。对 "筛选出受到资产冻结或其他制裁的法人的支付报文" 这项操作来说，LEI 将提高其可靠性和成本效益。这样就能更多地为合规性监控提供支持，并且降低延迟支付的风险，使各种规模的公司都能从 LEI 中真正获益。CPMI 建议 "应在当前相关支付报文中可选择性地使

---

① 见 2018 年 4 月 CPMI – IOSCO《重要 OTC 衍生品的数据元素（除 UTI 和 UPI）协调技术指南》。CPMI 和 IOSCO 认为报送给 TRs 的 OTC 衍生品交易中使用统一 LEI，对于报送给 TRsOTC 的衍生品交易实现全球一致性和有意义的汇总至关重要。因此，CPMI 和 IOSCO 强烈鼓励有关部门要求使用 GLEIF 发布的 LEI 来识别向 TRs 报告的数据中的法人。第 2.7 和 2.8 节明确规定，有资格获得 LEI 的交易对手方不允许使用 LEI 以外的值。阿根廷、巴西、中国、印度尼西亚、沙特阿拉伯和南非尚未在衍生品报告中使用 LEI。澳大利亚、中国香港、日本、韩国、墨西哥、俄罗斯、新加坡和瑞士在某些情况下请求或要求使用 LEI，但还没有要求所有符合 LEI 条件的实体使用 LEI（包括无须报告的交易对手方），即使他们确实还没有 LEI（除以商业身份行事的自然人外）。

② 参见 FSB 报告：《关于唯一交易识别码（UTI）的治理安排：结论和实施计划》（2017 年 12 月）。

③ 参见 2018 年 11 月《FSB 评估和应对代理银行业务下滑行动计划：G20 峰会进展报告》和 2016 年 7 月 CPMI《代理银行——最终报告》。

用 LEI 作为支付报文中的附加信息，而且，作为未来可能向基于 ISO 20022 标准的报文格式迁移的一部分，鼓励相关机构（ISO 和 SWFIT）考虑开发专用代码或数据项，以便将 LEI 包含在这些支付报文中"。

在支付报文中嵌入 LEI 等事项即将完成，这为制定支付报文中应用 LEI 的国际时间表提供了良好契机。SWIFT 委员会建议，应从 2021 年 11 月开始将代理银行支付报文迁移到 ISO 20022 标准，并指出 LEI 正在纳入 ISO 20022 标准的过程中。该迁移时间表可能为业界在支付报文中选择性应用 LEI 提供契机。FSB 与其代理银行协调小组的其他成员以及诸如沃尔夫斯堡集团（Wolfsberg Group）、支付市场实务规范工作组（PMPG）①、LEI ROC 和 GLEIF 等行业机构合作，对其使用 LEI 的效率和收益进行记录跟踪，以此来确定目前在 GLEIS 中或通过 GLEIS 获得的信息是否足以协助尽职调查，以及是否存在应优先考虑使用 LEI 的法人类型。同样重要的是，因为可能涉及大量不断更新的 LEI 数据，该报告也建议 LEI 发行和维护过程中的任何改进都应及时考虑 ISO 20022 的迁移。如英国在最近的磋商中所设想的那样，及时提供有关法人因开展此类改进使 LEI 成本可能降低的信息十分重要，特别是某些司法管辖区考虑在支付领域使用 LEI。FSB 将通过与 SSB 和行业机构合作，促进在支付报文中有效实施 LEI 选项，以帮助解决代理

---

① 在其 2017 年 11 月的讨论报告《支付市场的 LEI 编码》中（https：//www. swift. com/about - us/community/swift - advisory - groups/payments - market - practice - group/document - centre/document - centre），PMPG 指出，"对合规和风险管理职能来说，使用 LEI 能清楚识别发起方和受益方（因此各方具有更多的透明度），可以在战略上带来重大的定量和定性效益"，例如，"消除付款处理过程中可能出现的延误，避免在合规和制裁筛查中出现虚假打击；优化和更准确地反洗钱控制、可疑活动检测、识别订货和受益客户的能力，为代理银行在支付链中充当中间人提供了有用的信息。"

银行关系数量下降的问题（建议 2c）。

LEI 可以支持 FSB 实现许多监管目标。在适当的情况下，当监管部门必须处理破产金融机构及其所有相关法人时，LEI 可以有助于数据的及时处理。此外，LEI 还可在金融创新相关的问题中发挥作用，如 RegTech 和 Suptech。[①]

● FSB 还将探讨 LEI 在其工作中的潜在作用，例如在金融机构处置方案和金融创新问题方面的作用（建议 2a）。

● 一般而言，相关 SSB（BCBS、IAIS、CPMI、IOSCO）和国际组织（IMF、OECD、世界银行）应评估并考虑如何在其政策和实施工作中纳入或加强对 LEI 的应用，以促进主管监管部门和市场参与者应用 LEI。例如，指导法人将 LEI 纳入其数据披露中，以及促进 LEI 在证券交易和跨境支付中的使用（建议 3）。

市场参与者已经确定了几个 LEI 能够产生收益的领域，这些领域不一定与监管用途有关。其中一些新用途与数字化经济转型有关，在这种情况下，准确识别非面对面交易者身份以及有效管理大量数据至关重要，例如：

● LEI 能够支持法人数据更有效地披露，这些数据根据广泛接受的标准进行了结构化处理，易于在自动化流程中使用，而不是以文本形式提供。在法人披露数据中引入 LEI 能够使这些披露具

---

① RegTech 系指金融科技在监管、合规要求以及接受监管金融机构报告等方面的任何应用。它也可以指提供此类应用的公司。此外，它与"SupTech"（监管机构对金融科技的使用）有密切联系。

有可操作性。① 例如，在 XBRL（可扩展商业报告语言）② 分类标准中引入 LEI，将有助于法人在监管报告、商业登记、财务披露、税务报告、合规性、智能合约和数字识别编码等领域实现其引用方式的标准化。在分类标准中加入 LEI 将鼓励 XBRL 用户使用 LEI 识别法人。另一种可能的应用是，电子财务报表用 LEI 识别报表发布机构及所有相关机构，出具报表证明的审计师和接收报表的监管部门的电子签名中也包括 LEI。市场主管部门、IOSCO 和市场监管部门可以和会计师事务所、行业机构一道促进 LEI 在这方面的应用，例如在使用 IFRS③（国际财务报告准则）分类标准中编制结构化报告时。LEI 与其他编码（如 BIC 和最近的 ISIN）之间建立的映射可用性，④ 有助于 LEI 成为访问多源法人数据的核心，同时应当鼓励 GLEIF 及其映射伙伴的工作。根据对 ISDA 和 GFMA 少数成员的调查，在排除私有专用编码后，LEI 参考数据中包含的商业登记编号等映射都是金融机构最常需要的映射。⑤ 一些 FSB 成员鼓励将供应商编码映射到 LEI（见附录 6）。

---

① 见美国证券交易委员会投资者利益代表人 Rick A. Fleming，2016 年 10 月 24 日的演讲《用智能数据改进披露》，https：//www. sec. gov/news/speech/improving – disclosure – with – smart – data. html。

② 大约 70 个国家使用 XBRL，142 项授权覆盖了 2000 万家公司。参见 https：//www. xbrl. org/the – standard/what/taxonomies/。

③ 例如，CFA 研究所表示，所有公司都应维护并上报注册人及其主要子公司的 LEI，因为这将提高投资者识别和分析注册人及其子公司风险的能力。然而，即使目前只进行 LEI 上报这个初始操作，也将有利于市场，并给注册者带来的负担最小。CFA 研究所还希望，在整个报告中应使用 LEI，以帮助投资者。例如，一家公司在提及另一个法人时，应要求其使用适当的 LEI。参见 https：//blogs. cfainstitute. org/marketintegrity/2018/01/23/requiring – the – use – of – the – legal – entity – identifier/。

④ 第一个 ISIN 映射于 2019 年 4 月开始发布，尽管这些映射最初只覆盖了几个编号机构。参见 https：//www. anna – web. org/standards/lei/。

⑤ 根据 GFMA 和 ISDA 对其 21 名成员的调查，2/3 的情况下 LEI 映射到内部生成的机构识别编码或由交易报告库分配的代码（LEI 除外），大约一半的情况下 LEI 映射到 BIC。大约 20% 的情况使用 ISIN 映射 LEI，与此比例类似的是，使用工商登记编号和税号映射 LEI。

● LEI 可用于支撑更加安全的线上交易。LEI 已经开始包含在数字证书中，[①] 数字证书越来越普遍地成为安全网站和电子交易的一个主要特征。数字证书通常引用法人的名称，这意味着，由于证书的各要素之间有加密链接，当法人名称变更时（或合并时），证书也需要随之变更。[②] LEI 可以避免这个问题，它允许将法人使用的所有证书与法人标识上的参考数据进行可靠连接。与之相关的是，与报告库级别的安全应用相比，文档的签名和加密能够提供更小粒度（如文档或披露）级别的安全应用，这可以提高备案平台和相关注册人备案的安全性。这就需要 GLEIS 提供最新的、高质量法人标识数据，同时对使用 LEI 的法人来说，定期做好数据确认工作也将获得更为切实的收益。

● LEI 可以促进贸易的无缝处理，包括贸易融资、发票开具以及海关报告合规。LEI 将为金融机构及其业务客户提供完整、集成的审计跟踪。例如，麦肯锡和 GLEIF 已经说明了 LEI 在贸易融资中的好处。[③] 从行业角度来看，如果包括海关部门在内的所有参与者都统一使用这个编码，那么 LEI 在贸易中的好处将会更大。目前拥有 LEI 的法人很可能包含了大多数进出口商（当前拥有 LEI 的法人可能与进出口商群体大量重叠），因为进出口商经常使用衍生工具对冲风险，而这些衍生工具需遵守包含 LEI 的监管报告要求。至少，将 LEI 与交易中使用的其他编码进行映射，可以避免手工对账，从而支持更高效的数据管理。

---

① 例如，参见 InfoCert（https：//infocert. digital/）。

② 关于这一问题的讨论，以及"在公司详细信息发生变化后更改数字证书，是如何成为成本和风险的可能来源"问题，参见《为什么证书颁发机构部门应采用法人识别编码》，第二部分，https：//www. ubisecure. com/legal－entity－identifier－lei/lei－is－live－legal－entity－data/。

③ 参见麦肯锡和 GLEIF，法人编码：唯一对手方 ID（同上）的值。

LEI ROC 和 GLEIF 应当与行业和公共部门合作，通过编制现有用案例，或支持有前景的新用途试点项目和研究项目等方式，提高公众对 LEI 的认识，以进一步鼓励机构自愿使用 LEI（建议 4c）。

另一个需要解决的挑战是，LEI 覆盖率仍然太低，无法有效支持某些监管用途，或无法获取整个市场高覆盖率带来的效益。正如 FSB 在其 2012 年报告中所强调的，随着越来越多的参与方获得 LEI，整个体系带来的好处也在不断增加。然而，在 LEI 启动初期，与其他网络产品的例子一样，激励潜在的先行者申请 LEI 的措施不足，并且决策者无法全面考虑到应用 LEI 给第三方带来的好处（正外部性）。推动 LEI 应用的一种方法是将工作重点放在全球金融体系中发挥核心作用的某些法人群体上，以使收益最大化。例如，虽然所有全球系统重要性银行（G–SIBs）的母公司都有一个 LEI 编码，但其大多数子公司或主要交易对手方却并非如此。这既阻碍了这些公司之间的相互关联和常见共同风险的分析，也阻碍了这些公司在进行方案规划时使用 LEI。

● 为此，FSB 将与 SSB 和行业机构合作，推动 G–SIFIs 的所有集团法人和主要交易对手以及中央对手方（CCP）的清算成员及其集团母公司采用 LEI，以支持对风险敞口和相互依赖性的及时分析（建议 2b）。

● 出于同样的原因，FSB 成员应考虑在报告或披露框架中要求使用和及时更新 LEI，以便识别主要金融集团的所有机构、更大范围的金融市场参与者和基础设施、其交易对手和相关机构（包括直接和最终母公司），尤其是在跨境的情况下（建议 1b）。

● FSB 成员还应探索促进进一步应用 LEI 的措施，例如，制定全国性的实施战略，以最大限度地发挥 LEI 的跨部门效益；通过公共交流活动，宣传 LEI 的好处；通过案例引导中央银行和其他公共部门机构，特别是公共债务发行方使用 LEI；在引入新的编码之前先考虑使用 LEI 的潜力（建议 1c）。

推进 LEI 应用实施的其他阻碍还涉及 LEI 的内容、流程和业务模式。

首先，许多公共部门用户认为关系数据的可用性不足。[①] 为提高覆盖率而采取的措施，特别是针对母公司的措施，将有助于解决这一问题。LEI ROC 和 GLEIF 可以推动母公司报送报告，在法人和集团层级引入确认关系数据完整性的标志，并与相关机构（如 OECD 和 BIS）合作，将制定识别集团公司（如大型跨国企业）关系的标准作为优先考虑的目标，以及开展自愿采用 LEI 的推广活动或制定可能适用于这些集团的新法规。

此外，收集更多关系数据（除会计并表、基金/集合投资工具和分支机构之外的信息）将扩大 LEI 的用途。例如，有关受益人所有的信息将会对 AML/CFT 有所帮助，也有助于编制基于最终投资国的外商直接投资统计数据。机构负责人的信息还将有助于 AML/CFT 和数字签名。通过数字签名，该签名与负责人所代表的法人之间的联系得以建立。行业部门信息将有助于交易监控，并在 IMF 的协调证券组合调查中，促进证券持有人和发行人的信息交换。然而，一些利益相关方担心，如果在全球 LEI 体系中增加更多信息，LEI 编码的发布和续期也将变得更加复杂。解决这一问题的一种方案是，在某些情况下，由第三方发布 LEI 数据，这样

---

① 第 5 节中强调的一些障碍表明，为了完善关系数据，可能需要采取几种途径，例如，使母公司更容易同意披露数据，或包括机密信息的收集；增加母公司机构的 LEI 覆盖率；记录除会计并表定义以外的其他定义关系，包括与自然人之间的关系。

可以更容易地检索数据，也无须将所有数据元素都包含在 GLEIS 数据库中并由 LOU 验证。在添加某些关系数据等保密信息时，可以与 GLEIS 之外的其他来源进行连接。①

● LEI ROC 和 GLEIF 应通过以下方式增强第二层级（关系）数据的范围和可用性：

▷考虑以经济、有效、可靠的方式添加可以增加 LEI 价值的关系数据（例如，有访问权限和适当控制的保密关系数据，受益所有人，母公司的其他定义）（建议 4d. i）。

▷扩大此类数据的覆盖范围，例如针对大型跨国公司开展有针对性的 LEI 推广活动，并推动其集团机构的母公司报送关系数据报告（建议 4d. ii）。

另一个问题与数据质量有关。虽然只有约 20% 的监管当局认为数据质量是一个问题（见第 5 节），并且问卷反馈指出，LEI 的数据质量优于许多其他数据源，但是，LEI 的数据质量仍在许多方面需要改进：例如提供的注册地址经常与总部地址相同，并且对用于确定法人司法管辖区的"域"，尚未达成共识。失效 LEI 的比例也是一个关注点，因为信息可能已经过时了。行业参与者还建议监管部门加大力度强制要求 LEI 续期。LEI ROC 可持续跟踪关于 LEI 参考数据更新的相关明确要求及鼓励编码续期的措施，并将此加入 LEI 监管规则清单。

● LEI ROC 和 GLEIF 应考虑加强数据质量流程管理（包括鼓

---

① FSB 在 2012 年已经指出，GLEIS "一些国家针对具有潜在重要性的参考数据制定了保密和隐私限制要求，对这些限制要求所涵盖的数据，还必须提供适当保护，特别是关于公司关系和所有权结构的信息"。见 http：//www.fsb.org/2012/06/fsb－report－global－legal－entity－identifier－for－financial－markets。LEI ROC 的目标之一是确保 "机密数据得到保护，并适当考虑任何可行的数据保护立法" ［LEC ROC 章程第 2（a）（1）（iii）条］。

励和监控 LEI 参考数据更新的流程），增强 LEI 数据可靠性，从而提高数据对于市场参与者和监管部门的可用性（建议 4b）。

另一个关键问题是当前的业务模式不能使参与者在 LEI 使用的收益成本完全匹配。一些学术文献已经指出，不需要监管强制要求，"净利润回报是应用的最有力理由"，并与 GS1 条形码采用情况进行比较①："各个公司在应用和使用这些标准时有强烈的私人动机，因为不采用这些标准，它们就不能作为供应商或客户参与全球供应。"该体系的运行不需要监管强制要求。LEI 必须为批发金融市场的参与者提供类似效益。②

• LEI ROC 和 GLEIF 应考虑改进 LEI 业务模式，以降低机构申请和维护 LEI 编码的成本和管理负担，例如调整财务方法使用户收益和成本更加匹配，探索如何促进 LEI 发展维护与涉及类似任务的其他流程之间的互补（如颁发国内编码和数字证书、金融机构的客户尽职调查等）（建议 4a）。

最后，可以最大限度地减少 GLEIS 的活动与市场参与者类似业务之间的潜在重复。例如，允许银行对 LEI 记录上的客户信息进行验证（他们为满足监管要求已经在开展相关工作），或与工商登记机构进行更大程度地整合（例如，他们已经要求报送名称和地址的变更）。这将改进（而不是取代）当前的业务模式，例如，LOU 可以将一些验证工作外包给银行，而有些 LOU 已经成为工商注册机构。此外，国家类型和法人类型不尽相同，各种业务模式可能会并存。

---

① 参见 https：//www.gs1.org/standards/barcodes。

② Ka Kei Chan 和 Alistair Milne，《全球法人识别编码体系：如何交付?》，《风险与财务管理》杂志，2019 年 3 月 7 日，https：//www.mdpi.com/1911 – 8074/12/1/39/htm。

附录1：报告所述 FSB 司法管辖区成员金融当局的英文缩写

澳大利亚

ASIC   澳大利亚证券和投资委员会

欧盟

EBA   欧洲银行管理局

ECB   欧洲中央银行

EIOPA   欧洲保险和职业养老金管理局

ESMA   欧洲证券和市场管理局

SRB   欧洲单一处理委员会

中国香港

HKMA   香港金融管理局

SFC   香港证券及期货事务监察委员会

印度

RBI   印度储备银行

日本

JFSA   日本金融服务管理局

韩国

FSC   韩国金融服务委员会

新加坡

MAS   新加坡金融监管局

美国

CFTC   美国商品期货交易委员会

FDIC   联邦存款保险公司

FRB   美国联邦储备委员会

FSOC   美国金融稳定监管委员会

OFR   美国金融研究办公室

SEC   美国证券交易委员会

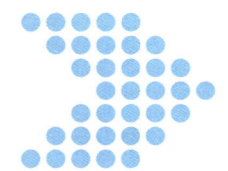

附录2：各司法管辖区使用的非 LEI 识别编码

除 LEI 以外，各司法管辖区还使用了多种识别编码。一些司法管辖区（如巴西、法国、意大利、瑞士、土耳其和西班牙）已拥有一种全国性的主要识别编码，覆盖了所有或大多数法人，而且用途很广。其他一些司法管辖区有多种识别编码，但没有明确的"主要"识别编码（如印度、沙特阿拉伯和美国）。

这些识别编码通常没有与 LEI 进行链接，但也有一些例外。例如，ECB 最近建立的细粒度信贷数据库（Anacredit）中的贷方和借方识别编码与其机构及分支机构注册数据库（RIAD）中的 LEI 建立了映射。EIOPA 的编码与 EIOPA 的参考数据库建立了法人层级的链接。在美国，OCC 已经将其许可证 ID、FDIC 证书号和美联储 RSSD 号映射到了对应金融机构的 LEI。与 LEI 建立映射可以访问更丰富的数据集。① 工商注册机构（机构注册中心）的法人识别编码（如适用）是 GLEIS 强制收集的数据项的一部分。然而，在 GLEIF 处理该问题的过程中，似乎各本地系统对"如适用"这一限定词的理解有所不同，进而导致了不同的做法。许多

---

① 例如，SEC 工作人员发布投资顾问信息报告，其中包含在 SEC 注册或作为免税报告顾问向 SEC 提交报告的投资顾问的信息，如果顾问有 LEI，LEI 包含在文件中。

FSB 成员认为，这种分歧所导致的国内识别编码不完全映射是一个重要的障碍，一些成员（如巴西）在 GLEIS 之外开发了自己的映射。巴西、德国、中国香港、西班牙、瑞士和美国则已将其他识别编码映射到了 LEI。

在外国司法管辖区注册或成立的机构使用的识别编码各不相同，包括专有识别编码和其他识别编码。最常用的一些识别编码分别是银行和账户使用的 BIC 和国际银行账号（IBAN）。欧洲监管当局提到了 LEI、Le（一种发给外国机构的国家识别编码）、金融监管部门专有编码和金融机构专有客户编码。交易报告库数据和 EMIR 数据使用了 LEI 和市场识别编码（MIC）。对于 EMIR 数据报送，一些市场参与者被要求在过渡时期接受 BIC，但分析显示，使用 BIC 报告的交易比例很小或可以忽略不计，而且这类交易中有很大一部分来自已经实施了 LEI 的司法管辖区。2017 年 11 月，欧盟要求衍生品报告普遍使用 LEI，此举导致约 13 万家法人中的 9362 个 BIC、国家编码和客户编码被替换。在俄罗斯，有 LEI、法人名称和税号。在美国，如果需要遵守外国法律，CFTC 允许报告使用隐私法识别编码（PLI），这是由报告对手方创建的专有客户编码。FDIC 使用法人的法定名称和原籍国家识别编码。在墨西哥和沙特阿拉伯，国外的法人则是通过公司章程或商业登记证的副本来识别的。

如果 LEI 能够在整个司法管辖区以及司法管辖区内的所有机构中得到更广泛的应用，那么许多识别编码都可以取消。一些已在用的识别编码正在被 LEI 替换或补充。

表 A2：已被 LEI 替换、将被 LEI 替换或已映射到 LEI 的识别编码

司法管辖区	已被替换/计划被替换的识别编码	已映射到 LEI 的识别编码	备注
巴西		全国法人注册中心（CNJP），国家税务局指定的唯一 ID 号	凡持有 LEI 的巴西机构必须将 LEI 纳入 CNJP
法国	BIC		LEI 完全取代了 BIC 编码，用于识别参与 MiFIR 监管范围内交易的投资公司
法国	CIB		2018 年 11 月，就 ACPR 报告使用 LEI 替换 CIB 一事征求了银行意见，预计将于 2020 年底实施
法国	SIREN		2018 年 10 月，就 ACPR 报告使用 LEI 替换 SIREN 一事征求了银行意见，预计 2020 年底实施
德国	中央信贷登记机构的债权人 ID 和借款人 ID		由德国央行映射
德国	RIAD 编码		由德国央行映射
中国香港	HKTR 会员编码		对于 OTC 衍生品交易报告，在刚开始强制实施 LEI 的第一阶段时（2019 年 4 月 1 日），HKMA 和 SFC 从《补充报告指引》（SRI）的识别编码优先级序列中删除了 HKTR 会员编码（其目前的优先级与 LEI 相同）
中国香港		HKTR 会员编码	TR 会员在 HKTR 登记时必须提供其所有的第三方编码（如有），并负责定期审查和更新这些识别编码。HKTR 将把所有这些第三方识别编码映射到 HKTR 系统对应的 LEI 上
西班牙	RIAD 中的所有识别编码（NIF、REN、BIC、RIAD）		NIF 是西班牙税务局提供的唯一法人识别编码。REN 是西班牙银行向金融机构提供的官方编码

续表

司法管辖区	已被替换/计划被替换的识别编码	已映射到 LEI 的识别编码	备注
瑞士		UID	当某个瑞士企业向联邦统计局（也管理 UID 注册中心）管理的瑞士本地系统申请 LEI 时，UID 编号会自动映射到 LEI。在发放 LEI 时，LOU 还可以通过将 UID 包含在参考数据中来实现映射
美国	CFTC 临时合规识别编码（CICI）		由于 CFTC 掉期交易数据报告规则先于 GLEIS 建立之前生效，因此掉期交易的对手方最初被要求使用 CICI 来识别。GLEIS 建立后，CFTC 就要求掉期交易对手方必须用 LEI 进行识别
美国		OCC 的许可证 ID、FDIC 的证书号，以及美联储的 RSSD 号	OCC 已将这些识别编码映射到相应金融机构的 LEI（如果银行/银行控股公司的财务报告提供了 LEI）

附录3：各司法管辖区的 LEI 实施战略

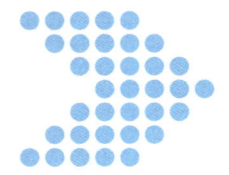

司法管辖区	战略特征			
	应用级别（国家级、超国家级、主管部门级）	实施方式	动机/目标	说明
澳大利亚	国家级	主管部门与金融机构和本地注册机构之间对话协商	促进机构层面交易数据的汇总，以评估和监控交易清算活动与重大风险	推动采用 LEI 的方式是：要求将 LEI 作为 OTC 交易报告的识别编码（AVID 或 BIC 作为备用），要求受监管机构按照市场诚信规则（证券市场）、清算规则和重大风险审慎标准规定报送的报告中将 LEI 作为必填项
巴西	国家级	主管部门间对话	为税务及其他国家主管部门提供信息	持有 LEI 的法人必须将其报送给国家注册机构
加拿大	国家级	主管部门间对话	促进机构层级的交易数据整合，以评估和监控不同机构之间的交易活动，促进机构之间互联	要求 OTC 衍生品、交易所交易衍生品、证券市场都使用 LEI

司法管辖区	战略特征			
	应用级别（国家级、超国家级、主管部门级）	实施方式	动机/目标	说明
中国	主管部门级（中国人民银行上海总部及部分市场基础设施管理机构，包括中国外汇交易中心/全国银行间同业拆借中心、上海清算所和中央国债登记结算有限责任公司）	主管部门与金融机构间对话和协商	防范宏观系统性金融风险，加强对参与中国市场的境外机构的识别	境外机构在报送债券市场准入记录系统（BMARS）、中国银行间债券市场（CIBM）、银行间市场金融衍生品CCP清算报告（从2020年开始）中需使用 LEI（如适用）
欧盟（EBA）	超国家级	欧盟决策程序	保障报告质量，更好地进行数据分析，以及便于进行风险分析	促进 LEI 使用
欧盟（ECB）	超国家级	欧盟决策程序	更好地进行数据分析	要求使用 LEI 来识别进入 RIAD 的机构
欧盟（EIOPA）	超国家级	欧盟决策程序	通过提升数据质量提高监管效率	促进 LEI 使用
欧盟（ESMA）	超国家级	利益相关方对话＋欧盟决策程序	实现所有 ESMA 授权的行业立法方式一致	对于 OTC 衍生品合约的金融和非金融对手方、进行金融工具交易的投资公司、交易平台、信用评级机构、中央证券存管结算内部机构，强制要求使用 LEI（即使该机构尚未注册 LEI）。上述机构报告的数据必须包括下列机构的 LEI

续表

司法管辖区	战略特征			
	应用级别（国家级、超国家级、主管部门级）	实施方式	动机/目标	说明
欧盟（ESMA）	超国家级	利益相关方对话＋欧盟决策程序	实现所有 ESMA 授权的行业立法方式一致	（即使该机构尚未注册 LEI）：投资公司的客户、CCPs、报告机构的中介机构和对手方、已授予信用评级的机构、金融工具发行人、参与 CSD 系统及结算银行的机构
中国香港	国家级	利益相关方对话	跟随国际趋势，有益于整体金融行业	自 2019 年 4 月起，分阶段强制要求在 OTC 衍生品交易报告中使用 LEI
印度	国家级	协商（跨监管技术小组，IRTG）	有助于实现金融稳定目标，更好地进行风险管理（特别是跨司法管辖区）	分阶段强制要求在 OTC 衍生品交易中和具有较大信用风险的机构使用 LEI。无 LEI 申请计划的机构将在银行信贷中受到限制
日本	主管部门级（JF-SA）	利益相关方协商	促进交易量汇总，加强跨境交易	JFSA 向金融工具业务运营商宣传 LEI 的好处并鼓励使用 LEI
韩国	主管部门级（FSC）	利益相关方协商	遵循 G20 要求，提升系统性风险管理水平	要求在 OTC 衍生品合约定期报告中使用 LEI，并将很快分阶段推进金融机构在交易数据库中使用 LEI 作为唯一识别编码

续表

司法管辖区	战略特征			
	应用级别（国家级、超国家级、主管部门级）	实施方式	动机/目标	说明
墨西哥	国家级	国家金融主管部门（金融稳定理事会）	同时提高金融机构和主管部门的风险识别能力	要求在金融市场操作的各方及其对手方都使用 LEI，并逐步在监管中要求将 LEI 作为向墨西哥银行提交金融市场运营报告的唯一识别编码
沙特阿拉伯	国家级	国家金融主管部门	不适用	分阶段要求注册 LEI，首先是金融机构，其次是特定金融交易
新加坡	主管部门级（MAS）	公共协商	使主管部门能更好地观察和分析潜在系统性风险（特别是涉及多个法人的业务）	监管要求报告机构和对手方（如有）在衍生品合约报告中使用 LEI
瑞士	国家级	利益相关方参与立法程序（主管部门和业界）	金融数据质量的提高有利于系统性风险评估和增强金融稳定	参加 LEI ROC；修改立法以使联邦统计局（FSO）成为 LOU；将 LEI 纳入 OTC 衍生品和证券交易报告中
土耳其	主管部门级	国家金融主管部门	遵循其他国家做法，以提高数据质量	要求在 OTC 衍生品交易报告中使用 LEI 作为唯一识别编码

续表

司法管辖区	战略特征			
	应用级别（国家级、超国家级、主管部门级）	实施方式	动机/目标	说明
英国	主管部门级	欧盟决策过程，利益相关方协商	通过一致、高效、有效的监管活动，来确保高质量、可靠、可比的数据，打通数据筒仓以及更好地监测系统性风险	支持欧盟法规中关于LEI的监管要求，如CRR、Solvency Ⅱ、MiFID Ⅱ/MiFIR 和EMIR；尽可能将LEI纳入监管报告和其他数据收集中
美国	主管部门级（OFR, OCC, FRB, CFTC, SEC）	利益相关方参与	降低监管合规成本，提高数据质量	鼓励在新的美国及全球金融监管中使用LEI（OFR）；强制要求所有掉期交易对手方机构必须使用LEI（CFTC）；要求所有证券掉期交易参与者使用LEI进行报告（SEC）；要求投资顾问机构如有LEI，应进行报告（SEC）；要求注册投资公司注册并报告LEI（SEC）；包括在FSOC年度国会报告中建议在监管中使用LEI
尚未制定战略的司法管辖区：阿根廷、印度尼西亚、俄罗斯、南非。				

附录4a：场外衍生品交易中采用LEI识别报告机构或对手方的百分比

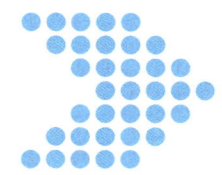

	存量交易		增量交易		存量交易		增量交易	
	按交易数量	按总持有名义金额	按交易数量	按总名义余额	按交易数量	按总名义余额	按交易数量	按总名义余额
司法管辖区	所有OTC衍生品交易中，采用当前LEI识别报告机构的百分比				所有OTC衍生品交易中，采用当前LEI识别报告机构对手方的百分比			
澳大利亚	100	100	100	100	90	不可用	87	87
加拿大	96	97	98	96	94	98	86	98
欧盟	99	96	100	100	90	99	97	99
法国	100	100	100	100	79	100	74	100
德国	99	100	100	100	93	100	99	100
中国香港	100	100	100	100	92	98	89	97
印度	100	100	100	100	89	98	96	97
意大利	99	99	100	100	97	NA	100	100
日本	100	100	100	100	67	94	63	94
墨西哥	100	100	100	100	3.8	6	4	47
荷兰	100	100	100	100	100	100	100	100
俄罗斯	NA	NA	100	100	NA	NA	100	100
新加坡	100	100	100	100	75	86	77	90
西班牙	99	100	100	100	90	99	93	100
英国	100	100	100	100	93	99	96	99
美国	100	100	96	100	98	100	92	100
土耳其	100	100	100	100	89	89	86	86

资料来源：FSB同行评估问卷调查反馈。阿根廷、巴西、中国、印度尼西亚、韩国、沙特阿拉伯、南非和瑞士的数据不详。对于俄罗斯来说，目前还没有存量交易的数据，但据俄罗斯当局估计，存量交易的数据在90%～100%。

附录 4b：FSB 司法管辖区内证券发行人的 LEI 覆盖率（2018 年 9 月底）*

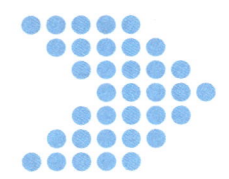

	非金融公司			金融机构			广义政府机构			经济体**		
	LEI 覆盖率（%）			LEI 覆盖率（%）			LEI 覆盖率（%）			LEI 覆盖率（%）		
	发行人	金融工具	持有金额	发行人	金融工具	持有金额	发行人	金融工具	持有金额	发行人	金融工具	持有金额
阿根廷	6	4	75	22	24	75	55	87	99	9	10	90
澳大利亚	9	3	39	25	73	90	43	96	100	13	23	71
巴西	0	1	25	8	54	42	10	99	100	0	24	50
加拿大	6	5	84	16	57	90	6	24	97	7	25	89
瑞士	3	3	91	18	90	96	6	23	65	5	42	91
中国	1	2	5	6	27	68	2	24	42	2	15	36
德国	14	14	99	47	99	99	94	66	100	19	97	99
西班牙	18	8	93	61	92	100	100	100	100	27	29	98
欧盟	17	12	94	48	98	97	38	78	100	22	88	97
法国	8	8	99	21	86	99	62	95	100	10	33	99
中国香港	9	8	43	53	84	91	100	100	100	22	50	63
印度尼西亚	7	4	30	18	71	85	100	100	100	10	20	62
印度	5	14	85	7	45	81	5	5	3	5	22	58
意大利	45	50	93	69	93	97	12	28	100	47	69	98
日本	7	14	56	44	88	87	2	12	92	9	46	77
韩国	1	3	53	2	90	81	4	13	96	1	48	70
墨西哥	9	10	54	26	65	59	25	95	100	13	35	61
荷兰	26	32	100	83	100	100	89	95	100	56	97	100
俄罗斯	1	4	66	32	46	91	0	58	93	4	11	75
沙特阿拉伯	6	1	60	62	68	97	100	100	100	21	8	78

续表

	非金融公司			金融机构			广义政府机构			经济体 **		
	LEI 覆盖率（%）			LEI 覆盖率（%）			LEI 覆盖率（%）			LEI 覆盖率（%）		
	发行人	金融工具	持有金额	发行人	金融工具	持有金额	发行人	金融工具	持有金额	发行人	金融工具	持有金额
新加坡	12	3	65	44	82	92	100	100	100	18	28	80
土耳其	8	3	65	34	5	92	67	100	100	14	7	88
英国	25	4	91	57	99	94	42	85	100	34	84	94
美国	6	4	92	21	40	61	13	43	95	10	24	83
南非	2	4	48	10	46	69	13	82	99	3	24	64
FSB 总量 ***	9	6	75	26	80	76	15	44	89	12	58	79
世界其他地区总量 ****	3	4	49	29	53	76	61	22	86	7	30	64
全球总量	8	6	73	27	78	76	17	38	89	11	55	78

备注：

* LEI 覆盖率统计数据是根据 ESCB 中央证券数据库（CSDB）的微观数据计算的。CSDB 是一个多源的证券记录数据库，它自动组合来自多个数据源的证券和发行人信息，并为每只证券及其发行人派生一个"黄金副本"。它由欧洲央行和 27 家 ESCB 央行共同运营，有明确定义的数据质量管理框架。应当指出的是，非欧盟 FSB 司法管辖区的数据不能像欧盟国家那样进行深度核查，而且非欧盟 FSB 司法管辖区可能存在一定的覆盖空白。因此，对非欧盟 FSB 成员的 LEI 覆盖率统计数据应视为近似估计，并在解释时考虑到这些情况。

** 数据涵盖除货币市场基金和非货币市场投资基金（SNA 部门 S.123 和 S.124）以外的所有子行业。

*** FSB 总量包括欧盟所有成员国，为欧盟总量的一部分。

**** 世界其他地区指的是非 FSB 司法管辖区（非 FSB 的欧盟成员包括在 FSB 总量中，为欧盟总量的一部分）。

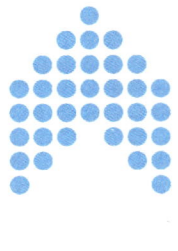

附录4c：机构不提供其直接和最终母公司信息的原因

已发布及已失效最终母公司的LEI的百分比（最近的除外）	阿根廷	澳大利亚	巴西	加拿大	瑞士	中国	德国	西班牙	法国	英国	中国香港	印度尼西亚	印度	意大利	日本	韩国	墨西哥	荷兰	俄罗斯	沙特阿拉伯	新加坡	土耳其	美国	南非	欧盟	全部FSB成员	ROW（世界其他地方）
最终母公司																											
已报告最终母公司的	18	12	14	10	9	22	6	4	7	6	14	27	10	4	5	23	22	3	14	22	19	26	6	16	6	6	6
其中：已失效的	1	8	30	11	8	12	9	11	13	38	13	14	0	7	2	10	8	10	8	11	11	7	10	22	14	13	14
未报告最终母公司但给出例外原因的	62	76	70	64	86	59	84	91	81	92	78	66	78	83	90	69	66	84	53	55	67	69	58	56	86	80	87
其中：																											
未获同意或有其他障碍的	12	32	23	15	8	18	2	1	6	4	18	14	3	2	2	12	12	1	6	11	19	5	22	7	4	7	14
自然人	11	8	7	12	19	7	7	1	27	11	18	7	54	39	1	26	7	0	26	13	14	33	6	10	21	19	25

续表

已发布及已失效LEI的百分比（最近的除外）	阿根廷	澳大利亚	巴西	加拿大	瑞士	中国	德国	西班牙	法国	英国	中国香港	印度尼西亚	印度	意大利	日本	韩国	墨西哥	荷兰	俄罗斯	沙特阿拉伯	新加坡	土耳其	美国	南非	欧盟	全部FSB成员	ROW（世界其他地方）
非合并母公司	8	16	7	17	14	14	8	84	32	37	19	14	10	11	6	16	29	78	5	21	13	14	14	11	32	28	23
其中：基金	2	7	1	6	5	1	0	3	8	1	6	1	0	0	1	9	2	0	0	1	3	1	4	3	2	3	3
无明确控制人的机构（如分散持股）	17	14	27	12	40	8	64	3	9	37	11	11	5	27	81	10	11	1	11	6	10	7	9	11	25	22	18
其中：基金	0	3	22	2	5	0	5	0	1	0	2	1	0	0	0	3	0	0	0	0	1	0	2	3	2	2	2
母公司无LEI	14	6	6	7	5	12	2	2	7	3	13	20	5	3	1	6	7	3	6	5	11	9	7	19	4	5	8
直接母公司																											
已报告有直接母公司的	16	11	12	9	7	17	5	3	8	5	12	20	9	4	3	19	17	3	18	19	16	29	5	13	5	6	5
其中：已失效的	1	1	1	0	0	2	0	0	1	0	1	2	0	0	0	2	1	0	1	2	2	2	0	1	0	0	0
未报告有直接母公司但给出别的原因的	65	77	72	64	87	64	85	91	81	93	80	73	79	82	92	73	70	85	50	57	70	66	60	59	86	81	88
其中：未获同意或有其他障碍的	13	32	23	15	8	19	2	1	6	4	18	14	3	2	1	13	15	1	6	12	21	5	22	8	4	7	14
自然人	10	8	7	12	20	6	7	1	26	10	15	7	54	39	1	26	6	0	18	13	13	30	6	10	21	18	24
非合并母公司	10	17	8	17	16	16	9	84	32	38	20	17	11	11	6	19	30	79	6	21	14	12	15	12	32	28	24
其中：基金	2	6	1	6	5	1	0	3	8	1	6	0	0	0	1	9	2	0	0	1	3	1	4	2	2	3	3

续表

	阿根廷	澳大利亚	巴西	加拿大	瑞士	中国	德国	西班牙	法国	英国	中国香港	印度尼西亚	印度	意大利	日本	韩国	墨西哥	荷兰	俄罗斯	沙特阿拉伯	新加坡	土耳其	美国	南非	欧盟	全部FSB成员	ROW（世界其他地方）
无明确控制人的机构（如分散持股）	16	14	27	12	37	8	64	3	9	37	10	11	5	27	81	10	11	1	8	6	10	6	9	10	25	22	18
其中：基金	0	3	22	2	5	0	5	0	1	1	2	1	0	0	0	3	0	0	0	0	1	0	2	2	2	2	2
母公司无LEI	15	6	8	7	6	15	2	2	7	4	15	23	6	3	1	6	8	3	12	5	13	14	8	19	4	5	8
未报告母公司且未给出例外原因的	9	11	15	27	5	15	10	5	11	2	6	5	0	14	5	7	12	10	33	15	12	5	35	11	8	12	6
无须报告的会计并表母公司的情况																											
独资公司	10	1	1	0	1	4	0	1	0	0	0	2	12	0	0	0	0	2	0	6	1	0	0	12	0	1	1
分支机构	1	0	0	0	0	0	0	0	0	0	0	0	0	0	0	0	0	0	0	2	0	0	0	5	0	1	0
已发布和失效的LEI总数*	511	12175	1663	28872	14409	1668	114019	94646	67914	133677	5031	649	19924	98926	8084	1054	3299	97622	1266	381	4716	1598	179668	1239	914554	1200761	126835

资料来源：GLEIF。文件"Reporting Exceptions v1.1"，LEI-CDF v2.1 链接文件，截至2019年1月3日的RR-CDF v1.1，可在http://www.gleif.org/en/lei-data/gleif-concatenated-file/download-the-concatenated-file#calculation fab查阅。计算时只考虑了"已发布的""失效的"或"待迁移"状态的LEI（以及那些没有最近记录处于"待归档状态"的记录）。对于同一关系，可能会报告几个例外原因。

ROW：世界其他地方。

附录 4d：全球金融市场协会与国际掉期和衍生品协会成员的样本客户群 LEI 覆盖率

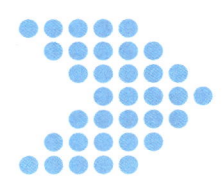

北美调查对象	持有 LEI 的欧洲客户（％）	持有 LEI 的北美客户（％）	持有 LEI 的亚太客户（不包括日本）（％）	持有 LEI 的日本客户（％）
最低值	10	3	5	1
最高值	100	99	100	100
平均值	58	52	42	33
众数	不适用	不适用	不适用	不适用
中值	70	65	20	19

日本调查对象	持有 LEI 的欧洲客户（％）	持有 LEI 的北美客户（％）	持有 LEI 的亚太客户（不包括日本）（％）	持有 LEI 的日本客户（％）
最低值	8	4	1	5
最高值	100	100	100	100
平均值	87	81	59	59
众数	100	100	不适用	82
中值	100	100	90	67

　　备注：全球金融市场协会（GFMA）和国际掉期和衍生品协会（ISDA）于 2019 年 3 ~ 4 月进行了该项调查，调查结果来自 21 份问卷反馈（大部分来自卖方）。没有收到欧洲的反馈，亚太地区（日本除外）的一个机构被认为可能不具有代表性，其问卷被排除了。LEI 实施完成的主要业务领域是衍生品（约 80％，其中 LEI 是强制要求的）。1/3 的调查对象在未受到强制要求的情况下在衍生品业务中实施了 LEI，另有 1/4 的调查对象正在实施过程中。LEI 在客户注册方面的实施情况也很好（约占样本的 40％），但在贸易融资、银行同业支付和证券交易方面的实施情况非常差，有 2/3 的调查对象甚至还没有实施计划。

附录 5：公开征求意见反馈情况 和市场参与者圆桌会议摘要

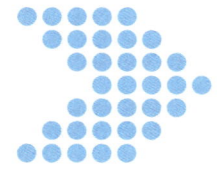

　　FSB 就同行评估的有关内容公开征求了意见，共收到 20 多份书面答复。绝对多数的受访者支持 LEI 和 FSB 同行评估。许多受访者建议采取措施提高应用率以及新用例的应用，其中大多数都呼吁出台监管强制要求（包括 LEI 续期）。下面总结了公众书面反馈意见的主要观点，以及 2018 年 12 月 10 日伦敦圆桌会议的主要内容。在该次圆桌会议上，同行评估小组与 50 多个利益相关方进行了对话，包括银行、信用社、证券交易商、投资顾问、证券交易所、数据供应商、支付行业、GLEIS 参与者、其他类型识别编码或数字证书发行机构以及监管机构的代表。

一、LEI 实施情况：达到的覆盖率、取得的进展及实施战略中的经验教训

　　到目前为止，LEI 主要是依靠法规来实施，主要用于支持金融交易报告和风险汇总。总体而言，虽然对 LEI 的认识在不断提高，但其实施主要还是靠监管的强制推动；书面反馈的结果表明，凡没有受到监管强制要求去获取和维护 LEI 的司法管辖区（和行业），其使用 LEI 的意识都较低。在某些情况下，受访者强调参与者不清楚他们是否需要 LEI。

圆桌会议与会者认为，LEI 已经在衍生品市场参与者中得到了使用，并且还在证券市场得到了小范围使用，这已经是一个相当不错的成绩。大型金融机构认为 LEI 对它们自身业务流程非常有用，比如确保与它们交易的机构能够被充分识别并且拥有最新的合同文件，以及用于管理机构的限额。然而，以本地客户为主的小型银行仅能从 LEI 中看到很少的好处。

大多数与会者认为，监管强制是一种必要和首选的方法，至少在达到采用率临界点之前是这样。否则，机构没有动力去改造他们的流程，特别是考虑到只有当所有参与者都共同使用才能带来更多好处时。一位与会者指出，所有国家或地区都强制实施 LEI 无论如何都不太可能，因此有必要采取其他激励性的方法。

主要的实施困难：

（一）不同司法管辖区要求的时间和范围不同。美国和欧盟要求衍生品在同一时限内使用 LEI，这对于这些主要市场实施 LEI 非常有效。无论如何，这些法规都要求来自其他司法管辖区的市场参与者持有 LEI，即使那些司法管辖区并非总是强制要求衍生品使用 LEI。对于衍生品以外的领域，一些要求也是如此规定，这些要求往往更专属于某个司法管辖区，例如欧盟要求证券发行人持有 LEI。当强制要求持有 LEI 的国家的被监管机构与期望其拥有 LEI 的国外机构之间没有合同关系时，问题就会变得更加复杂：例如，任何经纪商都可以不经发行人同意即在德国证券交易所上市证券。教育和说服这些参与者获取 LEI 的重担落在了该行业身上。由于一些亚洲司法管辖区要求使用 LEI 的范围较小，因此说服亚洲机构的困难曾多次被提及。时间要求上的差异也使最先采取行动的国家的金融机构处于不利地位。因此，一些行业参与者建议，在

商定的范围内，比如衍生品和上市证券，持有 LEI 的监管要求应在全球范围内适用于所有法人。

（二）说服小型机构申请 LEI 的困难。一些与会者想知道，在所有情况下，特别是对于交易不频繁的小型机构，要求持有 LEI 是否合理。对于非常小的账户，申请 LEI 的成本可能与其不相称，并且这些机构看不到 LEI 的任何用处。不过，大多数与会者都认为，LEI 最好覆盖所有机构，因为所有机构最终都将受益于运营效率，例如，如果 LEI 能支持跨境支付的直通处理，并能减少制裁机构筛查中的误报（这会导致支付延误），那么效率将大大提高。在金融危机中，小型机构也可能是最先受到影响的机构，而 LEI 有助于评估冲击的影响，或确保客户提交的抵押品能够得到适当追踪。一些监管机构指出，从传导性看，小额交易可能是相关的，大量小风险可能汇聚成系统性的风险。此外，一个监管机构指出，如果没有 LEI，所收集的数百万条记录将无法管理。

（三）操作问题。LEI 发放或状态更新的不及时会导致一些问题并延迟交易。

（四）与会者关于提高 LEI 采用率的建议。

与会者关于提高 LEI 采用率的建议包括：

- 强制使用 LEI。

- 通过线上及线下研讨会和行业协会论坛等途径，在接受率不高的行业，监管机构和行业开展联合教育工作。过去大家认为 GLEIF 和 LOU 在这方面很有帮助，多种语言的行业 FAQ 也是，但立法者和商业注册机构也应当参与外联工作。在这方面，FSB 的国家同行评估、决策者的专题报告也都产生了积极的影响，例如英格兰银行关于支付问题的咨询文件。

● 尽可能将 LEI 用于更多的用途，包括税收用途。

● 在 GLEIS 中纳入更多数据：一些与会者建议增加在每笔交易中都不会改变的数据元素（不会给当前交易报告带来负担）。例如，某个实体是否是美国人，或增加机构的行业分类，以支持 AML/CFT。另一种解决办法是由第三方使用 LEI 发布机构数据，这将使数据检索更加容易，无须将所有数据要素包含到 GLEIS 数据库中并由 LOU 验证。

● 减少费用和重复的流程，特别是与其他识别编码的（如在本地商业登记机构嵌入发布的），最好使用 LEI 替换其他识别编码。银行可以在发布和维护方面发挥作用，但一位与会者强调，这不应取代机构更新其数据的责任，另一位与会者提醒说，不应再出现银行在未经客户授权的情况下为客户申请 LEI 的情形，这会导致为同一机构申请多个编码。

● 解决失效 LEI 的问题。对失效的 LEI 缺乏更新是一个问题。例如，如果机构的名称没有更新，这可能导致为该同一机构发放一个新的 LEI。一些与会者强调，监管机构有必要明确强制续期。

● 公共和私营部门在新领域开展合作，例如在支付和 KYC 方面，一些与会者建议先与沃尔夫斯堡集团等行业组织协商后，再采用新的监管要求。

二、采用 LEI 给市场参与者带来的好处和挑战

除监管目标外，LEI 还可用于帮助改进内部流程，并为市场参与者带来其他好处。在书面反馈中，已确定的用途包括客户/对手方识别、数据整合和分析、系统风险识别、高效的供应链管理、政府与企业关系、支付和 AML/CFT 合规。

（一）好处

圆桌会议与会者列举了 LEI 的下列好处：

• 免去了人工核对机构数据的成本，因为名称各式各样、不同语言和字符集的翻译或音译也五花八门，这些都使得人工核对非常复杂；

• 为 ISDA 文档更新提供了便利；

• 使结算指令能够更准确地识别机构；以及

• 使得复杂的大型机构内部可以利用同一实体的其他数据点。

（二）未来可能的用途

在 XBRL 分类标准中引入 LEI，将有助于在监管报告、工商注册机构注册、财务披露、税务报告以及合规等领域实现机构引用方式的标准化。大约有 70 个国家在使用 XBRL，出台了 142 项强制要求，覆盖 2000 万家公司。将 LEI 引入该分类标准，将鼓励 XBRL 用户在需要识别机构时考虑使用 LEI。圆桌会议与会者指出，我们可以想象一下，财务报告使用 LEI 来识别发布报告的机构和报告中涉及的相关机构，审计报告的审计机构、接收报告的监管机构使用的电子签名中也包含 LEI，这意味着什么。

与会者指出，LEI 已开始被纳入数字证书，数字证书是安全网站和越来越普遍的电子交易的关键特征。数字证书通常涉及机构名称，这意味着当机构变更名称或兼并时需要变更证书。LEI 可以避免这个问题，并且可以在机构使用的所有证书与关于机构身份的可靠数据之间建立可靠连接。在数字签名中嵌入 LEI 将有助于合同的管理。

LEI 还会给会计师事务所识别与其客户相关的机构带来便利，目前这些流程依赖于供应商的多源数据以及大量的手工操作。

（三）挑战

书面反馈提出的主要障碍有：缺乏影响覆盖面和续期的监管要求，不同司法管辖区的要求存在差异，成本以及数据质量问题。圆桌会议讨论了其中一些挑战：

LEI 的覆盖率差异很大，在一些地区仍然很低：一家大型国际银行指出，其欧洲客户的 LEI 覆盖率达到 69%，美国客户覆盖率为 29%，亚太地区客户覆盖率仅为 4%。尽管部分覆盖也能实现 LEI 的一些好处，但高覆盖率能够为流程改造所需的额外投资给出正当理由。此外，只要 LEI 不能用于所有机构，就需要维护其他识别编码。

LEI 的数据质量虽然优于许多其他来源，但在很多方面仍可改进：例如，LEI 所提供的法人地址往往与总部地址相同，并且对于使用统一字段来确定机构所在的司法管辖区还没有达成共识。此外，工商注册号仍然经常缺失。

LEI 的失效率太高会对某些用途（如 KYC 要求）构成障碍。一些与会者想知道，如果数据没有变化，两次续期间隔时间较长是否可以接受。但是，这样一来就无法告知用户数据是否是最新的。其他途径可能有助于实现更高的续期率：例如，在西班牙，许多 LEI 由当地工商注册机构管理，LEI 的续期（续期率超过了 90%）被视作机构向登记处提交年度财务报告的流程的一部分。

三、推广战略

在收到的书面反馈中，大多数受访者呼吁使用更多的监管强制措施。其他建议包括降低 LEI 申请和续期的成本，将 LEI 与其他识别编码（如 ISIN）关联起来，以及提高对 LEI 及其好处的认识。

圆桌会议与会者讨论了如何借鉴其他领域的案例来推动 LEI 应用，以及促进 LEI 应用的其他方式：

● 一些司法管辖区对数字证书进行了强制要求，例如意大利强制所有与政府通信的公司使用数字证书，这就有助于在私营部门推广 LEI。

● 大型零售商要求使用条形码，因为这有助于其更有效地管理销售和库存。这一市场要求迫使那些想要通过大型零售商销售的公司使用条形码来标记他们的商品。

与会者建议让所有数据供应商在其提供的机构数据中包含 LEI 将有助于 LEI 的采用。

来自正在申请和维护 LEI 的机构的观点：为了促进 LEI 得到更广泛的应用，需要解决成本、用户体验和其他挑战。

一些行业参与者认为 LEI 成本太高，注册流程太烦琐，这可能影响 LEI 的推广，并说明了法人每年确认 LEI 参考数据的各种困难。

书面反馈提出的主要成本是申请 LEI 以及将其整合进内部系统的成本。一些反馈意见认为，费用完全由申请 LEI 的机构承担，但好处却大家都有（包括公共和私营部门）。一份反馈意见建议，应当把建设一个不向 LEI 申请机构收费的系统作为目标。一些受访者提到了强制申请 LEI 但不强制续期的情况，他们怀疑，考虑到成本，许多未被强制要求续期的机构会让其 LEI 失效。一名受访者指出，续期费用一直在下降，另一名受访者认为费用本来就低；相比之下，基金组织则指出，基金管理人为其基金申请 LEI 的成本很高。

与会者讨论了应对这些挑战的可能方法。

一些其他机构开展与 LOU 类似的工作，例如：银行（对客户进行尽职调查）、数字证书发行机构、税务机关以及工商注册机构。对于其中的一些重复操作可以精减，例如：

● 允许 LOU 通过银行对 LEI 记录进行验证：银行已经进行了此类验证，通常频率为一年、两年或三年一次，验证范围甚至超出了 GLEIS 所要求的信息。银行将不会取代 LOU，因为他们不太可能想要管理 LEI 记录、应对挑战等；或者

● 与工商注册机构进行更深入的整合。当工商注册机构的记录发生变化时，LOU（同时也是工商注册机构）通知机构的联系人，以便能够一并修改其 LEI 记录。与会者指出，工商注册机构无法完全取代 LOU，并非所有机构都在工商注册机构进行了登记，有些工商注册机构不够资格，或对此类活动没有兴趣。

竞争降低了 LEI 成本，但也可能影响质量：重要的是 GLEIF 质量监控不仅要监控 LEI 记录的质量是否正常，而且还要监控与公共部门的对应关系。GLEIS 中的成本回收原则避免了与成本不符的过高价格，该原则也得到 LOU 的认同，不要指望他们会亏本运营。

探索 LEI 在支付和 KYC 中的应用：

一些市场参与者和公共部门已经注意到在代理银行业务中使

用 LEI 的潜在好处。这些好处包括：在支付报文中使用 LEI（如 SWIFT）来提升对支付发起人/受益人的识别准确性和支付信息筛查的可靠性；支持客户尽职调查流程。目前对文本字符串的筛查还不可靠。LEI 适合作为金融机构之间交换机构信息的媒介。例如，LEI 可以用于高风险的司法管辖区，以解决代理银行业务下滑的问题，尤其是在可以通过支付报文传送其他信息［如交易是否具有外国资产控制办公室（US）的许可证］的情况下。

将 LEI 纳入 ISO 20022 的变更申请正在进行中。将代理银行信息迁移到 ISO 20022 为在支付报文中使用 LEI 提供了机会，考虑到空间限制，这比在当前格式中采用 LEI 选项的方式更容易实现。从 2021 年 11 月开始，安排了四年的共存期，但预计大部分支付流量将提前迁移。在全部报文都能处理 LEI 之前，报文必须同时包括 LEI、名称和地址。

在英国，LEI 将成为金融机构之间支付的强制性要求。免除人工核验、方便对账和提高效率的好处也同样体现在零售支付中，但要面临机构数目太多的挑战。一名与会者还指出，LEI 将支持信用卡支付流程，特别是在识别互联网商户方面。

圆桌会议与会者讨论认为，可能需要更多的信息来支持支付方面的尽职调查，如行业部门、受益所有权、机构是否受监管以及由谁来监管等。举例来说，如果监管机构使用 LEI 来公布其监管的机构名单，则可以降低此类信息的成本。这也可用于其他数据，如审计机构签署的财务报告等。

使用 GLEIS 作为银行验证地址的可信赖工具更具挑战性。本地法规（如在英国）要求，银行在（与公司）建立关系之前，必须提供公司的组成文件。如果要依赖 LEI，则需要修改法规。

附录6：标准制定组织和国际组织对调查表的反馈

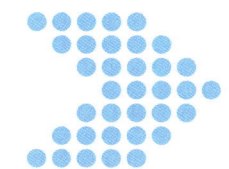

巴塞尔银行监督委员会（BCBS）、国际清算银行（BIS）、全球金融体系委员会（CGFS）、支付和市场基础设施委员会（CP-MI）、国际保险监管者协会（IAIS）、国际会计准则理事会（IASB）、国际货币基金组织（IMF）、经济合作与发展组织（OECD）、世界银行和国际证监会组织（IOSCO）均对调查做出反馈。

标准制定组织（SSB）和国际组织（IO）报告称，LEI 被用于有关提高金融市场信息透明度的政策文件中，特别是用于 OTC 衍生品报告、银行的数据整合和风险报告、客户识别［尤其是国际支付（代理银行）和信贷业务中客户识别］报告。由于最近增加了关于母公司机构的信息，GLEIS 也被认为有助于理解和传播有关集团结构的信息，从而支持保险监管，并更好地了解资本、商品和服务的跨境流动的情况。

LEI 已用于数据收集，以支持获取 G – SIB 对手方和中央清算相互依赖关系的信息，同时也被 IAIS 用于获取保险集团结构信息，以支持保险资本标准的制定。它还被 OECD 用于一个涉及 100 多个跨国企业的试点项目。

LEI 的其他用途旨在支持 IMF 组织的协调投资证券调查（特别

是有助于检索持有和发行证券的机构的行业信息）、收集外商直接投资（FDI）统计数据和更好掌握不同属性企业贸易情况的统计数据。

LEI 的价值在于，有利于跨境情况下更明确地识别机构，以及充分利用 LEI 非专有性质更方便地获取机构直接和最终母公司的信息。LEI 也开始提供与其他识别编码的映射，但迄今为止仅限于 BIC 和国家工商注册号，以及最近的 ISIN。

LEI 最主要的局限性是其覆盖范围不足。虽然 LEI 对欧盟大型企业贷款的借款人的覆盖率接近 100%，但在其他地区，特别是亚洲的覆盖率不足。LEI 被提供给参与 IAIS 数据收集的保险集团范围内 73% 的法人，但只有 1/3 的保险集团覆盖了几乎所有的机构。在银行部门，G－SIB 向 BIS 报告其顶级机构的 LEI，但只有少数公司向其对手方报告 LEI。在几个针对非金融公司的项目中，低覆盖率阻碍了 LEI 的应用。

其他不足包括：与其他识别编码的映射不足，尤其是与数据供应商（它们仍然需要访问机构的其他信息）的映射。对额外的专有信息的需求也减少了 LEI 数据开放性带来的好处。集团结构信息也不够完备，要么是因为报告不完整（部分源于母公司 LEI 缺失），要么是因为母公司的定义不满足要求（例如，缺乏关于公众可获得的受益所有人的信息，包括个人）。最后，在 LEI 应用更为成熟的领域（如衍生品），其他障碍阻碍了 LEI 的充分利用。

一、LEI 在 SSB 政策管理中的应用

根据 2018 年 4 月 LEI ROC 进度报告的描述，BCBS 在两份政策文件中提到了 LEI：《有效风险数据整合和风险报告原则（2013

年)》，以及《开户通用指南》，见《与洗钱和资助恐怖主义有关的风险健全管理》（2017 年）附录 4。

BCBS 解释说，LEI 可以促进客户识别和数据整合，从而有助于改善银行的风险管理和风险评估。

CPMI 和 IOSCO 也认为 LEI ROC 进度报告中的政策用途清单是全面的，并提到了以下文件中有关于 LEI 的内容：《关于统一 UTI 的 CPMI – IOSCO 技术指南》（2017 年 2 月）、《关于统一关键场外衍生品数据元素（UTI 和 UPI 除外）的 CPMI – IOSCO 技术指南》（2018 年 4 月）、《CPMI 报告，代理银行业务》（2016 年 7 月），以及 FSB – CPMI《向 G20 提交的关于评估和应对代理银行业务下降所采取行动的报告》（2015 年 11 月）中的建议。

LEI 支持 CPMI 通过提高金融市场信息和 IOSCO 的透明度来应对系统性风险，促进实现金融稳定的目标。例如，CPMI – IOSCO 关于 OTC 衍生品数据报告和加总要求的报告（2012 年）建议"LEI 标准能够实现报告中讨论的数据整合目标，应迅速制定和执行"。[1]

世界银行还在两份有关代理银行业务的出版物中提及 LEI，涉及 CPMI 建议和 FSB 行动计划。[2] 在第二份出版物中，国际金融公司指出，许多利益相关方认识到利用新兴技术可以提高金融机构的风险管理能力。目前，（金融体系）正在向以客户为中心的架构

---

[1] 参见 https：//www. bis. org/cpmi/publ/d100. htm。

[2] 世界银行集团，《从代理银行退出的地点、原因和对策》，2015 年 11 月，http：// documents. worldbank. org/curated/en/113021467990964789/pdf/101098 – revised – public – cbr – report – november – 2015. pdf；世界银行集团，《新兴市场金融部门的去风险和其他挑战：国际金融公司对代理银行业务的调查结果》，2017 年 9 月，http：//documents. worldbank. org/curated/en/ 895821510730571841/pdf/121275 – WP – IFC – 2017 – Survey – on – Correspondent – Banking – in – EMs – PUBLIC. pdf。

转型，多种颠覆性技术被运用在增强身份验证领域，其中就包括生物识别技术和 LEI。各国中央银行提出了多项具体的改进措施来提升全球支付体系的安全性和降低进入门槛，包括建立机构唯一识别编码标准，这可在交易中正确识别交易应答方及其客户，帮助代理银行管理风险和确保合规。此类标准的应用可以考虑使用 LEI，因其已经是国际标准化组织（ISO）的一个标准。

世界银行还研究了 LEI 在信贷报告中的使用。一些信贷报告服务提供商（CRSP），包括德国和西班牙的信贷登记机构，使用 LEI 来识别公司；但是，这些 CRSP 机构只是全球的一小部分。更广泛地使用 LEI 将使公司识别更容易和更准确，从而为国内和国际上的中小企业（SME）、信贷发行人和监管机构带来好处。① 世界银行还注意到，由于 LEI 提供了一种可以识别和匹配每个数据库中的数据主体的机制，因此它不仅有助于国内数据库的关联，而且尤其有助于跨境数据库的关联。② 世界银行在其 2018 年《开展业务、获得信贷、信贷登记调查》③ 中列入了一个关于 LEI 的问题，并在其关于《在政府中实施具有唯一性的业务编码，从业人员指导说明和九个国家案例研究》④ 的报告中对 LEI 应用进行了探讨。

---

① 世界银行集团，《改善中小企业融资难，信贷报告、担保贷款和破产实践提供的机会》，2018 年 5 月，http：//documents. worldbank. org/curated/en/316871533711048308/pdf/129283 − WP − PUBLIC − improving − access − to − finance − for − SMEs. pdf。

② 世界银行集团，《信贷报告在支持金融部门监管和监督方面的作用》，2016 年 1 月。http：//pubdocs. worldbank. org/en/954571479312890728/CR − 2016 − role − credit − reporting − in − supporting − financial − regulation. pdf。

③ 参见 http：//www. doingbusiness. org/content/dam/doingBusiness/media/Methodology/Survey − instruments/db18/db18 − credit − public − question − en. pdf。

④ 参见 http：//documents. worldbank. org/curated/en/471531468196759403/pdf/103570 − REVISED − Implementing − a − unique − business − identifier − in − government. pdf。

由 BIS 主管的欧文·费希尔中央银行统计委员会（IFC）在《IFC 交易报告库数据公报》中提到了 LEI。[①] 报告讨论了 LEI 在管理交易报告库数据方面的潜在用途。各国央行一致认为，在许多情况下，无法通过 LEI 识别对手方，降低了其制定政策在机构中推广应用 LEI 的兴趣。

IAIS 强调，在收集了大量数据的情况下，LEI 有利于理解集团结构随时间的演变情况。

IASB 回复称，IFRS 标准是以准则为基础的，不包含 LEI 这样细节层面的内容。IFRS 准则主要适用于上市公司的合并财务报表，会计准则并不要求在这类财务报表中披露附属机构的详细信息。有关 LEI 的要求可以由国家或者地区的公司法或者上市规则规定。CGFS 没有报告与 LEI 相关的活动。

二、LEI 在数据收集或研究项目中的应用

（一）LEI 当前的用途

国际清算银行货币和经济部门的一些研究项目正在使用 LEI，主要用于跟踪公司在资本市场的活动。

LEI 还被用于：

● FSB – CPMI – IOSCO 研究小组关于中央清算相互依赖性的研究项目。

● IAIS 自 2014 年以来开展年度数据收集，旨在支持保险资本标准的制定，该标准作为国际活跃保险集团共同框架的一部分，

---

① 参见 https：//www. bis. org/ifc/publ/ifc_report_cb_trade_rep_deriv_data. pdf。

将于 2019 年底被采用。这些数据收集过程的定量分析（称为现场测试）要求保险集团志愿者提供其集团 LEI（如果 LEI 可用），并通过 LEI 识别其数据传输过程中涉及的法人。

● 在 OECD 的试点项目 ADIMA① 中，汇编了关于 MNE 国际活动规模和范围的公开统计数据，从而提供了一张独特的 "MNE 全景" 视图。ADIMA 为销售额最大的前 100 家 MNE 制定了三组不同的数据：每个 MNE 及业务所在国家（地区）的一系列经济指标、MNE 母子公司结构登记册以及一个旨在及时提供有关 MNE 重组信息以帮助各个国家编制工作的监测工具。LEI 是 ADIMA 的一个不可或缺的数据源，用于识别母子公司之间的关系，还可以分配 LEI（以及 ISIN、国家商业标识编码、网站和其他创新标识编码），改进对现有各个国家和国际层面（通常是保密）数据库内 MNE 机构的识别，并与这些数据库建立联系。

BCBS 没有在数据收集中使用 LEI。通过 BCBS 定量影响研究（QIS）过程收集的所有数据都是匿名的，因此没有必要使用 LEI。

（二）未来可能的用途

● 参与 IMF CPIS 的司法管辖区使用 LEI，将为基于包含来源和目的地信息的集中数据交换提供支持。IMF 统计部门计划建立一个发行商行业信息的 CPIS 实验性数据库，该数据库允许报告机构能够按照（非居民）发行商行业细分其投资组合资产，并最终向用户提供按照经济体以及持有人和发行商行业分类的包含来源和目的地信息的 CPIS 头寸。预计一些报告机构将使用 LEI。②

---

① 参见 OECD 关于单个跨国公司及其附属公司的分析数据库（ADIMA）。

② 参见 https：//www.imf.org/external/pubs/ft/bop/2018/pdf/18 - 08.pdf。

● 只要 LEI 包含有关集团结构的细化信息，IAIS 就打算在未来的任何数据收集中包含 LEI。

● OECD 认为，LEI 可能有助于收集和汇编统计数据，特别是国际投资和贸易统计数据。

OECD 一直在研究 LEI 的这些潜在用途。对于国际投资统计数据，关系信息有助于改进统计数据和地理属性的完整性。外商直接投资（FDI）统计数据是在直接投资者基础上编制的（与投资企业有直接影响/联系的统计数据）。GLEIS 中的第二层级数据可用于识别当前统计数据无法确定的直接投资关系，以及明确直接投资者的国家（地区）。此外，有关最终投资者的信息有助于对按照最终投资国家（地区）分类的统计数据进行补充说明。MNE 内所有权结构的复杂性往往妨碍对公共 FDI 统计数据的正确解释，因为它掩盖了 FDI 的最终来源和目的地。OECD 第四次基准定义①建议，各国根据最终投资国编制外来投资头寸，以确定实际控制本国投资的投资者所在国家。沿着直接投资者的所有权链往上溯源，直到出现一个不受其他机构控制的机构（此机构即为投资的最终受益人），即可实现这一点。LEI 信息有助于确定最终投资国。

应当指出，FDI 统计数据中使用的定义与目前的第二层级数据并不完全一致，因为这些定义仅基于会计并表准则，而忽略了个体和少数群体的信息。因此，所有受益人的整合信息将是汇编

---

① OECD 的《外商直接投资基准定义，第 4 版》（BD4）于 2008 年出版。它就外商直接投资统计数据的覆盖范围、收集、汇编和传播提供了最完整和详细的指导。除了提供与 IMF《国际收支和国际投资头寸手册》第 6 版相一致的外商直接投资汇总统计数据收集指导外，还提供了关于汇编补充 FDI 系列的指导，以提高 FDI 统计数据的有用性和相关性。

按照最终投资国分类的 FDI 统计数据的有用工具。这类关系信息将有助于解答对 FDI 统计数据的一些质疑，并促进国家统计机构和国际组织之间的数据共享。

外国分支机构统计数据（FATS），也称为跨国公司活动（AMNE）统计数据，是另一个可以从 LEI 关系数据中受益的统计领域。对于 FDI 统计数据，这些信息可用于改进统计数据的覆盖范围和地理属性，但与 FDI 统计数据不同，LEI 中使用的会计并表概念与 FATS 中使用的概念和定义更为接近。

如下文进一步讨论的那样，FDI 统计数据和 FATS 都将受益于 LEI 在非金融机构覆盖范围的扩大。

按所有权分类的贸易数据统计（外国 MNE/国内 MNE/非 MNE）是一项与统计相关的领域。如果上述提到的利用 LEI 来确定所有权关系的能力得以改善，则此类统计也会从中受益。这些数据是一个更大的统计领域（按企业特征划分的交易统计①）的一部分，该领域依赖于国家海关数据与国家工商统计数据（通常是来源于中央工商登记统计机构）之间的联系。因此，OECD 对 GLEIF 与国家主管和统计部门之间合作建立 LEI 和海关数据之间的联系非常感兴趣。

三、LEI 对数据收集和研究项目的价值

在 BIS 项目中，LEI 被用作通过公司贷款在资本市场上借款的机构的标识编码。对于每个机构，BIS 还确定了其直接母公司和最终母公司及其相应的 LEI。然后，BIS 在机构层面综合汇总贷款。

---

① 参见 http：//www. oecd. org/sdd/its/trade－by－enterprise－characteristics. htm。

BIS 设法建立了机构与其母公司的关系。

在 IAIS 的现场测试中，收集 LEI 是为了以明确的方式，对本次测试收集的数据与其他来源数据进行交叉检查。IAIS 还指出，为集团范围内的机构添加 LEI 请求并未增加任何具体成本，而这些信息可用性高，可帮助了解兼并和收购操作后的副作用在集团范围内逐年变化情况。

对于 IMF 而言，如果 LEI 在参与 CPIS 的经济体内可用，则其可以成为按照国际公认标准有效识别证券持有人所属行业系统的重要组成部分。对于该项目，一直期望中的 ISIN/LEI 标识编码与各个国家标识编码之间的联系将是有益的。

对于 OECD 的 ADIMA 项目，LEI 是开放数据方面的关键数据源。在用于对比和共享时，这些数据很有用。可访问性/开放性的数据在汇编 MNE 数据方面发挥着重要作用，这也是 OECD 的 ADI-MA 项目的主要关注点。

四、LEI 的局限性

LEI 主要局限性包括：

（一）LEI 覆盖面不足

BIS 报告说，一篇探索如何通过大型公司贷款建立银行—公司风险敞口方法论的文章，得出的主要结论是并非所有公司都能获得 LEI，特别是，很少亚洲的公司持有 LEI。因此，截至今天，LEI 不能用作全球编码，这意味着该项目从 LEI 受益很少，并导致 LEI 在其他项目也不能用。相比之下，商业数据服务商（汤森路透永

久 ID 或彭博 FIGI）生成的通用编码却非常有用。[1]

在 BIS 研究关于通过大型公司贷款建立银行—公司风险敞口的项目时，市场上借款机构仅半数使用 LEI，因此在实际中没有多大用处。然而，LEI 在欧盟企业的覆盖率较好，在许多国家覆盖率高达 100%，BIS 认为 LEI 有助于跟踪欧盟境内的发展，但 BIS 的关注点通常更多的是全球。此外，BIS 研究了市值最高的 10000 家公司的 LEI 可用性，得出了类似的 LEI 没有实用价值的结论，同时还发现同一区域 LEI 的可用性也不平衡。BIS 没有发现行业方面存在的差异。

作为 BIS 对手方的中央银行也没有完全覆盖。

在 IAIS 最近的一次数据收集中，参与数据收集的法人约 73% 持有 LEI。1/3 的集团机构能够提供其集团中全部或几乎全部法人的 LEI，而 40% 的集团机构没有提供任何 LEI，其余的集团机构处于中间情况，即 LEI 仅可用于集团内部分机构。

对于 IMF 协调证券投资调查（CPI），LEI 所面临的问题主要来自报告机构，因为报告机构没有在试点中使用 LEI 的义务。普遍缺乏 LEI 可能对建立一个具有高度可操作性的集中数据库带来挑战。

LEI 将不能为 OECD 的 ADIMA 项目提供足够的覆盖范围。尽管非金融公司在参与金融交易时注册了 LEI，由于对这些公司本身缺乏监管要求，LEI 覆盖 ADIMA 项目中集团机构中所有母公司和子公司的可能性降低。另一个相关的挑战是，通过 LEI 确定同属一个母公司的子公司之间以及子公司与其母公司之间的关系（当

---

① 瑟琳娜·加拉尔达，J. M，《跨国银行公司风险：我们能从公开的数据中学到什么？》。

关系尚未确定或者当母公司没有 LEI 时）。尽管存在覆盖空白点，但 LEI 对数据可访问性的关注对于项目非常有价值。

同样，对于 FDI 统计数据，OECD 有一个研究项目探讨 MNE 复杂的所有权结构，然后合并 FDI 头寸并按照最终投资国分类呈现。该项目的一部分工作是研究这些结构并了解它们为公司发挥的作用。如果覆盖率有所提高，关系信息将来可能对该项目有用，但目前还不能使用。

（二）与其他识别编码的映射不足

上面提到的 BIS 的 IFC 研究文章的作者在汤森路透使用了 LEI，发现对数据共享、发布和分发具有重要限制。BIS 无法使用 GLEIF 提供的 LEI 进行分析，因为 GLEIF 没有建立 LEI 与非金融公司使用的其他公开通用标识编码之间的联系。特别是，LEI 与汤森路透永久 ID（这是开源的）的联系是有用的，但这些映射由汤森路透构建，并且只能通过其系统访问。BIS 指出，尽管 GLEIF 拥有 LEI 映射服务认证，但 BIC – LEI 映射是唯一可用作开源的映射。

OECD 还指出，将 LEI 映射到其他标识编码（如汤森路透 Permid），加强身份识别以及与其他数据库之间的连接，对 OECD 的 ADIMA 项目非常重要。因此，这已经纳入 ADIMA 项目中。

（三）关于集团结构的信息不足

如果进一步考虑将 LEI 用于将来的数据收集，BCBS 指出，将需要更多关于集团结构的信息（如关于分支机构的信息），以支持对银行集团的风险评估。

FDI 统计数据中使用的定义与目前的第二层级数据并不完全一致，因为这些定义仅基于会计并表准则，而忽略了个体和少数群体的信息。因此，所有受益人的整合信息将是汇编按照最终投资国分类的 FDI 统计数据的有用工具。

（四）LEI 仍然太新，尚未建立有意义的时间序列数据

BCBS - CPMI - IOSCO - FSB 衍生品评估小组试图使用 LEI 数据了解 OTC 衍生品市场构成随时间的演变发展情况。[①] 不幸的是，这是不可能的，因为 LEI 使用相对较晚，无法构建时间序列（还有其他挑战）。

（五）其他

在 BIS 银行部看来，LEI 可以支持在交易进入和交易确认的对账时更容易识别交易机构。BIS 的银行部门将 LEI 信息纳入自己的风险系统中，并认可了 LEI 带来的好处，例如管理机构的基本身份信息。但是，目前，BIS 银行部觉得 LEI 的使用还很有限，例如，LEI 没有出现在 SWIFT 确认中，而这在技术上是可行的。

世界银行财政部也在 Markitwire 交易中使用 LEI，并把 LEI 登记在 Markitwire 对手方经理系统中。

---

① 衍生品评估小组于 2018 年 11 月发布了一份评估报告，评估对集中清算场外衍生品激励机制改革的影响。参见 http：//www. fsb. org/2018/11/fsb - and - standard - setting - bodies - publish - final - report - on - effects - of - reforms - on - incentives - to - centrally - clear - over - the - counter - derivatives/。

FINANCIAL
STABILITY
BOARD

Thematic Review on Implementation of the Legal Entity Identifier

Peer Review Report

28 May 2019

The Financial Stability Board (FSB) is established to coordinate at the international level the work of national financial authorities and international standard-setting bodies in order to develop and promote the implementation of effective regulatory, supervisory and other financial sector policies. Its mandate is set out in the FSB Charter, which governs the policymaking and related activities of the FSB. These activities, including any decisions reached in their context, shall not be binding or give rise to any legal rights or obligations under the FSB's Articles of Association.

Contacting the Financial Stability Board

Sign up for e-mail alerts: www. fsb. org/emailalert Follow the FSB on Twitter: @ FinStbBoard

E-mail the FSB at: fsb@ fsb. org

Foreword

Financial Stability Board (FSB) member jurisdictions have committed, under the FSB Charter and in the *FSB Framework for Strengthening Adherence to International Standards*,① to undergo periodic peer reviews. To fulfil this responsibility, the FSB has established a regular programme of country and thematic peer reviews of its member jurisdictions.

Thematic reviews focus on the implementation and effectiveness across the FSB membership of international financial standards developed by standard-setting bodies and policies agreed within the FSB in a particular area important for global financial stability. Thematic reviews may also analyse other areas important for global financial stability where international standards or policies do not yet exist. The objectives of the reviews are to encourage consistent cross-country and cross-sector implementation; to evaluate (where possible) the extent to which standards and policies have had their intended results; and to identify gaps and weaknesses in reviewed areas and to make recommendations for potential follow-up (including through the development of new standards) by FSB members.

This report describes the findings of the peer review on implementation of the Legal Entity Identifier, including the key elements of the discussion in the FSB Standing Committee on Standards Implementation (SCSI). It is the fifteenth thematic review conducted by the FSB, and it is based on the objectives and guidelines for the conduct of peer reviews set forth in the April 2017 version of the *Handbook for FSB Peer Reviews*.②

The draft report for discussion by SCSI was prepared by a team chaired by Amir Zaidi (US Commodity Futures Trading Commission), comprising Khaled H. Alshammary (Saudi Arabian Monetary Authority), Vinicius Brandi (Banco

---

① See http://www. fsb. org/2010/01/r_100109a/.
② See http://www. fsb. org/2017/04/handbook-for-fsb-peer-reviews-2/.

Central do Brasil), Olaf Kurpiers (German Federal Financial Supervisory Authority), Franck Lasry (French Autorité des marchés financiers), Kirill Markov (Bank of Russia), Tim Pinkowski (IOSCO General Secretariat), Beju Shah (Bank of England), Wolfgang Sommerfeld (European Central Bank), Antonio Tiberio (Bank of Italy) and Robert Michael Willis (US Securities and Exchange Commission). Stéphane Mahieu, Gianmatteo Piazza (until June 2018), Michael Januska (since July 2018) and Costas Stephanou (FSB Secretariat) provided support to the team and contributed to the preparation of the peer review report.

Definitions of key terms used in the report

"**Beneficial owner**" – a single individual with significant responsibility to control, manage or direct a legal entity.

"**Central counterparty**" – an entity that interposes itself between counterparties to contracts traded in one or more financial markets, becoming the buyer to every seller and the seller to every buyer and thereby ensuring the performance of open contracts.

"**Child**" – entity that is owned or otherwise controlled by another entity within a corporate group.

"**Counterparty**" – entity that takes the opposite side of a financial contract or transaction-for example, the borrower in a loan contract, or the buyer in a sales transaction.

"**Current LEI**" – an issued LEI that is actively maintained by the entity through a contract with an accredited LEI issuer (LOU), so that changes in the entity data (e. g. name, address, parent entities) are reported on a timely basis by the entity, challenges by third parties are addressed by the LOU and the entity, and the accuracy of the entity data is recertified by the entity and validated by the LOU at least yearly. This excludes LEIs that are duplicates, lapsed, retired, annulled or merged. ①

"**Digital authentication**" – the process of establishing confidence in user identities presented digitally to a system.

"**E-invoicing**" – the exchange of an electronic invoice document between a supplier and a buyer. An electronic invoice (e-invoice) is an invoice that has been issued, transmitted and received in a structured data format which allows for its automatic and electronic processing.

"**Gross notional outstanding**" – gross notional value of all derivatives

---

① Accepted statuses for current LEIs are "issued" and "pending transfer". An LEI with a registration status "pending_archival" may also be considered as current when the same LEI is not published with an "issued" registration status by another LOU, which may happen in rare cases.

contracts concluded and not yet settled on the reporting date.

"**Know your customer**" – the process of verifying the identity of one's customer.

"**Lapsed LEI**" – an LEI that is overdue for annual renewal.

"**LEI**" – The Legal Entity Identifier (LEI) is a 20-character, alpha-numeric code that uniquely identifies legally distinct entities that engage in financial transactions.

"**Level 2 data**" – the reporting of parent information by legal entities. Level 2 data provides the answer to the question of 'who owns whom'. Specifically, legal entities that have or acquire an LEI report their 'direct accounting consolidating parent' as well as their 'ultimate accounting consolidating parent'.

"**Local Operating Unit**" (LOU) – an organisation accredited by the GLEIF to issue LEIs. They supply registration, renewal and other services, and act as the primary interface with registrants for LEIs. An LOU may issue LEIs to legal entities in any country where it is accredited to do so.

"**Optional**" – situation where the LEI does not have to be reported as part of a transaction, irrespective of whether the entity has one.

"**Parent**" – entity that owns or otherwise controls other entities within a corporate group. In the GLEIS, the "ultimate accounting consolidating parent" of entity X is the highest level legal entity preparing consolidated financial statements that consolidate entity X, based on the accounting definition of consolidation applying to this parent.

"**Payment messaging**" – communication of instructions to credit and debit accounts to transfer money between financial institutions, for instance through the messaging services of the Society for Worldwide Interbank Financial Telecommunication (SWIFT).

"**Reinsurance**" – a mechanism that an insurer uses to obtain protection against some or all risks associated with the insurance policies it issues. Typically, this process involves an assuming reinsurer who, for a consideration, indemnifies the ceding or direct insurer against some or all of the loss it may incur under a policy or policies it has issued.

"**Renewal**" – annual confirmation by the entity of its LEI reference data (e. g. name, address, parent entity) and verification by the Local Operating Unit of that data against authoritative sources, where available. A Local Operating Unit generally charges a fee.

"**Reporting entity**" – the entity that is reporting a transaction (e. g. to a trade repository).

"**Requested**" – situation where the LEI is to be provided/reported if the entity already has one, but the entity is not required to acquire one.

"**Required**" – situation where the LEI is required to enter into a transaction.

"**Resolution (of a financial institution)**" – the exercise of resolution powers, including in particular the exercise of a resolution power specified in the FSB *Key Attributes of Effective Resolution Regimes for Financial Institutions* (Attribute 3), ① by a resolution authority in respect of a bank that meets the conditions for entry into resolution, with or without private sector involvement, with the aim of achieving the statutory objectives of resolution set out in Key Attribute 2. 3.

"**Subsidiaries**" – entities that are controlled by another entity.

"**Supply chain**" – network of providers from which a company buys products and services to produce and deliver a final product.

"**Trade finance**" – the financing of international trade flows.

"**Unique Product Identifier**" – the UPI's purpose is to uniquely identify any OTC derivative product that an authority requires to be reported to a trade repository.

"**Unique Transaction Identifier**" – the primary purpose of the UTI is to uniquely identify individual OTC derivatives transactions that are required by authorities to be reported to trade repositories.

---

① See http://www. fsb. org/2014/10/key-attributes-of-effective-resolution-regimes-for-financial-institutions-2/.

Abbreviations[1]

ADIMA   Analytical Database on Individual Multinationals and their Affiliates (OECD)

AML/CFT   Anti-money laundering and combating the financing of terrorism

AnaCredit   Analytical Credit Datasets

AVID   Avox International Business Entity Identifier

BCBS   Basel Committee on Banking Supervision

BIC   Bank identification code

BIS   Bank for International Settlements

BMARS   Bond Market Access Record System (China)

CCP   Central counterparty

CDS   Credit default swaps

CGFS   Committee on the Global Financial System

CIBM   China interbank bond market

CLO   Collateralised loan obligation

CPIS   Coordinated Portfolio Investment Survey (IMF)

CPMI   Committee on Payments and Market Infrastructures

CRILC   Central Repository of Information on Large Credits (India)

CSDB   Centralised Securities Database (ECB)

EMIR   European market infrastructure regulation

EU   European Union

---

[1]   See Annex 1 for the abbreviations of national authorities mentioned in this report.

FATS	Foreign Affiliate Statistics, also called Activities of Multinational Enterprise (AMNE) statistics
FDI	Foreign Direct Investment
FSB	Financial Stability Board
GLEIF	Global LEI Foundation
GLEIS	Global LEI System
G-SIB	Global systemically important bank
G-SII	Global systemically important insurer
IAIS	International Association of Insurance Supervisors
IASB	International Accounting Standards Board
IBAN	International bank account number
IFC	Irving Fisher Committee on Central Bank Statistics (BIS)
IMF	International Monetary Fund
IOSCO	International Organization of Securities Commissions
ISIN	International Securities Identification Number
ISO	International Organization for Standardization
KYC	Know your customer
LEI	Legal Entity Identifier
LEI ROC	LEI Regulatory Oversight Committee
LOU	Local Operating Unit (of the Global LEI System)
MIC	Market Identifier Code
MiFID II	Markets in Financial Instruments Directive II (EU)
MiFIR	Markets in Financial Instruments Regulation (EU)
MNE	Multinational enterprise
OECD	Organisation for Economic Cooperation and Development

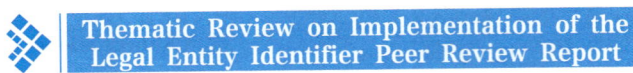

OTC	Over-the-counter (derivatives)
PLI	Privacy law identifier (US)
QIS	Quantitative impact study (BCBS)
Repos	Repurchase agreements
RIAD	Register of Institutions and Affiliates Database
RSSD ID	Research Statistics Supervision Discount ID (US)
S-b-s	Security-by-security
SCSI	Standing Committee on Standards Implementation (FSB)
SWIFT	Society for Worldwide Interbank Financial Telecommunication
UCITS	Undertakings for Collective Investments in Transferable Securities
UIC	Ultimate Investing Country
UK	United Kingdom
UPI	Unique Product Identifier
US	United States
UTI	Unique Transaction Identifier
VAT	Value-added tax
XBRL	eXtensible Business Reporting Language

Executive Summary

Since its endorsement by the G20 in 2012, the Global LEI System (GLEIS) has been successfully brought into operation, with over 1. 4 million entities uniquely identified by an LEI in more than 200 countries. Widespread coverage has been achieved in some financial market segments, with LEIs identifying reporting entities for close to 100% of the gross notional outstanding for over-the-counter (OTC) derivative trades in most FSB jurisdictions, and securities issuers for around 78% on average of the outstanding amounts of debt and equity securities in FSB jurisdictions. In these areas, the LEI has come the closest to meeting the G20's objective to "encourage global adoption of the LEI to support authorities and market participants in identifying and managing financial risks" .

Most FSB jurisdictions have implemented rules mandating LEI use in at least one area. Adoption has been most successful when the LEI has been mandated by regulators as part of an international standard-setting effort (such as reporting of OTC derivatives, where the LEI is used by regulators in some jurisdictions as a reporting entity or counterparty identifier), or across multiple market segments in the same region (European Union, EU).

The regulatory uses of the LEI are multiple and the benefits can be substantial. The LEI standardises identification of legal entities at the global level, to support the management and analysis of large datasets. Benefits derived from LEI implementation include enhancing regulators' surveillance by tracking market abuse across institutions, products and jurisdictions. The LEI can also assist regulators' and market participants' aggregation and more flexible retrieval of granular data on entities from multiple sources (e. g. security-by-security databases), as well as the analysis of counterparty risks, interconnectedness (e. g. through the identification of common exposures or funding sources) and complex group structures (due to the recent addition of so-called "Level 2" data on 150, 000 parent relationships). In some jurisdictions, the LEI is also used in reporting to credit registries, and for supporting the resolution of banks.

Many in the financial industry are supportive of the LEI, citing substantial existing and potential benefits stemming from its use. Several financial institutions and trade associations have called on authorities to mandate the use (and renewal by entities) of the LEI, both to facilitate regulatory reporting and to increase the efficiency and lower the costs of customer identification, transaction processing and data aggregation.

Notwithstanding this progress, the LEI has far to go to meet the G20's objective. LEI adoption remains low outside securities and derivatives markets, which limits the ability to effectively support further regulatory uses or to capture positive externalities and maximise network effects to the market as a whole. More efforts should be made both at national and international levels to promote LEI adoption and enhance the benefits to authorities and market participants from its use by addressing identified obstacles.

LEI adoption remains uneven across countries. LEI coverage is concentrated in Canada, the EU and the United States (US), where it spans from 2% to 7% of all eligible legal entities, and is much lower elsewhere. Several FSB jurisdictions-particularly in Asia and emerging economies-have not taken steps to mandate use of the LEI in any area, or have adopted rules requiring LEI use only if the entity already has one. Few jurisdictions have plans for new strategies to increase adoption. Standard-setting bodies have only recommended the LEI in their policy making for certain areas to date and, in most of those cases-for anti-money laundering and combating the financing of terrorism (AML/CFT), risk data aggregation and correspondent banking-they have not proposed timelines for adoption and the use of the LEI was left as an optional element.

LEI coverage remains too low to encourage new industry or regulatory uses or to reach a tipping point where voluntary take-up by market participants would suffice to propel further adoption. Higher LEI coverage (including for non-financial corporations) would support regulatory uses such as for AML/CFT, as well as other business and industry uses such as know your customer (KYC) processes and the transfer of funds, especially across borders.

In addition, while the parent entities of all global systemically important banks (G-SIBs) have an LEI, this is not usually the case for all of their subsidiaries or major counterparties. Without higher LEI coverage of G-SIBs' group entities, for example, the effectiveness of regulators' and market participants' analysis of interlinkages and common exposures across these firms, as well as the potential use of LEI in resolution planning for them, may be limited.

A number of obstacles to further LEI adoption and implementation should be addressed. These include the current business model, which does not clearly align the current benefits and costs of LEI use for participants; a lack of LEI coverage for Level 2 (relationship) data; and insufficient links with other (in particular, business registry) identifiers. Enhancing the business model by minimising the cost and administrative burden of LEI registration and maintenance for registrants, for instance through a greater reliance on third parties such as banks or business registries for data verifications and updates, may help to address some of these challenges. Exploring further use cases, improving relationship data availability and quality, and mapping to other identifiers would also expand LEI adoption.

Jurisdictions' approaches and strategies to implement the LEI (section 3)

- All FSB jurisdictions except one have implemented the LEI in at least some contexts. Almost all FSB jurisdictions have regulations referring to the LEI, although the number of rules varies widely. Out of the 101 rules published by FSB members, roughly half (49) mandate all or some of the entities subject to the rules to have an LEI. In other cases, the LEI is to be reported only if the entity already has one, or LEI reporting is optional. Only in 12 FSB jurisdictions is LEI renewal mandatory for at least some uses.
- The evolution and composition of LEI issuance strongly suggests that adoption was driven by regulatory requirements rather than by voluntary or optional programmes. Where regulatory adoption and renewal mandates were absent, LEI adoption and maintenance rates have generally been significantly lower.

- Very few jurisdictions (typically those with large financial markets) have implemented the LEI beyond OTC derivatives and securities transactions. Commonly, priority is given by jurisdictions to the identification of parties to financial transactions.

- Most jurisdictions report having explicit strategies in place to implement the LEI, but the scope of such strategies differs. ① In some jurisdictions, the strategy is largely based on supporting voluntary LEI adoption (e. g. by increasing awareness of its benefits to market participants), while in others it includes specific rule setting. When jurisdictions report that they have a strategy in place, these strategies are evenly distributed between national and authority-specific strategies. Six jurisdictions do not have an LEI strategy. No jurisdiction plans for universal adoption of the LEI across all eligible legal entities.

LEI coverage (section 4)

- While LEI coverage in absolute terms is relatively low, it varies widely across FSB jurisdictions and is far higher for entities involved in OTC derivatives and securities transactions, for supervised financial intermediaries and for large non-financial companies. Coverage is also strong for the parent entities of large financial and non-financial groups, but is not complete for their subsidiaries.

- All but three FSB jurisdictions' central banks have an LEI, and all jurisdictions reported having at least one other public sector body with an LEI (typically, the main public debt issuer).

Achievements and benefits (section 5)

- The LEI is currently used for regulatory and other public sector tasks such as: monitoring financial risks; exposure aggregation in data reporting; statistical analysis; understanding the structures of multinational

---

① A "strategy" is defined here as a structured approach or action plan that would generally include a set of measures supporting LEI adoption (e. g. coordination between relevant authorities, communication with other stakeholders, preparation of laws and regulations).

companies, market structure and trading networks; and facilitating market surveillance and compliance assessments.

- Benefits derived from LEI implementation include improved data analysis and, in some cases, cost savings. A significant proportion of FSB jurisdictions report that the use of LEI has led to improvements in data quality and analysis. Cost reductions resulting from regulatory LEI implementation were only cited by the FSB jurisdictions with the largest number of uses (EU members and US).

- Other LEI benefits include a uniform identification method for both foreign and domestic entities, and facilitating data aggregation and coordination across multiple jurisdictions and authorities.

- Several commercial market stakeholder responses highlighted the benefits associated with the use of the LEI in KYC and AML processes.

Obstacles to adoption and implementation (section 5)

- The usability of relationship data still falls short of authorities' expectations, as information on parent entities based on accounting consolidation, which was collected more recently, is inhibited by the absence of LEIs for 56% of the ultimate parent relationships (46% for child entities located in FSB jurisdictions). This is in part due to the fact that parent entities that do not trade certain types of products are outside the remit of financial regulators, which may need to be addressed by legislation, as was done for instance in Mexico. Other issues include the fact that this information cannot currently be collected by the GLEIS when it is confidential and that accounting consolidation rules do not always meet all the needs for relationship data.

- The perceived asymmetry of financial burden and benefits seems to be an issue across jurisdictions. This reflects a view from many in the private sector that those who benefit the most (i. e. financial authorities and some large financial institutions subject to reporting obligations) contribute marginally to the financing of the system, whereas the entities that have to pay for LEI issuance and renewal-many of which are smaller

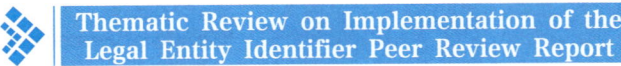
in size-fail to see clear current benefits on their side, especially given the existence of low-cost business registries and the lack of other process enhancements enabled by having an international standardised identifier (e. g. digital authentication/identity).

- The existence of other identifiers-in particular, no-cost or low-cost national identifiers and of systems built around those identifiers-is seen by several jurisdictions as a barrier to LEI implementation, in the sense that it reduces incentives for jurisdictions to promote mandatory LEI adoption, especially in markets where firms undertake limited cross-border activities.

Way forward in advancing LEI adoption (section 6)

- Prospective LEI use case examples identified by jurisdictions and market participants include digital authentication, KYC, payment messaging, trade/supply chain finance efficiencies, e-invoicing and financial institution resolution.

Recommendations

The FSB remains committed to a broader use of the LEI globally in order to meet the G20's objective. To accomplish this, and in light of the above findings, there are four sets of recommendations addressed to: FSB member jurisdictions, the FSB itself, relevant standard-setting bodies and international organisations, and the LEI Regulatory Oversight Committee (LEI ROC) and Global LEI Foundation (GLEIF).

1) FSB jurisdictions should:
   a. Follow-up on CPMI-IOSCO guidance that strongly encourages authorities to require the use of LEIs for the identification of legal entities in the data reported to trade repositories for OTC derivatives.
   b. Consider requiring the use and timely renewal of the LEI in reporting or disclosure frameworks, for the identification of all entities in major financial groups, a wider set of financial market participants and infrastructures, their counterparties, and related entities (including direct and ultimate parents), especially in a cross-border context.
   c. Explore ways to promote further LEI adoption, for instance by fostering nationwide implementation strategies to maximise the cross-sectoral benefits of the LEI; communicating on LEI benefits through public outreach initiatives; leading by example in obtaining LEIs for the central bank and other public sector bodies, especially issuers of public debt; and considering the potential for LEI use before introducing new identifiers.

2) The FSB will:
   a. Explore the potential role of the LEI in its work, for instance in the resolution of financial institutions and on financial innovation issues.
   b. Work with standard-setting and industry bodies to facilitate adoption of the LEI for all group entities and major counterparties of global

systemically important financial institutions, as well as for the clearing members of central counterparties (CCPs) and their ultimate parents, in order to support the timely analysis of risk exposures and interdependencies.

c. Facilitate, by working with standard-setting and industry bodies, the effective implementation of the LEI option in payment messages to help address the decline in the number of correspondent banking relationships.

3) The relevant standard-setting bodies (BCBS, CPMI, IAIS, IOSCO) and international organisations (IMF, OECD, World Bank) should review and consider ways to embed or enhance references to the LEI in their work, in order to facilitate the implementation of relevant LEI uses for authorities and market participants. This could involve, for example, guidance on the inclusion of the LEI in disclosures of data on entities as well as promoting LEI use in securities transactions and cross-border payments.

4) The LEI ROC and GLEIF should:

a. Consider enhancements to the LEI business model to lower the cost and administrative burden for entities acquiring and maintaining an LEI. These could involve, for instance, adjusting funding approaches to align the benefits and costs for users more closely, and exploring ways to foster complementarity between the issuance and maintenance of the LEI and other processes involving similar tasks.

b. Consider data quality process enhancements to increase the reliability of the LEI data so as to improve its usability by market participants and regulators, including processes to encourage and monitor updates of LEI reference data.

c. Work with industry and the public sector to raise awareness of the benefits of the LEI and encourage voluntary adoption by documenting existing uses, or by supporting pilot programs or research projects on promising new uses.

d. Enhance the scope and usability of Level 2 (relationship) data by:

i . considering cost-effective and reliable ways to add relationship data that would increase the value of the LEI (e. g. confidential relationships subject to access rights and appropriate controls; beneficial owners; other definition of parents) ; and

ii. expanding the coverage of such data, for instance by conducting targeted LEI adoption campaigns for large multinational firms and by facilitating relationship reporting by parents of their group entities.

1. Introduction

The global financial crisis showed the difficulty of identifying counterparties to financial transactions across borders with accuracy and speed. To address this problem, in 2011 the G20 supported the creation of an LEI and called on the FSB to take the lead in helping coordinate work among the regulatory community to prepare recommendations for the appropriate governance framework for the GLEIS. At the June 2012 Los Cabos Summit, the G20 Leaders endorsed the FSB report *A Global Legal Entity Identifier for Financial Markets* and encouraged "global adoption of the LEI to support authorities and market participants in identifying and managing financial risks". [①] Since then, the FSB has continued to support the LEI implementation, including by establishing in 2014 the GLEIF as the operational arm of the system that federates local LEI issuers under the oversight of the LEI ROC.

This thematic review offers a timely opportunity to evaluate the progress made by FSB members-both national authorities and international bodies-in response to the G20 Leaders' call. In particular, the objectives of the peer review are to:

a. Take stock of the approaches and strategies used by FSB members to implement the LEI, including its adoption for regulatory requirements by FSB member jurisdictions.

b. Assess whether current levels and rates of LEI adoption are sufficient to support the ongoing and anticipated needs (particularly financial stability objectives) of FSB member authorities.

c. Identify the challenges FSB members face in further advancing the implementation and use of the LEI, and make recommendations (as appropriate) to address common challenges.

In order to avoid duplication with the LEI ROC and GLEIF work, the peer

---

① See http: //www. fsb. org/wp-content/uploads/g20 _ leaders _ declaration _ los _ cabos _ 2012. pdf and http: //www. fsb. org/2012/06/fsb-report-global-legal-entity-identifier-for-financial-markets/.

review does not examine the governance or technical functioning of the GLEIS but rather focuses, across the FSB membership, on LEI implementation approaches and uses for financial stability purposes and on possible strategies to further global adoption.

The primary source of information for the peer review was responses to a questionnaire by FSB member jurisdictions. In addition, the review team collected information from SSBs and international financial institutions on areas in the scope of the review (see Annex 6). In terms of stakeholder outreach, the FSB issued a call for public feedback in August 2018 on the areas covered by the review. The team also held a roundtable with stakeholders in London in December 2018 to exchange views on the benefits/uses of the LEI and related strategies and challenges with respect to global LEI adoption. Annex 5 provides a summary of the main takeaways from the written public feedback and from the roundtable.

The report is structured as follows:

- Section 2 provides some background on the LEI, including its governance and certain key features;
- Section 3 describes the approaches and strategies of FSB members in implementing the LEI, including regulatory and non-regulatory tools and areas of coverage;
- Section 4 examines LEI coverage in areas relevant for financial stability, describing the evolution of LEI issuance over time and the current rates of issuance by jurisdiction and across sectors;
- Section 5 highlights achievements and challenges in further advancing LEI adoption; and
- Section 6 identifies possible ways to address challenges in advancing LEI adoption.

Annex 1 provides a list of abbreviations of financial authorities in FSB jurisdictions; Annex 2 describes identifiers other than the LEI used by jurisdictions; Annex 3 summarises jurisdictions' strategies to implement the LEI; Annexes 4a and 4b provide details on LEI coverage for parties to OTC derivatives transactions and for securities issuers, Annex 4c describes the reasons that entities do not provide information on their direct and ultimate parents, and Annex 4d presents LEI coverage in the customer base of a sample of 21 members of the Global Financial Markets Association (GFMA) and the International Swaps and Derivatives Association (ISDA). Annex 5 provides a summary of public feedback regarding the LEI. Finally, Annex 6 summarises the uses (current and projected) by SSBs of the LEI in policy work, data collection or research projects, as well as any limitations they identified.

2. Background

The LEI is a 20-character, alpha-numeric code that uniquely identifies legally distinct entities that engage in financial transactions. LEIs are linked to reference data which provide basic information on the legal entity itself, such as the name and address, and its ownership (direct and ultimate parent entities). The LEI is the result of joint public and private sector efforts and the structure and fundamental features of the LEI code were defined in a standard set by the International Organization for Standardization (ISO). [1]

The governance of the GLEIS, recommended by the FSB in 2012, has three layers:

- LEIs are issued by 33 Local Operating Units (LOUs), some of which are from the public sector (e. g. business registries, national statistical offices) or the private sector [e. g. numbering agencies issuing the International Securities Identification Number (ISIN), stock exchanges]. Any organisation can apply for accreditation. Some LOUs operate in multiple countries, while others specialise in their domestic jurisdiction.
- These LOUs are accredited by the GLEIF, a non-for profit organisation established by the FSB in 2014, which also monitors LOU compliance with LEI standards, collects LEI codes in a centralised database and publishes LEI data.
- The LEI Regulatory Oversight Committee (LEI ROC), a group of more than 70 member public sector authorities (including the FSB and 34 FSB member agencies) and 18 observers, oversees the GLEIF and establishes policy standards for the GLEIS. [2]

As recommended by the FSB, the LEI is a non-proprietary system with free use of LEIs and related reference data for regulators and the public, and

---

① See https://www.iso.org/standard/59771.html.
② See https://www.leiroc.org/.

portability of LEIs between competing LOUs, among other features. ① The GLEIS relies on self-registration, whereby registrants are responsible for the accuracy of their data (see Box 1).

Box 1: Self-registration of LEIs

Only an entity eligible to receive an LEI or its authorised representative may apply for an LEI code. The permission of the LEI registrant to perform an LEI registration on its behalf by a third party is considered to satisfy the requirements of self-registration only if the registrant has provided explicit permission for such a registration to be performed. This feature is meant to reduce the risk that several LEIs could be requested for the same entity, and ensure that entities have the primary responsibility for the accuracy of their data. LOUs are also required to check data against reliable sources (public sources such as a business registry, private legal documents) prior to publishing the LEI and associated reference data, and to encourage updates.

The contractual relationship between LOUs and the entity supports the provision of accurate and up-to-date information by registrants. In particular, entities commit to provide true, full and authentic information, review the accuracy of this information at least annually and promptly submit any changes. These commitments are for the life of the entity, unless the entity chooses to abandon any use of the LEI and terminates the contract without porting its LEI to another LOU.

The GLEIS is funded by fees paid by entities when registering and renewing annually their LEI registration, on a cost-recovery basis: a portion of the fee ($11 in 2019) funds the GLEIF (paid by LOUs to the GLEIF). LOU fees vary from around $55-220 for new issuance of an LEI, and $35-125 for LEI renewals. In almost all jurisdictions, users can acquire an LEI for $65 (first issuance) and $50 (renewals) or less, including a zero fee in China (but only for Chinese entities). This is a significant reduction from earlier years, with

---

① See https://www.gleif.org/en/lei-data/access-and-use-lei-data.

prices more than halving in many jurisdictions: for instance, in May 2016, the three largest issuers at the time, which were available in most jurisdictions, charged between $160-219 for first issuance and $103-159 for renewals, plus VAT where applicable. Prices are expected to be further reduced in 2019 due to the reduction of the GLEIF fee to $11, from $17 in 2018.

3. Approaches and strategies to implement the LEI

This section describes the implementation approaches adopted by FSB members, including whether sectoral rules have been issued or whether other approaches have been chosen, and the main areas covered by those rules. It also discusses whether rulemaking was part of a comprehensive strategy at the jurisdiction level or by individual authorities. As almost all regulations in EU member states result from EU-level rulemaking, the EU is presented as a single jurisdiction in this section, except where something specific to a member jurisdiction is described. ①

Implementation approaches

Almost all FSB jurisdictions have regulations referring to the LEI, although the number of rules in each varies widely (see Graph 1). The EU and US have each adopted more than 20 rules, while Canada and Australia have implemented six and four respectively. Twelve other jurisdictions② have issued up to three rules that have been implemented. Two jurisdictions (Indonesia and South Africa) have issued no final rules to date, although South Africa has published a draft rule.

These regulations have differing expectation of entities. Under some rules, entities must have an LEI ('required'). Under other rules, use of the LEI is mandatory only if the entity already has one ('requested'). ③ Under

---

① Some other LEI regulations, in addition to those issued at the EU level, were adopted in the United Kingdom.

② Argentina, Brazil, China, Hong Kong, India, Japan, Korea, Mexico, Russia, Saudi Arabia, Singapore and Turkey.

③ The "requested" category includes cases, such as Australia's OTC derivative transaction reporting rules, where the LEI is mandated as the first of a "waterfall" of the three global standard identifiers (the other options being AVIDs or BICs) for non-natural entities that are parties to a reportable OTC derivative transaction. In practice, Australia noted that parties without one of the three standard identifiers will obtain an LEI to comply. However, entities that have an AVID or BIC are not mandated to obtain an LEI. A similar framework exists in Korea.

other rules, the use of the LEI is optional.

Roughly half (49) of the 101 rules published by FSB members mandate some or all entities subject to their rules have an LEI. In other cases, the LEI is requested to be reported only if available or LEI reporting is optional. Argentina, Australia, Brazil, China, Japan and Korea have implemented the LEI in their regulations exclusively through provisions that do not mandate entities to acquire an LEI (described as "requested" or "optional" in Graph 1).

Number of rules implementing the LEI

Graph 1

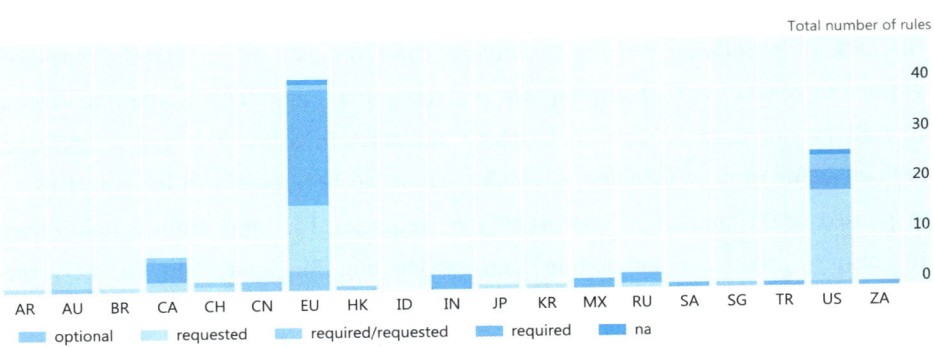

Notes: "optional" means the LEI does not have to be reported as part of a transaction, irrespective of whether the entity has one; "requested" means that entities have to provide an LEI only if they already have one; and "required" means that entities are mandated to have an LEI. Required/requested means that the regulation combines both approaches depending on the entities. N/A refers mainly to cases where the regulation does not apply to the entities, but to the information provided by regulators in public disclosures or for cooperation between regulators.

Jurisdiction acronyms here and through the remainder of the report are as follows: AR = Argentina, AU = Australia, BR = Brazil; CA = Canada; CH = Switzerland; CN = China; DE = Germany; ES = Spain; EU = European Union; FR = France; HK = Hong Kong SAR; IN = India; ID = Indonesia; IT = Italy; JP = Japan; KR = Korea; MX = Mexico; NL = Netherlands; RU = Russia; SA = Saudi Arabia; SG = Singapore; TR = Turkey; UK = United Kingdom; US = United States; ZA = South Africa.

Source: LEI ROC and survey of FSB members.

The figures in Graphs 1 and 3 suggest that adoption was driven by mandatory regulatory requirements rather than by voluntary or optional programmes. Where regulatory adoption and renewal mandates were absent, LEI

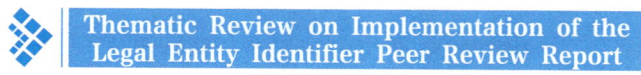

adoption and maintenance rates were significantly lower (see section 4). This is consistent with views expressed in public feedback (see Annex 5).

Rationales differ for choosing whether the use of the LEI in a particular sector should be required, requested or optional. Three authorities sought to minimise the burden: one authority (US SEC), by requiring filers in certain cases to report an LEI only if the entity already has one, and two authorities (Australia-ASIC, Japan) permitting AVID or bank identification code (BIC) as alternatives. Other authorities are of the view that mandatory reporting may be necessary to increase the coverage (Mexico, UK). The analysis of costs and benefits of requiring versus requesting an LEI were reported as taken into account in Canada, Hong Kong, Germany, Italy, Switzerland, and the US. Korea notes the lack of regulatory powers to impose strict obligations on certain types of entities to obtain an LEI, opting for a "requested" approach (although Korea intends to move to an approach where financial investment business entities, collective investment schemes and CCPs would all be required to have an LEI). A phased or differentiation approach (i. e. requiring LEI only from certain types of entities) has been adopted in Hong Kong and Singapore. In the US, the rationale for requiring or requesting an LEI depends on the authority. ①

The scope of LEI implementation has primarily focused on the identification of parties to financial operations (OTC and exchange-traded derivatives, investment activities, equity markets, repos, securities transactions, securities financing transactions, etc). This is in large part due to international efforts in this area. International SSBs identified early on that the LEI was

---

① The CFTC and the OFR called for mandatory LEI adoption to improve data quality; the SEC mandated LEI reporting in certain cases; and the FRB, OCC, FDIC and other members of the Federal Financial Institutions Examination Council implemented a requested approach. The FRB reported adopting the requested approach given the existence of another, more comprehensive identifier (Federal Reserve's Research Statistics Supervision Discount ID), while the FDIC and OCC noted the regulatory burden on reporting entities in their decision to adopt this approach, given the existence of nearly 5,000 small community banks as well as over 2,700 credit unions under $100 million in total assets.

needed for OTC derivatives aggregation, ① and requirements were subsequently introduced in major markets. ② The CPMI-IOSCO final technical guidance to authorities on UTIs③ has selected the LEI as the code to identify the party generating the UTI. The EU requires use of the LEI in reports of both exchange-traded and OTC derivatives.

- The high correlation between international standard-setting, subsequent national implementation, and the relatively high number of LEIs issued for market participants active in the transactions covered by regulatory requirements, suggests that this has been an effective approach to promote global adoption of the LEI.

Jurisdictions suggested other additional reasons for this focus in scope. Two jurisdictions (China, Indonesia) note that authorities should prioritise LEI implementation in markets with high share of international participation (or where international participation is desirable) and systemic importance. The US Office of Financial Research (OFR) observes that its strategy seeks the adoption of the LEI as the principal identifier for legal entities engaging in financial market transactions in the US, with a priority placed on those actively engaging in such transactions and which may pose, contribute to, or be endangered by financial stability risks. The European Securities and Markets Authority (ESMA) notes that it is easier to require the LEI for the entities under direct supervision of an

---

① The FSB noted in its September 2014 *Feasibility study on approaches to aggregate OTC derivatives data* (http://www.fsb.org/wp-content/uploads/r_140919.pdf) that "counterparty identifiers (LEI) are required to accumulate accurate position data across TRs. The LEI with hierarchy (for consolidation purpose) is also needed for some mandates at least in a second step when the fully fledged LEI is in place". This study concluded that "it is critical for any aggregation option that the work on standardisation and harmonisation of important data elements be completed, including in particular through the global introduction of the Legal Entity Identifier (LEI), and the creation of a Unique Transaction Identifier (UTI) and Unique Product Identifier (UPI)". Subsequently, in September 2015, CPMI and IOSCO have proposed use of the LEI for the identification of the primary obligors and the payer of payment streams of reportable derivative contracts (http://www.bis.org/cpmi/publ/d132.htm).

② For example, EMIR and MiFID II in the EU.

③ See http://www.bis.org/cpmi/publ/d158.pdf. The final guidance on the UPI was published in September 2017.

authority (i. e. regulated entities). ① A progressive approach, where LEI is first implemented for the financial sector and then to other sectors, is deemed preferable by Italy. The UK notes that a holistic approach to implementation should be considered as some rules may affect others, and prefers a progressive approach like Italy. The US notes that it is easier to implement LEIs in new regulations rather than in existing regulations, where other identifiers already are used to comply with these existing regulations. **Only Australia, Canada, the EU, India, Mexico, Russia, Switzerland and the US have implemented rules on the LEI beyond OTC derivatives (see Table 1).** Argentina, Brazil and China have not implemented rules on derivatives, but have used the LEI in other areas.

Many jurisdictions are following or foresee a step-by-step approach with phased LEI implementation. Moreover, no jurisdiction plans to fully replace existing entity identifiers with the LEI, but the US-OFR noted that the expanded use of the LEI may gradually result in the phase-out of other identifiers, where these identifiers are repetitive and the LEI demonstrates its superiority vis-à-vis data quality and cost (see Annex 2 for more information on other identifiers used by FSB members).

A few jurisdictions have issued rules involving LEI use that is not related to financial regulation, such as with respect to energy markets in the US② and customs in China,③ where the LEI is also used in the area of movable property pledge financing. ④

The extent to which LEI renewal is mandatory differs across jurisdictions. In 12 jurisdictions [Canada, EU member states, India, Mexico, South Africa, Switzerland, and the US (FDIC, OFR, and FRB)] renewal of

---

① In the absence of direct supervision, ESMA suggests clarifying the consequences for a regulated entity failing to report the LEI code of a third party: for example, by clarifying that the regulated entity is no longer allowed to provide a service that would trigger the obligation to submit a report where the LEI of the third party is required, prior to the LEI being obtained from that third party.

② Use of LEIs for the reporting of connected entities by electric market participants.

③ LEI as one of the enterprise identifiers that are to be provided when products pass through customs.

④ The People's Bank of China is leading the role to facilitate the issuance and use of LEI in China, and reports developing an implementation strategy and action plan, expected to come into effect in the second half of 2019, covering most banking institutions and many non-bank financial institutions.

the LEI is mandatory for at least some uses. Some jurisdictions and authorities note that there are implicit requirements that do not directly ask for yearly renewal or reject the reporting if the LEI is lapsed, but require or encourage entities to keep their information up to date (Australia, Hong Kong, Japan, Singapore, US-CFTC and US-SEC ①). Some other jurisdictions and authorities are considering implementation of renewal requirements in the future (Australia, China, Korea, Russia, Saudi Arabia and US-OFR②). The proportionality principle is often considered in this respect [European Insurance and Occupational Pensions Authority (EIOPA), ESMA, and Italy]. ESMA distinguishes between entities that are subject to the reporting obligation, which are always obliged to renew their LEI (including the 350,000 financial and non-financial counterparties to derivative contracts, where the proportion of lapsed LEIs in reporting is below 1% for both the reporting counterparty and the other counterparty, some 10,000 investment firms,③ and 40 credit rating agencies) and entities that are required to be identified in the report by reporting entities (41, 000 issuers of financial instruments, potentially several millions of customers). For the latter, reporting entities are not required to ensure that the LEI of these third parties are duly renewed, but ESMA and the EU National Competent Authorities have clarified that, while the legal requirements cannot oblige reporting entities to renew the LEI of third parties, additional contractual obligations can be envisaged between the LOUs and the entity registering for an LEI. Given that it is one of the fundamental principles of the GLEIS, renewal is always part of those contractual arrangements. ④

---

① The SEC noted that reporting entities should not knowingly submit inaccurate LEIs to the Consolidated Audit Trail (CAT), Order Approving the National Market System Plan Governing the Consolidated Audit Trail, Release No. 34-79318 (15 November 2016) at 200, available at https: // www. sec. gov/rules/sro/nms/2016/34-79318. pdf.

② As of publication date of this report, US-OFR has made renewal mandatory with effect in February 2019.

③ Many of which are captured in the previous figure, as counterparties of derivative contracts.

④ See ESMA clarification at GFMA webinar on LEI (https: //www. esma. europa. eu/press-news/ esma-news/webinar-new-update-use-lei-now-available) and the general Briefing note on LEI on ESMA website: "to ensure that the reference data related to its own LEI code is up-to-date, each legal entity is asked to pay an annual maintenance fee" (https: //www. esma. europa. eu/sites/default/files/library/ esma70-145-238_lei_briefing_note. pdf).

Table 1: Areas covered by published rules and regulations

Jurisdiction	derivatives	securities regulations	asset management	credit rating agencies	securitisation	securities financing transactions	bank supervision	insurance supervision	resolution	payment services	credit registries	other	total
AR	0	0	0	0	0	0	1	1	0	0	0	1	3
AU	2	1	0	0	0	0	1	0	0	0	0	0	4
BR	0	0	0	0	0	0	0	0	0	0	0	1	1
CA	3	4	0	0	0	0	0	0	0	0	0	0	7
CH	1	1	0	0	0	0	0	0	0	0	0	0	2
CN	0	0	0	0	0	0	0	0	0	0	0	2	2
EU	1	23	2	2	1	1	4	3	1	1	1	2	42
HK	1	0	0	0	0	0	0	0	0	0	0	0	1
ID	0	0	0	0	0	0	0	0	0	0	0	0	0
IN	1	1	0	0	0	0	1	0	0	0	1	1	5
JP	1	0	0	0	0	0	0	0	0	0	0	0	1
KR	1	0	0	0	0	0	0	0	0	0	0	0	1
MX	1	0	0	0	0	0	0	0	0	0	0	1	2
RU	1	1	0	0	0	1	0	0	0	0	0	1	4
SA	0	0	0	0	0	0	1	1	0	0	0	1	3
SG	1	0	0	0	0	0	0	0	0	0	0	0	1
TR	1	0	0	0	0	0	0	0	0	0	0	0	1
US	5	5	4	1	1	1	6	1	1	0	0	2	27
ZA	1	0	0	0	0	0	0	0	0	0	0	0	1
Total	21	36	6	3	2	3	14	6	2	1	2	12	108

Note: the same rule can cover several areas, for instance one rule in Argentina covers three sectors. Hence, totals may differ from Graph 1. Rules adopted by individual EU jurisdictions are not shown here.

Similarly, there are large differences in renewal rates across FSB jurisdictions, including within the EU (see Table 2).

Table 2: LEI renewal rates in FSB jurisdictions

Jurisdiction	Renewal rate （%）	Jurisdiction	Renewal rate （%）
India	93	France	69
Japan	92	Turkey	66
Switzerland	81	South Africa	58
Spain	78	Mexico	57
Netherlands	77	Saudi Arabia	57
Germany	76	China	57
Hong Kong	74	Canada	56
Indonesia	71	Russian Federation	53
Australia	70	United Kingdom	52
Italy	70	United States	46
Korea	69	Argentina	45
Singapore	69	Brazil	41

Source: GLEIF, file 3 January 2019. The renewal rate is the proportion of LEIs with a legal address in the given jurisdiction that were due for renewal and have been renewed.

The LEI ROC progress report of April 2018 summarises the data quality concerns associated with lapsed LEIs, notably the risks that a second LEI could be issued to the entity (if for instance a name change was not timely recorded), confusion about the surviving LEI in case of mergers, difficulties in reconciling LEI data with other databases (e. g. different addresses), lack of management of challenges to LEI data by third parties (as LOUs cannot generally update a record without the agreement of the entity). Another concern is that data enhancements are not implemented for lapsed LEIs, for instance the collection of relationship data which is progressively rolled out.

LEI implementation strategies (*see Annex 3*)

Most jurisdictions (**20**) **report having explicit strategies in place to implement the LEI.** However, in some jurisdictions, the strategy is largely based on supporting voluntary LEI adoption (e. g. by increasing awareness of its benefits to market participants), while others have implemented more concrete measures (e. g. rule setting) as elements of their strategy. Likewise, some EU members refer to the EU as the relevant jurisdiction to issue regulations/laws and have therefore not reported an explicit strategy at the national level, whereas other EU members have described as their strategy their LEI promotion activities, e. g. the organisation of public conferences targeting the non-financial sector.

National① and authority-specific② strategies are approximately evenly distributed. Argentina and Russia have implemented one or several LEI rules without defining a strategy, while Saudi Arabia reports having a strategy but have not yet issued any rules.

Four jurisdictions do not have an LEI strategy and only two of them are in the process of developing one. Argentina notes it is not a priority because of the relatively small depth of the local capital and OTC derivatives markets, and because relevant entities are in any case getting an LEI when required by foreign rules. Indonesia notes that domestic identifiers are sufficient. Russia included the development of incentives to use LEI by market participants and implementation of the national standard, identical to ISO 17442 on the LEI, into the draft *Roadmap on implementation of the key priorities for the development of financial market of the Russia Federation for 2019-2021*, although detailed measures are yet to be developed. In South Africa, a public consultation has been launched, the outcome of which has to be awaited before implementation can start. ③

Many of the strategies in place include regulatory mandates for reporting, while others involve encouragement and support for voluntary LEI adoption.

Many FSB jurisdictions (Canada, EU, India, Mexico, Switzerland, Turkey and US) made the LEI mandatory for certain transaction reporting purposes via adoption of legal acts or regulations. Most jurisdictions (in particular Canada, France, Germany, India, Italy, Japan, Mexico, Singapore, Switzerland, UK, and the US) highlighted as objectives the improvement of data quality in statistical and regulatory reporting, data analysis, facilitation of risk

---

① Brazil, Canada, France, Hong Kong, India, Italy, Mexico, Saudi Arabia and Switzerland.
② China, EU, Germany, Japan, Korea, Russia, Singapore, Spain, Turkey, UK and US.
③ See https://www.fsca.co.za/Regulatory%20Frameworks/Documents%20for%20Consultation/Discussion%20pap er%20on%20the%20implementation%20of%20Legal%20Entity%20Identifiers%20-%2019%20November%202018.pdf.

assessment (for both financial entities and authorities) for financial stability purposes, and/or reduction of the reporting burden by financial institutions. Hong Kong refers generally to benefits for the financial sector as a whole and the international trend towards adopting LEI as a global standard, as well as to the FSB's recommendation to actively promote the use of the LEI reporting for OTC derivatives reporting. ①

Many jurisdictions (Brazil, Canada, Hong Kong, India, Italy, Japan, Mexico, Saudi Arabia, Switzerland, Turkey and US) report close cooperation between relevant national authorities when developing the strategy or drafting the respective legal acts or regulations.

Other jurisdictions perceive their strategy as providing general support for initiatives aiming at a voluntary adoption of the LEI. This was mainly explained by the lack of authority to set rules (e. g. in the case of EU member states the development of a strategy and the respective rule-setting are not at the national level but at the EU level).

The majority of jurisdictions are using meetings, seminars, and conferences to increase awareness and promote adoption of the LEI. Most jurisdictions (all but Argentina, Brazil, Hong Kong and Turkey) report having an ongoing dialogue between public authorities and the private sector. Furthermore, LOUs are striving to increase awareness and promotion via their own work and websites. Such efforts are not possible in some jurisdictions that do not have local LOUs.

Among those with a jurisdiction-wide strategy, only a few jurisdictions (Canada, Germany, Hong Kong, Italy, and Switzerland) mention that a cost-benefit analysis was carried out in the context of the development of the strategy. Even in those cases, the analysis was not specifically related to LEI adoption but rather concerned wider regulatory measures. In Hong Kong a non-quantitative cost-benefit analysis was undertaken when developing the strategy. Japan notes that, in spite of efforts to raise awareness and promote LEI implementation, entities not subject to trade reporting generally had difficulties in

---

① See the February 2018 FSB peer review report of Hong Kong for details (http: //www. fsb. org/ 2018/02/peer-review-of-hong-kong/).

recognising the benefits of a broad adoption of the LEI. Other cost-benefits analyses conducted as part of specific rulemaking, for instance in the EU and US, are described in section 5.

Implementation strategies most commonly cover OTC derivatives reporting and other reporting to securities regulators. In contrast, there have been fewer strategies covering identification in credit registries and payments or application for AML/CFT purposes (see Graph 2).

Areas covered (fully or partly) by LEI strategies in FSB jurisdictions

Graph 2

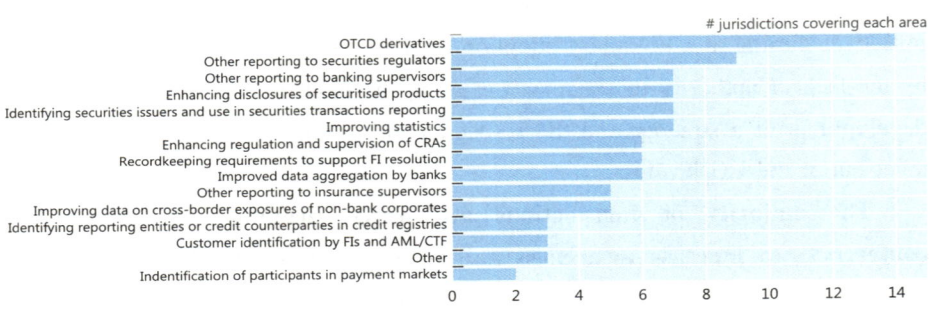

Source: Responses to peer review questionnaire

Almost none of the jurisdictions with an LEI strategy currently have plans to change their approaches. The UK intends to raise the profile of the LEI and its applications in the public and private sector to help support broader adoption and application as part of strategic initiatives. In the US, the CFTC has announced that its regulations relating to swap data reporting will be revised, and the revisions may include changes to the sections relating to LEI, though the CFTC expects to continue to require LEIs for the identification of swap counterparties. Many jurisdictions have begun to assess the success of their existing strategy by the number of LEIs issued or the degree and scope of coverage (e.g. France, Italy, Japan, Mexico, Switzerland, and US), or by compliance in reporting (India, Italy, and Mexico). Other jurisdictions are, however, still in a wait-and-see mode as they consider assessing the success of the chosen strategy as premature. This holds for jurisdictions that have developed their strategy recently (e. g. Saudi Arabia).

The LEI has replaced or been linked with existing identifiers in a few jurisdictions (see Annex 2), but no jurisdiction plans for universal adoption of the LEI (i. e. implementing the LEI for all eligible entities including those outside financial sector). Germany intends to discuss the issue as part of work to reduce the administrative costs in statistics, and Saudi Arabia is considering it as part of the process of introducing a unifying identification system (the 10 numeral identification system) that would be compatible with the LEI. Two jurisdictions (Mexico and Switzerland) considered, but decided against, implementing a plan for universal adoption. In Mexico, there have been discussions with the federal tax authority on incorporating the LEI into the tax registry, but no final decision has been taken and cost is one of the main issues. In Switzerland, the Unique Business Identification Number system is run by the Federal Government and is free of charge. Adopting the LEI as the (legal) universal identifier would require substantial amendments to existing legislation, processes, and existing infrastructure used by a large number of users and could entail data quality issues.

4. LEI coverage in areas relevant for financial stability

Evolution of LEI issuance

The evolution of LEI issuance reflects the large role played by regulations in promoting its adoption (see Graph 3). The number of issued LEIs, particularly but not exclusively in the EU, increased markedly with the adoption of EMIR (and its subsequent revision) and of MiFID Ⅱ in the EU. Similarly, the number of LEIs is the largest in the EU and US, which have adopted multiple rules referring to the LEI.

Cumulative issuance of LEIs by group of jurisdictions

End-of-quarter figures   Graph 3

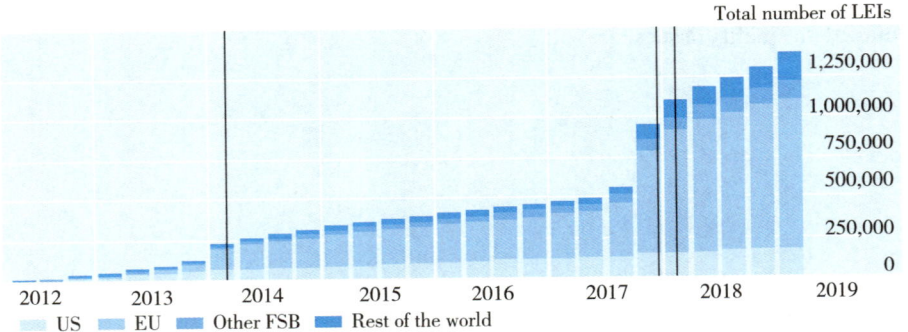

The vertical lines indicate the January 2014 EMIR reporting requirements, the November 2017 EMIR revision and the January 2018 MiFID Ⅱ implementation, respectively.

Source: GLEIF.

Overall rates of issuance

The issuance of LEIs, in terms of number of codes and percentage coverage of eligible legal entities, is mainly concentrated in Canada, the EU① and the US (see Graph 4). LEI codes have been issued for legal entities incorporated in more than 220 countries; however, more than 50% of the jurisdictions have less than 100 codes (see Graph 5).

LEI coverage in absolute terms is still relatively low and varies widely across FSB jurisdictions. It is estimated that coverage in Canada, the EU, and the US ranges from 2% to 7% of all eligible legal entities. ② A second group of jurisdictions (Australia, Hong Kong, Japan, Korea, Saudi Arabia, Singapore and Switzerland) has an estimated coverage between 0.2% and 2%; the remaining jurisdictions have a coverage lower than 0.1% (Brazil, Indonesia, Mexico, Russia and Turkey) or is unknown (Argentina, China, India and South Africa).

LEI adoption (by count and % of eligible entities) in FSB jurisdictions

As at November 2018   Graph 4

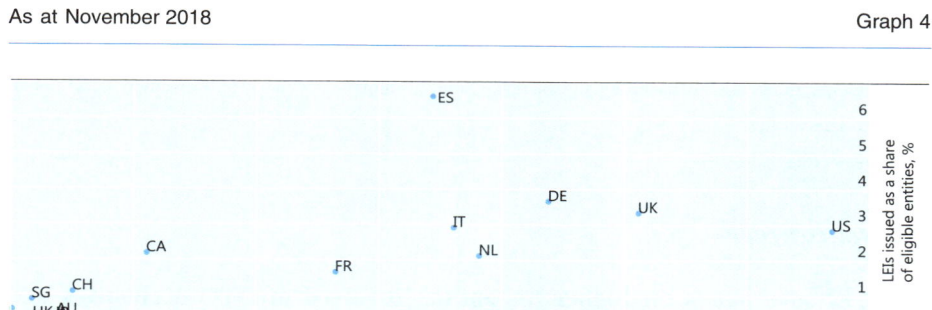

Source: GLEIF and responses to peer review questionnaire.

_____

① 10% of LEIs are from entities in the UK, 8.7% in Germany, 7.5% in Italy, 7.4% in the Netherlands, 7% in Spain and 5.4% in France.

② The total number of eligible entities has been calculated with reference to corporates only, i. e. excluding sole proprietors that may in some cases be LEI eligible but whose number is not always available at country level. Note that calculating precise coverage ratios does not always lead to exactly comparable results due to the different sources and methodologies used to identify the eligible entities population.

LEI issuance by jurisdiction as of 31 March 2019

Graph 5

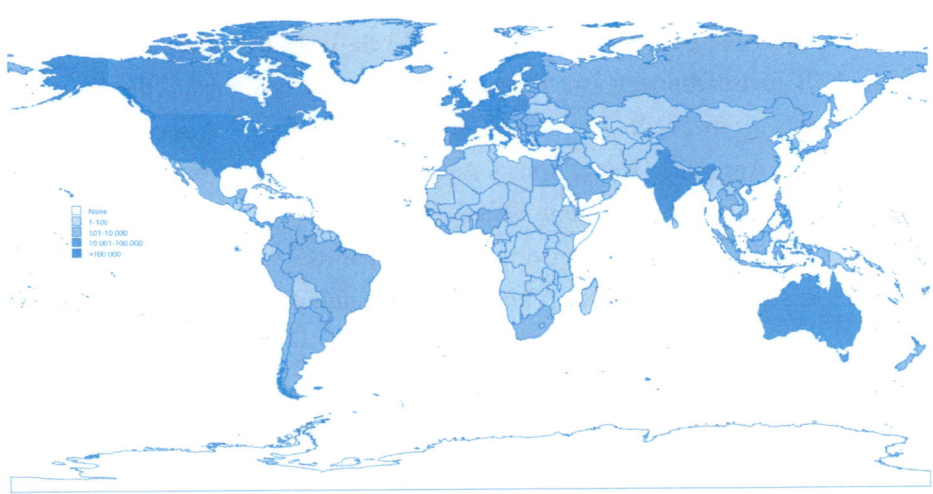

Notes: Graph shows LEI issuance by jurisdiction. Source: https: //www. gleif. org/en/lei-data/global-lei-index/lei-statistics.

Sectoral coverage

LEI coverage is far higher for entities involved in OTC derivatives and securities transactions, as well as for financial intermediaries. This is because, as noted in section 3, these sectors have been the focus of legislation mandating LEI adoption, largely driven by financial stability objectives.

With regard to OTC derivatives, many FSB jurisdictions report coverage close to 100% for trades where the reporting entity is identified with an LEI, although lower rates are reported by some jurisdictions for the LEI coverage of the transactions' counterparties (see Table 3).

Table 3: Percentage of new OTC derivatives trades (by gross notional outstanding)
where the reporting entity or counterparty is identified with an LEI

Transaction coverage	For reporting entities	For counterparties
96% – 100%	AU, CA, FR, DE, HK, IN, IT, JP, MX, NL, RU, SG, ES, UK, US, TR	CA, ES, EU, FR, DE, HK, IN, IT, NL, RU, UK, US
90% – 95%	—	JP, SG
80% – 89%	—	AU, TR
50% – 79%	—	—
<50%	—	MX
Unavailable	AR, BR, CH, CN, ID, KR, SA, ZA	AR, BR, CH, CN, ID, KR, SA, ZA

Source: Jurisdiction responses to peer review questionnaire. See Annex 4a for detailed figures.

In addition, a very large portion of securities issuers in terms of outstanding amounts is covered by an LEI. A detailed table produced by the European Central Bank (ECB) on the basis of its Centralised Securities Database (CSDB) suggests that, at the global level, more than 70% of securities in terms of outstanding amounts issued may be issued by entities with an LEI (79% for FSB jurisdictions vs 65% in the rest of the world). Based on these ECB estimates, FSB jurisdictions with the lowest overall LEI coverage for securities issuers (in terms of outstanding amounts) are Brazil, China, Hong Kong, India, Indonesia, Mexico and South Africa, with coverage between 36% (China) and 65% (South Africa), whereas other jurisdictions are assessed to have a coverage above 70%, including nine jurisdictions above 90% (see Table 4 below, and Annex 4b).

Table 4: Estimated percentage of LEI coverage for securities issuers in FSB jurisdictions, by outstanding amount

Outstanding amount	Non-financial corporations	Financial institutions *	General government	Total economy *
90% – 100%	CH, DE, ES, EU, FR, IT, NL, UK, US	AU, CA, CH, DE, ES, EU, FR, HK, IT, NL, RU, SA, SG, TR, UK	AR, AU, BR, CA, DE, ES, EU, FR, HK, ID, IT, JP, KR, MX, NL, RU, SA, SG, TR, UK, US, ZA	AR, CH, DE, ES, EU, FR, IT, NL, UK
50% – 89%	AR, CA, IN, JP, KR, MX, RU, SA, SG, TR	AR, CN, ID, IN, JP, KR, MX, US, ZA	CH	AU, BR, CA, HK, ID, IN, JP, KR, MX, RU, SA, SG, TR, US, ZA
< 50%	AU, BR, CN, HK, ID, ZA	BR	CN, IN	CN

Notes: LEI coverage is based on data from the ESCB's CSDB. For non-EU FSB member jurisdictions, the CSDB data cannot be checked with the same depth as for the EU countries, and there may be some coverage gaps for securities and their issuers. Thus, for non-EU FSB jurisdictions, the coverage information should be treated as approximate estimates.

* : Data cover all subsectors but money market funds and non-money market investment funds. See Annex 4b for detailed coverage by jurisdiction.

Coverage varies widely for other sectors and is skewed towards financial sector entities. Although very few jurisdictions report sectoral breakdowns, the coverage of the financial sector is reportedly not lower than 10%, and reaches 80% in the case of an EU jurisdiction. The coverage is even higher in some financial sub-sectors: for example, 91% of EU credit institutions (according to ECB)[1] and 88% of EU insurance companies (according to EIOPA)[2] have an LEI. In the US, out of the 1,261 national banks and federal savings associations

---

[1] See https://www.ecb.europa.eu/stats/financial_corporations/list_of_financial_institutions/html/daily_list-MID.en.html.

[2] See https://eiopa.europa.eu/publications/register-of-insurance-undertakings.

supervised by the OCC, only 330 have an LEI (26%).

The lower figures reported by jurisdictions for the overall coverage in Graph 4 (less than 7%) are due to the non-financial sector, which includes many more legal entities and is less impacted by the regulations adopted to date. In absolute terms, the ratio between non-financial and financial entities owning an LEI spans from 1: 1 to 10: 1 depending on the jurisdiction.

Similarly, **coverage appears higher among customers of cross-border financial institutions compared to the average of corporate entities**, perhaps because the former are more likely to use financial instruments subject to LEI requirements. For instance, a large international bank noted at the peer review roundtable that LEI coverage reached 69% for its European customers, 29% for its US customers, and 4% for customers in the Asia-Pacific region. A survey subsequently conducted by GFMA and ISDA confirmed this was not an isolated case. ①

Public sector LEI adoption is progressing slowly but is still incomplete. Twenty one jurisdictions noted that their central bank has an LEI (the exceptions being China, Hong Kong, and the US), while all jurisdictions reported having at least one other public sector body with an LEI. This often includes the issuers of general government debt and based on the estimates presented in Annex 4b, LEI coverage exceeds 90% of amounts outstanding for the general government in all FSB jurisdictions except India (3%), China (42%) and Switzerland (65%). ②

Coverage by size and type of institution

Firm size is another parameter influencing the LEI coverage. For Italy and Spain that reported size class distributions, large entities (i. e. more than

---

① Respondents in North America, Asia Pacific and Japan from 21 institutions reported that they had on average an LEI coverage of their corporate customers above 50% in Europe and North America and above 30% in Asia, with a few of those institutions having 100% coverage (see Annex 4d for more details).

② ESMA reports that China and India were among the three jurisdictions (as measured by the number of ISINs) with the largest number of sovereign securities traded in the EU without an LEI. For China, the Ministry of Finance obtained an LEI in August 2018.

250 employees), considering the aggregate of the financial and non-financial sector, show coverage of 40% and 77%, respectively. This is a much higher proportion than medium-sized firms in those jurisdictions (27% and 56% respectively).

LEI adoption is common among the top entities of large banks, insurers and non-financial groups (see Table 5), but most subsidiaries of these firms generally do not have an LEI. When considering the 20 largest domestic banks/deposit-taking institutions, 15 jurisdictions report 100% LEI coverage, seven jurisdictions report less than 100% coverage, while the remaining two were unable to provide data. On average across all jurisdictions, 94% of the 20 largest such entities have an LEI. For insurers, 10 jurisdictions report 100% LEI coverage for their 20-largest entities and 12 jurisdictions report partial coverage. On average across all jurisdictions, 75% of the 20 largest such entities have an LEI. For the 20 largest non-financial groups headquartered in their jurisdiction, eight jurisdictions report 100% LEI coverage, another 12 report partial coverage, while the remaining four were unable to provide data. On average across all jurisdictions, 78% of the 20 largest such entities have an LEI.

Table 5: Share of top entities of the 20 largest banks, insurers, and non-financial groups with an LEI

Jurisdiction	Banks / Deposit Taking Institutions		Insurers		Non-Financial Groups	
	LEI in place (count)	%	LEI in place (count)	%	LEI in place (count)	%
AR						
AU	20	100	12	60	7	35
BR	15	75	3	15	10	50
CA	17	85	19	95	18	90
CN						
FR	20	100	20	100	20	100
DE	20	100	20	100	20	100
HK	20	100	19	95	20	100
IN	20	100	3	15	18	90

Jurisdiction	Banks / Deposit Taking Institutions		Insurers		Non-Financial Groups	
	LEI in place (count)	%	LEI in place (count)	%	LEI in place (count)	%
ID	16	80	1	5		
IT	20	100	20	100	20	100
JP	20	100	20	100	20	100
KR	16	80	20	100	14	70
MX	20	100	8	40	17	85
NL	20	100	20	100	20	100
RU	18	90	12	60	8	40
SA	20	100	20	100	3	15
SG	20	100	16	80	11	55
ZA	12	60	15	75	11	55
ES	20	100	20	100	16	80
CH	20	100	19	95	19	95
TR	18	90	5	25	10	50
UK	20	100	20	100	20	100
US	20	100	20	100	20	100
Average	18. 7	94	15. 1	75	15. 6	78

Notes: These figures only show the top entities of these firms that have an LEI, but not their subsidiaries. Grey shading indicates no data available. Green shading indicates 100% coverage.

Coverage among the parent entity of G-SIBs and global systemically important insurers (G-SIIs) is especially strong. All G-SIBs identified in 2018 and headquartered in FSB member jurisdictions have an LEI. All but one of the G-SIIs identified in 2016 and headquartered in FSB jurisdictions have an LEI.

However, LEI coverage generally does not extend to all relevant entities of the large banks, insurers and non-financial groups. In the banking sector, G-SIBs have an LEI for the top entities within their group structure, but not necessarily for all their subsidiaries. The LEI was provided for 73% of the legal entities included in the group structure of the insurance groups participating in the IAIS data collection undertaken to support the development of the Insurance Capital Standard, but only one third of the insurance groups were covering almost all their entities. While all EU-located (insurance and reinsurance) subsidiaries of EU headquartered G-SIIs have an LEI, only 70% of their foreign (insurance and reinsurance) subsidiaries have an LEI. And although coverage was reported to be close to 100% for large corporate borrowers in the EU, the coverage is much lower in other regions, especially Asia. In several projects targeting non-financial companies, for instance an analysis by the Bank for International Settlements (BIS) of corporate loans, or the pilot project by the Organisation for Economic Cooperation and Development (OECD) on an Analytical Database on Individual Multinationals and their Affiliates (ADIMA), low LEI coverage is reported as an obstacle to LEI uses.

Similarly, there is evidence that larger entities more frequently have LEIs. In addition to the data on securities issuers, AnaCredit (which is a dataset providing detailed information on individual bank loans in the euro area) shows that while 7% of debtors have an LEI, these account for 48% of the total outstanding amounts. Although this is still preliminary data based on nine EU member states, 18% of the value of credits without LEIs is to entities from outside the EU, while these only represent 0.2% of debtors without an LEI. This is an indication that (i) non-EU debtors may represent a significant amount, and that the LEI, as a global unique identifier, is an appropriate tool to aggregate banks' exposures, and; (ii) these non-EU exposures may come primarily from large entities, such that there would be merit in promoting through international cooperation greater LEI coverage of large entities.

5. Achievements and challenges in further advancing LEI adoption

Regulatory uses

The LEI ROC progress report of April 2018 provides a comprehensive overview of regulatory uses of the LEI. ①

Implementation of the LEI has enabled a variety of uses by authorities, including:

i. **Monitoring financial risks** – The use of the LEI in regulatory reporting can significantly improve the ability of the public sector to understand and identify the build-up of risk across multiple jurisdictions and across complex global financial processes. For example, the LEI has allowed the US CFTC to identify the counterparties of the majority of swaps reported to the CFTC, permitting it to analyse the swap trading activity and exposure of entities via a single, harmonised and validated identifier.

ii. **Exposure aggregation/entity reporting to credit registries** – The LEI can facilitate the aggregation of data across all relevant entities. ② This information can then be used for various types of analysis such as in the case of the ECB for monetary policy (see Box 2). ③

---

① See the *Progress report by the Legal Entity Identifier Regulatory Oversight Committee* (April 2018, https://www. leiroc. org/publications/gls/roc_20180502-1. pdf).

② The consolidated exposures to key counterparty groups often involve multiple individual entities and, in some cases, a non-linear relationship between entity-level exposures and consolidated exposure. For aggregating simple risk exposures across these linked entities, a simple sum of exposure will provide the appropriate aggregate exposure. For more complex risk profiles such as derivative positions subject to netting arrangements, a simple sum of entity-level exposures will not suffice.

③ This is based on Cornejo Pérez and Huerga, *The Centralised Securities Database (CSDB) - Standardised micro data for financial stability purposes* (https://www. bis. org/ifc/events/ws _ micro _ macro/perez_ paper. pdf). This paper is part of the IFC Bulletin No 41 of May 2016 (http:// www. bis. org/ifc/publ/ifcb41. htm) on Combining micro and macro statistical data for financial stability analysis, which describes the proceedings of the IFC Workshop on "Combining micro and macro statistical data for financial stability analysis. Experiences, opportunities and challenges" Warsaw, Poland, 14-15 December 2015.

Another example is the use of credit exposure aggregation in risk analysis. For example, the ECB notes that supervisors need to identify and monitor risks stemming from significant borrower concentrations. In order to do so, the LEI code is used-when available-to uniquely identify the counterparties to supervised institutions. Exposures to a single counterparty can then be mapped across institutions in order to understand the overall exposure of each counterparty to the banking sector. This type of analysis can be useful, for instance, to assess the impact on the sector stemming from stress in a particular counterparty, or at a more aggregated level from economic sectors/countries to which counterparties are mapped (contagion risk). This is made possible because the LEI is globally available (compared to domestic identification codes) and consistently used across data reports. [1]

Australia uses the LEI in its large exposures reporting framework that came into effect from 1 January 2019. The reporting standard instructs banks and other deposit taking institutions to report the LEI of the counterparty for each exposure or the LEI of the principal counterparty if the exposure is to a group of connected counterparties (or N/A if the counterparty does not have an LEI). Canada is considering using the LEI for identifying counterparties under its new large exposures guideline.

Similarly, in India, the Reserve Bank of India (RBI) requires banks to make it mandatory for corporate borrowers to obtain an LEI if they have aggregate fund-based and non-fund based exposures above a certain threshold from any bank. The LEI will be captured in the Central Repository of Information on Large Credits (CRILC). The objective is to facilitate assessment of aggregate borrowing by corporate groups, and monitoring of the financial profile of an entity/group.

---

[1] In the EU, the LEI is requested, when available, to identify banks' counterparties in the credit registry held by the ECB (AnaCredit). See https://www.ecb.europa.eu/explainers/tell-me-more/html/anacredit.en.html.

Box 2: LEI use in the ECB's Centralised Securities Database (CSDB)

Operational since 2009, the CSDB is a security-by-security (s-b-s) database with the aim of holding complete, accurate, consistent and up-to-date information on all individual securities relevant for the statistical and, increasingly, non-statistical purposes of the European System of Central Banks (ESCB, comprised of the ECB and national central banks of all EU Member States). It contains reference data on securities (e. g. outstanding amounts, issue and maturity dates, type of security, coupon and dividend information, statistical classifications, etc.), issuers (identifiers, name, country of residence, economic sector, etc.) and prices (market, estimated or defaulted) as well as information on ratings (covering securities, issuance programmes, and all rated institutions independently of whether they are issuers of securities). The CSDB is a multi-source system that receives approximately 2. 5 million prices and 400,000 records of reference information per day. The compilation of s-b-s data requires the existence and application of unique identifiers, namely the International Securities Identification Number (ISIN) and the LEI.

Besides various statistical uses, including the compilation of securities holdings statistics, securities issues statistics, balance of payments statistics, investment fund statistics and financial vehicle corporation statistics, the CSDB supports the analytical and policy work of a number of central banking functions such as monetary policy, financial stability analysis, market operations, risk management, the monitoring of fiscal policy and economic research. For example, the CSDB supports the analysis of entities' refinancing needs, the funding structure of deposit-taking corporations, their cost of funding or changes in the credit ratings of financial instruments.

An s-b-s database, like the CSDB, offers a flexibility that cannot be matched by pre-aggregated data. Micro-data can be compiled on a multipurpose basis and be customised ex post for each specific analysis or used to produce new aggregates in a flexible way without multiple requirements to reporting agents. The CSDB also offers attributes not covered in aggregate data and the possibility to combine them.

The LEI is currently being introduced as a 'grouping identifier' in the CSDB, which is used to group securities under the same issuing entity. The use of the LEI significantly supports the linking of the CSDB with other micro databases. This linking with other data sets has in the past often been difficult due to the unavailability of an entity identifier that is universally applied across different data sets and jurisdictions. The LEI, as the only truly global entity identifier, significantly facilitates this linking of CSDB entity information with other ECB micro databases as well as other micro data sources.

iii. **Statistical analysis** – The LEI can facilitate a broad range of statistical analyses by providing explicit identification of legal entities. For example, the IMF is exploring the use of LEI in its Coordinated Portfolio Investment Survey (CPIS) database to provide users with from-whom-to-whom CPIS positions by economy and sector of holder and issuer. [1] The LEI has been used by the BIS in a methodological paper exploring how to construct bank-firm lending relationships through large corporate loans, although the insufficient LEI coverage has been an impediment. [2]

iv. **Understanding company structures** – The LEI can support the reliable identification of company structures. For example, the OECD's ADIMA leverages the LEI and other data sources to better understand multinational enterprise (MNE) company structures and activities for statistical and supply chain assessment purposes. [3] The Bank of Russia

---

[1] See the IMF Statistics Department paper on *Project on a Centralized Database of Issuers and Sectors for CPIS Reporting: What Comes Next?* (October 2018, https://www.imf.org/external/pubs/ft/bop/2018/pdf/18-08.pdf).

[2] Serena Garralda, J. M. *Cross-country bank-firm lending relationships: How can the Legal Entity Identifier help?* in *IFC Bulletin, Are post-crisis statistical initiatives completed?* volume 49 https://www.bis.org/ifc/publ/ifcb49_13.pdf.

[3] See the OECD Statistics Directorate paper on *Measuring MNEs using Big Data: The OECD Analytical Database on Individual Multinationals and their Affiliates* (ADIMA) (March 2018, http://www.oecd.org/officialdocuments/publicdisplaydocumentpdf/? cote = COM/STD/WPTGS/DAF/WGIIS (2018) 1&docLanguage = En).

used LEIs to build the accounting structure of Russian holding companies (including foreign subsidiaries, whose identification based on legal entity name had proved unreliable) and monitor the loans granted by Russian banks to entities at a group level.

v. **Understanding market structures** – The LEI enables better understanding of market structures through unambiguous identification of OTC derivatives market participants in trading networks and market structures. For example, the Monetary Authority of Singapore uses the LEI, along with other identifiers, to identify entities in the OTC derivatives market and to construct networks, facilitating a better understanding of the structure of those markets.

ESMA explained that the identification of clearing members across CCPs was highly improved with the use of LEIs in EU-wide CCP stress tests, which assess among other things interconnectedness among 900 clearing members identified with their LEI, as well as their liquidity providers and custodians. ① The stress tests assess for instance the degree of interconnectedness of CCPs through common clearing members.

ESMA also used the LEI to connect information from derivatives reporting to information from data vendors on features of investment funds in a paper analysing the use of Credit Default Swaps by Undertakings for Collective Investments in Transferable Securities (UCITS). ② Similar analysis by the European Systemic Risk Board presented in that paper used the LEI to show for instance that UCITS do not trade among themselves, but rely mainly on 13 dealers for their access to CDS markets. ③

---

① See http://firds.esma.europa.eu/webst/ESMA70-151-1154 EU-wide CCP Stress Test 2017 Report.pdf, in particular figure 22.

② *Drivers of CDS usage by EU investment funds*, in ESMA Report on Trends, Risks and Vulnerabilities, n° 2, 2018, https://www.esma.europa.eu/press-news/esma-news/what-drives-use-cds-eu-investment-funds.

③ See Figure V.27 of https://www.esma.europa.eu/sites/default/files/library/esma_50-165-632_report_on_trends_risks_and_vulnerabilities_no.2_2018.pdf#page=66.

ⅵ. **Market surveillance** – The LEI can facilitate market surveillance and compliance assessments. For instance, MiFIR mandates the use of the LEI to identify persons referred to in transaction reports. This has enhanced the UK Financial Conduct Authority's ability to monitor market abuse across different financial markets (e. g. cross-product manipulation, or in cases where orders are placed with multiple brokers) as the LEI provides a consistent and robust means to uniquely identify the entity involved in a transaction. Previously, an entity could be identified using multiple identifiers, making it difficult to reconcile information and hence the detection of potential instances of market abuse. The benefits of unique identification for the purposes of monitoring market abuse also apply to market participants. Similarly, the Netherlands has used the LEI as a primary key to join different transaction reports in order to get a full view of the order chain of a specific transaction, identifying all participants in the chain. France has also used the LEI in market surveillance. It is using the new MiFIR transaction reporting framework to instantly identify entities that engage in suspicious behaviour. The Autorité des marchés financiers created pattern detection algorithms that check whether an entity repeatedly tried to or did manipulate the market of a given financial instrument. Authorities note the LEI is of real added value for the surveillance work because of its universality (across Europe).

ⅶ. **Support transparency for the benefit of investors** – The LEI can augment the information provided to investors on securitised products and their underlying assets. For instance, in the United States, a rule issued jointly by six agencies requests that the LEI be used, if available, to identify the obligor of loans or assets held or to be held by an open market collateralised loan obligation (CLO), in the information provided to potential investors. The LEI also supports the transparency of credit ratings: for instance, in the EU the LEI is required for the identification of (i) credit rating agencies; (ii) entities for which credit ratings have been issued; (iii) in case of the subsidiary of a rated parent, the parent entity; and (ⅳ) in case of credit ratings on structured finance instruments, the identification of the originator. Publishing information on entities with an LEI makes it easier for market participants to retrieve the information and use it in their own analysis.

The LEI also underpins other transparency measures: ESMA uses the LEI in some cases to run calculations on liquidity of financial instruments in order to establish whether or not orders and/or transactions in financial instruments should be subject to real-time transparency. ① For instance, ESMA uses the LEI to identify underlying reference entity for single name Credit Default Swaps (CDSs) and to identify the issuers of the underlying bond for bond futures.

ⅷ. **Resolution of financial institutions** – To support the resolution of financial institutions, the EU authorities request that the LEI be included (when available) in the recordkeeping of designated financial contracts by certain financial institutions in financial groups, to facilitate access to information by competent authorities and resolution authorities. ② Similarly, in the US, certain insured depository institutions are required to have an LEI, and the counterparties of qualified financial contracts of these institutions are requested to be identified with an LEI if they have one. Having a unique identifier across entities, products and geographies supports a more comprehensive and faster analysis of contagion risks, and also a more timely analysis of the quality of the assets of the failed institution, e. g. by using a standardised international identifier for third party data on these assets without facing the delays of manually reconciling different proprietary identifiers.

---

① See https://www.esma.europa.eu/policy-activities/mifid-ii-and-mifir/transparencycalculations.

② 'Financial contracts' are defined in Article 2 (1) (100) of the Bank Recovery and Resolution Directive, and include securities contracts, commodities contracts, futures and forwards contracts, swap agreements, short-term inter-bank borrowing agreements, and master agreements for these.

Benefits

A significant proportion of jurisdictions report that the use of LEI has led to improvements in data quality and analysis, as shown in Table 6.

Table 6: Member views of LEI impact on data quality and analysis

	Yes	No	Incomplete, no response, or cannot assess yet
Is the implementation of the LEI or use of LEI data improving the quality, efficiency and/or accuracy of financial regulatory reporting, data analysis or other financial regulatory activities in your jurisdiction? Has it enabled new financial regulatory projects?	CA, CN, EU,① ES, FR, DE, HK, IT, JP, NL, SG, CH, UK, US	AU, MX	AR, BR, ID, IN, KR, RU, SA, ZA, TR

Other LEI benefits cited by jurisdictions include the improved identification of entities, data aggregation, and the provision of information on parent entities (see Table 7).

The most common benefit (reported by 20 jurisdictions) is the usefulness of the LEI in identifying foreign and domestic entities. For example, both China and Russia highlight the usefulness of the LEI in identifying foreign entities, while Russia notes that the LEI has provided a better means of mapping the foreign subsidiaries of Russian entities. Korea also indicates that the LEI eased risks in transacting with foreign entities. In Italy, the inclusion of the LEI in reporting templates has significantly improved the identification of non-resident banks' counterparties. Italy also reports significant improvements in the accuracy of identifying counterparties and of financial reporting/data aggregation, with use of the LEI reducing significantly the errors in the aggregation of data and the calculation of entities' positions (see Box 3). The US OFR highlights that the

---

① For Tables 6-8, the EU denotes one or several EU authorities, such as the ECB, the Single Resolution Board (SRB), the European Banking Authority (EBA), EIOPA and ESMA. EU member states are shown (and counted) separately.

LEI's principal value lies in its use across borders and across different types of transactions, and that the LEI is particularly valuable for non-bank corporates, which, as the 2008 financial crisis demonstrated, historically is an area with significant financial regulatory data gaps.

Box 3: Example of benefits to Italy

Before the introduction of the LEI, the Italian Central Credit Register relied on the company name and on the country of incorporation only for the unique identifications of banks' non-resident counterparties (while resident entities were easily identified by their tax code). Since the description of the same counterparties made by different reporting entities could vary-e. g. names as "ABC S. A. " and "ABC Société anonyme" could be considered as different entities-the duplication phenomenon was pretty frequent, causing underestimates when calculating the global risk position of the banking system vs. the counterparty, as the total loan amounts would be split between the duplicated entities. The opposite case (two different entities "merged" into one due to very similar company names) could also happen, with symmetric erroneous results in data aggregation.

The introduction of the LEI (where available) in the reporting requirements has reduced the risks of entity duplication or merging. Similarly, the introduction of the LEI in the AnaCredit and EMIR reporting allows a better identification of counterparties of loans contracts and OTC derivatives transactions at the European level.

Nineteen jurisdictions note that the LEI is useful in facilitating data aggregation and coordination across multiple regulators. Seventeen jurisdictions indicate that they benefit from the LEI's non-proprietary nature. Sixteen jurisdictions respond that they see benefit in the LEI being unique to an entity and remaining with the entity for its lifetime, including moving to any eventual successor entity.

In this context, Japan and the UK note that the LEI could play a key role in making it easier for firms to satisfy obligations under KYC or AML regulations. Several market participants also highlight the LEI benefits associated with KYC and AML processes (see Annex 5) , echoing BCBS guidance on customer due diligence, as well as FSB and CPMI recommendations on the use of the LEI in correspondent banking. ①

Lower costs of financial regulatory reporting, data analysis or other regulatory activities from LEI implementation were cited by a few jurisdictions (EU, France, Germany, Italy, Netherlands and the US). The US notes industry feedback suggesting efficiencies created by LEI work to lower compliance costs. Italy notes that in the context of AnaCredit the LEI reduced costs by rendering manual counterparty checks unnecessary. France notes that the requirement for clients to obtain an LEI reduces the costs by investment firms in maintaining multiple identifiers per client. Finally, Germany relays industry feedback suggesting that use of LEI reduces the burden of reporting other entity attributes (e. g. industry sector).

Table 7: Other LEI benefits

Benefit	Jurisdictions reporting benefits	% of responding jurisdictions
Support the identification of foreign and domestic entities	20	80
Support data aggregation	19	76
The LEI is a non-proprietary system	17	68
Uniqueness of the LEI; information on successor entities	16	64
The LEI provides direct and ultimate parent information	15	60
The LEI allows for recording of international branches	14	56
Support of multiple languages and character sets	10	40
The LEI is not locked in with a particular service provider	10	40

---

① ISDA and GFMA note that "banks perform due diligence as part of KYC processes and LOUs do the same as part of the LEI issuance process. As part of the client on-boarding as well as other due diligence processes, financial firms are generally required to use external sources to validate information about their clients, even if they have the client's LEI. If regulators were to permit reliance on LOU due diligence, the utility of LEI could be greatly enhanced and could help streamline the client on-boarding process". See https://www.isda.org/a/brvEE/ISDA_GFMA_FSB-Peer-Review_LEI-Implementation_3-October-2018_FINAL_Public.pdf.

Obstacles to adoption and implementation

FSB jurisdictions also highlighted various obstacles to further LEI adoption and implementation. These are displayed in Table 8, with the most notable ones summarised below:

i. **Lack of LEI coverage** – Ten jurisdictions report that a lack of LEI coverage is an obstacle to LEI use, and some (Canada, EU, France, India, and Italy) specifically note that a lack of LEI for foreign counterparties creates problems in their reporting regimes. Other jurisdictions (EU, China, and Singapore) cite a lack of coverage of parent entities, funds, and international branches respectively as obstacles. On the other hand, several jurisdictions report that LEI coverage is not an obstacle (Hong Kong, Japan, Mexico, and Switzerland), in particular following the implementation of MiFID II (UK).

ii. **Lack of Level 2 data**[1] – Many jurisdictions and authorities[2] report that Level 2 (relationship) data is insufficient for their needs due to a lack of coverage of entities or a lack of relevant information. Canada notes that only a small proportion of entities currently report direct and ultimate parent data, and that the level of corroboration of the information by the LOUs is lower than with the Level 1 data. China notes that fund relationship data is incomplete and that the quality of the data is not guaranteed.[3] Germany cites a lack of information for G-SIFIs as a problem, while Hong Kong notes that only 10%-20% of the relevant entities for its regime are reporting relationship data. Italy states that the lack of an LEI for the parent entity undermines the reliability of the data. Mexico notes inconsistencies in international branches (i. e.

---

① Where as 'Level 1' data refers to the business card information available with the LEI reference data, 'Level 2' data includes relationship data to answer the question 'who owns who', such as their direct and ultimate accounting consolidation parent.

② Australia, Brazil, Canada, China, EU authorities, Germany, Hong Kong, Italy, Mexico, Saudi Arabia, Spain, and the UK.

③ The LEI ROC issued in November 2018 a Second Consultation Document on Fund Relationships in the Global LEI System.

whether or not the branch has its own LEI) as a challenge and ESMA underlines that in some of its reporting regimes, entities are incorrectly reporting the LEI of the branch instead of the LEI of the headquarters, which underlines the importance of being able to connect reliably the two LEIs. The UK and US note that information about control, as opposed to accounting consolidation, would be more useful, while acknowledging the challenges of collecting such information. The US observes that currently joint ventures or companies with interlocking directors are currently not captured. The EU-EIOPA suggests that an approach based on Solvency II might be more useful to them. The US CFTC notes that the lack of non-public information limits the usefulness of the data.① Canada notes that it expects Level 2 data to be useful for understanding interconnectedness, and the US notes that more complete parent data would be useful.

Annex 4c shows that ultimate parent information is provided only for 6.2% of entities for all FSB members taken together and is below that level for Japan and the EU as a whole as well as for FSB members from the EU (except France). This information is provided in more than 14% of cases for 11 FSB members② but all have a small number of LEIs (less than 6,000) and tend to have less regulatory requirements mandating the LEI. It may be that companies with LEIs in these countries are more frequently subsidiaries of large groups.

The reasons provided by entities for not reporting parent information to the GLEIS (based on GLEIF data-see Annex 4c) vary significantly depending on the jurisdiction. The fact that the records have not been updated by the entity since the reporting of parent entities was introduced is the first cause of the absence of information in the US and

---

① The CFTC views the proliferation of opt-outs (to not reporting Level 2 data) as the biggest obstacle to improving overall quality of Level 2 data, and believes that action by LEI ROC to revise Level 2 data standards to reduce the allowable opt-outs will do the most to improve overall quality of Level 2 data

② Argentina, China, Hong Kong, Indonesia, Korea, Mexico, Russia, Saudi Arabia, Singapore, and South Africa.

Russia, affecting in both countries approximately one third of records (against 12% for FSB members as a whole). [1] Regarding ultimate parents, a lack of consent from the parent entities is by far the most significant reason in Australia and Brazil, representing a third of exceptions (though only 9% of exceptions for all FSB members taken together). This case is also very significant in the US (affecting 22% of records). The existence of other legal obstacles is cited by less than 1% of entities across FSB members, and below 10% for each of them. [2] The absence of an LEI for the parent is one of the main reasons in countries that have not adopted regulatory requirements, or have done so only recently (between 10 and 20% of LEIs in Argentina, China, Indonesia and South Africa). Other reasons given are the absence of a parent meeting the definition of accounting consolidation used in the GLEIS since, for example, control by natural persons is high in India (54% of LEIs) and Italy (39% of LEIs); that the controlling parent is not subject to consolidation (which can be the case of investment entities or government entities) is very high in the Netherlands (78% of LEIs) and Spain (84%); and that there is no parent controlling the entity according to accounting standards (e. g. a listed entity with diversified shareholders) is the most significant factor in Japan and Germany.

iii. **LEI costs** – Feedback on LEI costs was mixed, with 13 respondents[3] reporting that costs are a barrier to implementation, while 10 respondents[4] report that they are not an obstacle. In particular, eight

---

[1] These cases appear in Annex 4c under the line "No parent reported and no exception given".

[2] These other cases are a binding legal commitment not to disclose the information, the fact that disclosure would be detrimental or detriments are not excluded if the information was disclosed and other legal obstacles. They are presented together with the case where consent was not obtained in Annex 4c.

[3] Australia, Brazil, EU-EIOPA, Germany, Indonesia, Italy, Japan, Netherlands, Singapore, Spain, Switzerland, UK, and US.

[4] Canada, China, EU-ESMA, EU-SRB, France, Hong Kong, India, Korea, Mexico, and Saudi Arabia.

respondents[1] note that LEI fees (acquisition and renewal) may be a barrier for small entities. Some respondents note that the cost-benefit[2] analysis may focus on existing process and control issues (e. g. onboarding, credit assessments, and KYC) and thereby may not fully include those benefits associated with new capabilities and features afforded by a fully implemented LEI (e. g. digital identities, commercial smart contracts, etc.), particularly for entities outside of the financial sector. Further, the timing for realising these benefits may depend on more complete adoption and thereby provide relevant incentives in the longer term.

Cost-benefit analyses have tended to use the then current cost of the LEI, although in retrospect this cost has decreased sharply. For instance, the EBA recommendation on the LEI took into account the current average cost of registration, which was in effect in early 2014 of € 129 for the first issuance and € 74 for the annual maintenance fee. [3] In the adoption release of Regulation SBSR in 2015, the SEC also factored in the then current cost for registering a LEI, which it assessed (presumably for the US market, hence the difference with the EU estimate that included LOUs operating exclusively in Europe) at approximately $ 220, with an additional cost of $ 120 per year for maintaining an LEI. [4] As of early 2019, some LOUs offer annual maintenance fees of $ 50 or less in most jurisdictions. Therefore, although this may be a difficult exercise, there would be merits including in calculations the fact that given the steady expansion of the GLEIS, a further reduction in fees is likely, especially if the regulation being considered would lead to higher LEI issuance and renewals.

Double counting of costs should be avoided in cost-benefit analyses.

---

① Australia, Brazil, Germany, Indonesia, Italy, Japan, Korea, and Spain.

② See https://lei. info/portal/resources/lei-benefits/.

③ See https://eba. europa. eu/documents/10180/561173/EBA-REC-2014-01 + % 28Recommendation + on + the + use + of + the + Legal + Entity + Identifier% 29. pdf

④ See https://www. sec. gov/rules/final/2015/34-74244. pdf.

In the examples above, both the EBA and SEC took into account that many entities were subject to other regulations mandating the LEI or already had one, thereby reducing the cost attributable to the new regulations.

The administrative burden for entities is also a relevant cost. For instance, the reporting of Level 1 and Level 2 reference data was assessed to take two hours in the cost-benefit analysis for the Swap Data Recordkeeping and Reporting Requirements in the US. [1] Some LOUs aim at cutting the time required to obtain an LEI, for instance by pre-populating the forms with data extracted automatically from business registries. [2] By making sure that their national registry data is easily retrievable, authorities can contribute to reducing the administrative costs of LEI issuance.

Jurisdictions also report that cost and a perceived lack of benefits for the legal entities are the most important obstacles to voluntary adoption by market participants who are aware of the LEI (see discussion of private sector views below).

iv. **Existence of other identifiers**-Several jurisdictions (Australia, Brazil, Canada, Germany, Hong Kong, Indonesia, Italy, Korea, Netherlands, Singapore, Spain, Switzerland, Turkey, and EU-EBA) and some private sector respondents note that the existence of other identifiers-in particular, no-cost or low-cost national identifiers and of systems built around those identifiers (see Annex 2) -is a barrier to LEI implementation. Their existence also reduces incentives for jurisdictions to promote mandatory LEI adoption, [3] especially in markets where firms undertake limited cross-border activities. Two jurisdictions (Germany and Switzerland) noted that while these other identifiers exist, they might not be barriers because they can be used

---

[1] See https: //www. govinfo. gov/content/pkg/FR-2012-01-13/pdf/2011-33199. pdf, p. 41.

[2] For instance, https: //rapidlei. com/, and also some LOUs that are business registries.

[3] See, for example, the April 2017 FSB peer review report of Brazil (http: //www. fsb. org/2017/04/peer-review-of-brazil/).

alongside the LEI, establishing the appropriate links; nevertheless, some jurisdictions (Italy, Spain, and France) observed that establishing those links is only possible if the (mandatory) information on the Registration Authority Entity ID is correctly reported by the LOUs to the GLEIF database. At present, some LOUs seem to be not compliant with this obligation; this problem, if not quickly addressed by the GLEIF, represents a serious obstacle for LEI use. In this context, some stakeholders also noted that the proposed publication of a European unique identifier of companies and branches as part of a proposal on the use of digital tools and processes in company law① may inadvertently compete or distract from the global LEI initiative.

Table 8: Obstacles to LEI implementation

Question	Obstacle (%)	No Obstacle (%)	Other or Blank (%)
Is the lack of LEI coverage an obstacle to use?	55	17	28
Is the availability of parent relationship data sufficient for your needs?	55	17	28
Is cost an obstacle to LEI implementation?	45	34	21
Is the existence of other identifiers an obstacle to LEI implementation or use?	41	41	17
Is there need for relationship data beyond accounting consolidating parents?	28	38	34
Are there any other obstacles to LEI implementation?	28	34	38
Are there other issues related to the availability of relationship data?	24	38	38
Is LEI data quality an obstacle to LEI adoption?	21	52	28
Is there relevant information not currently captured in the LEI data?	17	45	38
Is the lapsed LEI rate an obstacle to LEI adoption?	14	62	24

---

① See *Proposal for a Directive of the European Parliament and of the Council amending Directive [(EU) 2017/1132] as regards the use of digital tools and processes in company law* (https: //eur-lex. europa. eu/legal-content/EN/TXT/? uri = COM%3A2018%3A239%3AFIN).

Uses, benefits and obstacles to LEI implementation-private sector view (see Annex 5)

Market participants indicate that LEI uptake in the OTC derivatives market, and to a lesser extent in securities markets, has been a considerable achievement. Large financial institutions consider the LEI as beneficial for their own processes. The main mechanism by which the LEI benefits such institutions is by reducing the costs of manually reconciling data on entities, which is otherwise complicated by variations in the use of names, the translation or transliteration of different languages and character sets, or the multiplicity of other identifiers. The LEI also facilitates the access to information on legal entities.

More specifically, the LEI reduces the costs associated with entity identification and verification by:

- reducing the likelihood of duplicative due diligence efforts being conducted multiple times on the same entity;
- making it easier to ensure that the relevant entity has been adequately identified and has up-to-date contractual documentation, especially if the LEI is included in transactions;
- providing a mapping with national business registries, making it easier to access business registry data. Industry associations estimated the time saving at up to 30 minutes per customer;[①]
- facilitating the management of information on group structures. For instance, Citi recorded in the GLEIS all the entities included in its consolidated US GAAP direct and ultimate parent structure, totaling approximately 700 LEIs, and has a process to keep this data up-to-date, for the benefit of their clients, counterparties and other stakeholders. This group also feeds LEI hierarchy information on other entities in its central client master data, providing visibility into other firms' accounting

---

① See the contribution by ISDA and GFMA to the FSB Thematic Peer Review on Implementation of the LEI. https://www.isda.org/a/brvEE/ISDA_GFMA_FSB-Peer-Review_LEI-Implementation_3-October-2018_FINAL_Public.pdf.

consolidated corporate hierarchies; and

- making it easier to identify which entity requires a contractual update, when regulatory changes affect only certain entities. Industry associations mentioned the example of margin requirements for non-centrally cleared derivatives: if the LEI had been embedded in the legal documentation, it would have been easier for financial institutions to identify cases where ISDA agreements had to be re-documented.

The LEI can also help to manage risks for market participants by:

- facilitating the aggregation of exposures to the same counterparty (or group of counterparties) across borders by use of a globally consistent and unique identifier;
- reducing operational risks, e. g. the use of the LEI in settlement instructions avoids ambiguity as to the entity the instructions are referring to; and
- monitoring limits applying to an entity, as well as various restrictions applying to trading on some entities (e. g. reducing false alerts that have to be cleared manually).

The LEI also supports straight-through processing and avoids delays for customers. If applied to payment messages, the LEI would support the screening of messages against sanction lists.

Thanks to reduced costs for customer identification and in middle-and back-office activities in the processing of capital and debt securities, McKinsey and the GLEIF have assessed that global LEI adoption could yield annual savings of over $150 million within the investment banking industry. ① As illustrated in section 4, LEI coverage is already high in this area, but fully reaping these benefits

---

① See McKinsey and GLEIF, *The Legal Entity Identifier: The Value of the Unique Counterparty ID* (October 2017) at https://www. gleif. org/en/lei-solutions/mckinsey-company-and-gleif-creating-business-value-with-the-lei. The report estimates that introducing the LEI into capital market onboarding and securities trade processing could reduce annual trade processing and onboarding costs by 10 percent. This would lead to a 3.5 percent reduction in overall capital markets operations costs, amounting to over $150 million in annual savings for the global investment banking industry alone. This does not take into account the cost of implementing the LEI, which presumably includes one-off costs (first issuance and introducing the LEI in systems and processes) but also annual costs (LEI maintenance fee).

would require an LEI for all counterparties, and not just the larger ones. The same study assessed that costs savings could reach up to $500 million for banks in the issuance of letters of credit. Another source assesses that the private benefits of the GLEIS (i. e. the direct "bottom line" benefits in terms of reduced costs or enhanced revenues) stem primarily from the implementation of the LEI in basic operational processes and are in excess of $1 billion per year. ①

However, a key obstacle to voluntary adoption by market participants is the lack of alignment between the perceived costs and the perceived benefits of having an LEI. In particular, there is a belief expressed by some private sector respondents to the peer review that those who benefit the most are large financial institutions (e. g. those subject to reporting obligations), while the costs accrue to all legal entities that have to pay for LEI issuance and renewal. Smaller entities with local customers see fewer benefits in the LEI because they either undertake fewer transactions where an LEI is used, or have less need for a unique and global identifier.

Many of the other challenges reported by market participants mirror those described by FSB jurisdictions. They include: insufficient coverage (e. g. the lack of regulatory mandates impacting coverage and renewals); differences in the timing and scope of requirements across jurisdictions; difficulties in accessing relationship data; and the high level of lapsed LEIs.

- Many noted that awareness of the LEI is growing but driven largely by regulatory mandates. Consequently, they considered such requirements as a necessary and preferred approach for increasing LEI take-up.
- Stakeholders agree that differences in the timing and scope of requirements across jurisdictions may complicate LEI adoption. A number of LEI uses (e. g. regulatory reporting, assessment of exposures for prudential supervision, resolution and financial stability work, and the identification of customers for AML/CFT) require not only the regulated entity to have an LEI, but also its counterparties domestically

---

① Ka Kei Chan and Alistair Milne, The Global Legal Entity Identifier System: How Can It Deliver? Journal of Risk and Financial Management, 7 March 2019, https://www.mdpi.com/1911-8074/12/1/39/htm.

and abroad to have one. Those counterparties themselves may not be required, by their principal regulator, to have an LEI, however. Indeed, not all authorities are in a position to mandate an LEI for entities in the scope that would be necessary, although in some cases mandating the LEI within their limited scope could be effective if other regulators do the same. ① Some authorities frequently require the LEI only if the entity already has one or opt for voluntary adoption of the LEI. As previously discussed, voluntary adoption is impeded by the lack of full alignment of the benefits and costs of LEI use for participants, in particular the belief that those who benefit the most are large financial institutions (e. g. those subject to reporting obligations), while the costs accrue to all legal entities that have to pay for LEI issuance and renewal.

On the high level of lapsed LEIs, a number of stakeholders expressed concerns relating to the maintenance of reference data over time and noted the absence of consistent guidance or requirements on renewals across regulatory agencies and jurisdictions resulting in diverse requirements for entities operating across multiple agencies and jurisdictions (see Section 3).

Recommendations received from public feedback included mandating LEI usage, pursuing joint education efforts by regulators and industry where take-up is low, using the LEI in as many areas as possible (including for tax purposes), incorporating additional data elements into the GLEIS, reducing costs and duplication of processes (especially with other identifiers), addressing the issues of lapsed LEIs, and increased public-private cooperation on new areas for LEI usage.

Ways to address these challenges are discussed in the next section.

---

① For example, in the EU a large number of sectoral rules at the regional level have achieved a good level of coverage. The EU are the only ones mandating the LEI for all issuers of financial instruments, and for non-EU financial instruments, the coverage achieved as of 17 October 2018 was approximately 60% (217,000 instruments with an LEI and 147,000 without) but the coverage was much higher when taking into account EU instruments, with a total of nine million instruments with LEIs.

6. Way forward in advancing LEI adoption

The feedback from member authorities, analysis of LEI data and discussions with stakeholders suggest three main common challenges that need to be addressed:

- LEI adoption across jurisdictions has been uneven and is low outside securities and OTC derivatives markets.
- LEI coverage remains too low to encourage further regulatory uses or to reach a potential tipping point where voluntary take-up by market participants would suffice to propel further adoption.
- Other obstacles to further LEI adoption and implementation, including the LEI business model, content and processes.

Concerning the first challenge, there is a recognition that not all jurisdictions or market participants have the same needs. While universal LEI coverage may remove the need to maintain multiple identifiers, some jurisdictions/markets may see less benefits in LEI use, especially if they have already invested in a domestic identifier. It would therefore be useful to focus efforts in those areas and markets that would benefit the most from broader LEI adoption.

Standard-setting bodies are well placed to support the identification of areas where coordinated LEI adoption would bring the most benefits, and propose appropriate timelines. With regard to identification, this has already been the case for OTC derivatives, although some regulators have yet to mandate the LEI for the identification of all legal entities in the data reported to trade repositories. ① For example, with regard to timelines, in December 2017 the FSB recommended that member authorities implement the UTI (which embeds the LEI) by end-2020. ② In addition to requiring the LEI as a component of the forthcoming UTI, among other things, CPMI-IOSCO critical data elements technical guidance recommended the use of LEIs for the identification of legal entities in the data reported to trade repositories for OTC derivatives.

- FSB member jurisdictions should follow-up on CPMI-IOSCO guidance that strongly encourages authorities to require the use of LEIs for the identification of legal entities in the data reported to trade repositories for OTC derivatives (**recommendation 1a**).

However, while standard-setting bodies have included the LEI in their policy making for certain areas, in most of those cases (AML/CFT, risk data aggregation and correspondent banking) LEI uses are left as an optional element and the standard-setting bodies have not proposed a timeline for adoption. For instance, the use of the LEI to support the unambiguous identification of originators and beneficiaries of cross-border wire transfers, as recommended by CPMI and FSB in their work on correspondent banking, ③ is an area with strong support from regulators and industry. The LEI

---

① See the April 2018 CPMI-IOSCO *Technical Guidance for the Harmonisation of critical OTC derivatives data elements (other than UTI and UPI)* "The CPMI and IOSCO consider the consistent use of LEI codes in OTC derivative transactions reported to TRs to be crucial to achieve global consistency and meaningful aggregation of OTC derivative transactions reported to TRs. Therefore, the CPMI and IOSCO strongly encourage authorities to require the use of LEI codes as published by the Global LEI Foundation (GLEIF) for the identification of legal entities in the data reported to TRs". Section 2.7 and 2.8 make clear that values other than the LEI are not allowed for counterparties that are eligible to obtain an LEI. Argentina, Brazil, China, Indonesia, Saudi Arabia and South Africa have yet to use the LEI in derivatives reporting. Australia, Hong Kong, Japan, Korea, Mexico, Russia, Singapore and Switzerland request or require the LEI in some cases but have yet to require the LEI for all LEI-eligible entities, including non-reporting counterparties, even when they do not already have an LEI (except for natural persons other than individuals acting in a business capacity).

② See the FSB report on *Governance arrangements for the unique transaction identifier (UTI): Conclusions and implementation plan* (December 2017).

③ See the November 2018 *FSB action plan to assess and address the decline in correspondent banking: Progress report to G20 Summit* and July 2016 CPMI *Correspondent Banking-final report.*

would increase the reliability and cost-efficiency of screening payment messages against lists of entities subject to asset freezes or other sanctions. This would more generally support compliance monitoring, and also reduce the risks of payments being delayed, making LEI benefits tangible for companies of all sizes. The CPMI recommendation is that "the use of the LEI as additional information in payment messages should be possible on an optional basis in the current relevant payment messages", and "also, as part of a potential future migration to message formats based on the ISO 20022 standard, relevant stakeholders (i. e. ISO and SWIFT) are encouraged to consider developing dedicated codes or data items for the inclusion of the LEI in these payment messages".

The upcoming completion of options to insert the LEI into payment messages may be an opportunity to propose an international timeline for the effective use of the LEI in payment messages. The SWIFT Board recommends that a migration of correspondent banking payment messages to ISO 20022 should start in November 2021, and the LEI is in the process of being embedded in ISO 20022. This migration timeline could be the opportunity for a coordinated adoption of the LEI, on an optional basis, in payment messages by the industry. The FSB, working with other members of its Correspondent Banking Coordination Group and industry bodies such as the Wolfsberg Group and Payments Market Practice Group (PMPG),[1] as well as LEI ROC and GLEIF, could document the efficiency gains to determine whether the information currently available in or through the GLEIS is adequate to assist with due diligence, and whether there are types of entities that should be given priority to

---

[1] In its discussion paper *LEI in the Payments Market* of November 2017 (https: // www. swift. com/sites/default/files/resources/swift_ paper _ pmpg _ lei _ paper _ industryupdate. pdf), the PMPG noted that "the ability to clearly identify the originating and beneficiary parties with LEI (and therefore having additional transparency on these parties) could bring significant quantitative and qualitative benefits on a strategic basis, mainly for compliance and risk management functions", for instance, "eliminating potential delays during payment processing from false hits in compliance and sanctions screening; optimized and more accurate AML controls and detection of suspicious activities and ability to identify ordering and beneficiary customer as meaningful information for correspondent banks acting as intermediary in the payments chain".

cover with LEIs. It is also important that any improvement in LEI issuance and maintenance processes recommended in this report be considered in time for the ISO 20022 migration, as a large number of LEIs would presumably be needed, and these would need to be kept up-to-date. Timely information on potential reductions in LEI costs for entities that would result from such improvements would be important especially if some jurisdictions were to consider requiring the LEI in the area of payments, as envisaged by the UK in its recent consultation. [75] The FSB will facilitate, by working with standard-setting and industry bodies, the effective implementation of the LEI option in payment messages to help address the decline in the number of correspondent banking relationships (**recommendation 2c**).

The LEI may support a number of regulatory objectives in FSB initiatives. Under the right circumstances, the LEI can facilitate timely data processing in the case of an authority having to deal with a failed financial institution and all of its related legal entities. It could also be useful in issues relating to financial innovation, such as RegTech and SupTech. [1]

- The FSB will also explore the potential role of the LEI in its work, for instance in the resolution of financial institutions and on financial innovation issues (**recommendation 2a**).
- More generally, the relevant standard-setting bodies (BCBS, IAIS, CPMI, and IOSCO) and international organisations (IMF, OECD, and World Bank) should review and consider ways to embed or enhance references to the LEI in their policy and implementation work, in order to facilitate the implementation of relevant LEI uses for authorities and market participants. This could involve, for example, guidance on the inclusion of the LEI in disclosures of data on entities as well as promoting LEI use in securities transactions and in cross-border payments (**recommendation 3**).

Market participants have identified several areas where the LEI would

---

① RegTech means any range of applications of FinTech for regulatory and compliance requirements and reporting by regulated financial institutions. This can also refer to firms that offer such applications. There is also a close link with "SupTech", or the use of FinTech by supervisory authorities.

provide benefits and that are not necessarily related to regulatory uses. Several of these new uses may relate to the transition to a more digital economy, where the certainty of identity for non-face-to-face transactions, and the efficient management of large amounts of data are paramount-for example:

- The LEI can support more efficient disclosures of data on entities, where data is structured according to widely accepted standards and easily usable in automated processes, instead of being provided as text. Including the LEI in disclosures on entities makes these disclosures interoperable with each other. [1] For instance, the LEI was introduced in the XBRL taxonomy, [2] which will help standardise how entities are referred to in areas such as regulatory reporting, registration in business registries, financial disclosures, tax reporting, compliance, smart contracts, and digital identifiers. Adding the LEI to the taxonomy will encourage XBRL users to use the LEI when they need to identify entities. Another possibility would be that electronic financial statements identify with an LEI the entity issuing the statements as well as all related entities, and that the electronic signature of the auditors that certified the statements and of the regulators that received them also include the LEI. Market authorities, IOSCO and market regulators could foster such use, along with accounting firms and industry bodies, for instance when implementing structured reporting with the IFRS taxonomy. [3] The availability of mappings with other identifiers, such as the BIC and more

---

[1] See Rick A. Fleming, SEC Investor Advocate, Improving Disclosures with Smart Data, speech 24 October 2016, https://www.sec.gov/news/speech/improving-disclosure-with-smart-data.html.

[2] XBRL is used in some 70 countries, with 142 mandates covering 20 million companies. See https://www.xbrl.org/the-standard/what/taxonomies/.

[3] For instance, the CFA Institute has stated that all companies should be required to maintain and report the LEI of a registrant and its major subsidiaries, as this would increase investors' ability to identify and analyse the risks of registrants and their subsidiaries. However, even taking an initial step of only those that currently maintain a LEI to report it would be beneficial to the marketplace and would impose minimal burden on registrants. The CFA Institute also noted that LEIs should be used in additional areas throughout the filing to aid investors; for example, a company should be required to use the appropriate LEI when referring to another legal entity. See https://blogs.cfainstitute.org/marketintegrity/2018/01/23/requiring-the-use-of-the-legal-entity-identifier/.

recently the ISIN,① supports the role of the LEI as a lynchpin to access entity data from multiple sources, and the work of GLEIF and their mapping partners should be encouraged. Together with the business registry number already included in the LEI reference data, these mappings are the ones most frequently needed by financial institutions, at least according to the survey of a small number of ISDA and GFMA members, when excluding proprietary identifiers. ② Some FSB members encouraged mapping the LEI with vendors' identifiers (see Annex 6).

- The LEI can be used as a building block for more secure on-line transactions. The LEI has already started to be included in digital certificates,③ which are a key feature for secure websites and for electronic transactions more generally. Digital certificates generally refer to names of entities, which means that, given the cryptographic link between the components of the certificate, the certificate needs to be changed when the name of the entity changes (or in case of mergers). ④ The LEI would avoid this issue and would allow connecting reliably all certificates used by an entity with reliable data on the entity's identity. Relatedly, the signature and encryption of documents providing the application of security at a more granular (e. g. document or disclosure) level than the application of security at the repository level can improve the security of filing platforms and related registrant filings. This would require high quality and up-to-date identity data in the GLEIS, and would also make the benefit of regularly confirming their data more tangible to

---

① The first ISIN mappings started to be published in April 2019, although these cover initially only a few numbering agencies. See https: //www. anna-web. org/standards/lei/.

② According to a GFMA and ISDA survey of 21 of their members, the LEI is mapped to an internally generated entity identifier or a code (other than the LEI) assigned by a trade repository in two thirds of cases and mapped with the BIC in around half of cases. Some 20% map the LEI with an ISIN, and a similar proportion map it with a local business registry number, and with a tax number.

③ See, for example, InfoCert (https: //infocert. digital/).

④ For a discussion of this issue, and how having to change digital certificates after a change in the details of the company can be a source of costs and risks, see Why the Certificate Authority world should embrace Legal Entity Identifiers, part ii, https: //www. ubisecure. com/legal-entity-identifier-lei/lei-is-live-legal-entity-data/.

entities using the LEI.

- The LEI can facilitate the seamless processing of trade, including trade financing, invoicing, and compliance with customs requirements. The LEI would allow a complete and integrated audit trail for both financial institutions and their business clients. McKinsey and GLEIF have, for instance, illustrated the benefits of the LEI in trade finance. ① From an industry perspective, the benefits of the LEI in trade would be magnified if it were used consistently by all participants including customs authorities. Entities that currently have an LEI are likely to overlap significantly with importers and exporters, which frequently hedge their risks with derivatives subject to reporting requirements that include the LEI. At a minimum, mapping the LEI with other identifiers used in trade would avoid manual reconciliation and support more efficient data management.

The LEI ROC and GLEIF should work with industry and the public sector to raise awareness of the benefits of the LEI to encourage voluntary adoption, by documenting existing uses, or supporting pilot programs or research projects on promising new uses (**recommendation 4c**).

Another challenge to address is that LEI coverage remains too low to effectively support some regulatory uses, or to capture the benefits of broader coverage to the market as a whole. As highlighted by the FSB in its 2012 report, the benefits from the system increase as more and more parties acquire an LEI. At the launch, however, as with other examples of network goods, the private incentives for potential early movers to acquire an LEI are low, and decision makers may not always be able to take into account the benefits that LEI adoption would have for third parties (positive externalities). One way to foster LEI adoption would be to maximise benefits by focusing efforts on certain populations of entities that play a central role in the global financial system. For instance, while the parent entities of all G-SIBs have an LEI, this is not the case for the majority of their subsidiaries or major counterparties. This prevents the analysis

---

① See McKinsey and GLEIF, *The Legal Entity Identifier: The Value of the Unique Counterparty ID* (ibid).

of interlinkages and common exposures across, as well as use of LEI in resolution planning for, these firms.

- To that end, the FSB will work with standard-setting and industry bodies to facilitate adoption of the LEI for all group entities and major counterparties of global systemically important financial institutions, as well as for the clearing members of CCPs and their ultimate parents, in order to support the timely analysis of risk exposures and interdependencies (**recommendation 2b**).

- For the same reasons, FSB members should consider requiring the use and timely renewal of the LEI in reporting or disclosure frameworks, for the identification of all entities in major financial groups, a wider set of financial market participants and infrastructures, their counterparties, and related entities (including direct and ultimate parents), especially in a cross-border context (**recommendation 1b**).

- FSB members should also explore ways to promote further LEI adoption, for instance by fostering nationwide implementation strategies to maximise the cross-sectoral benefits of the LEI; communicating on LEI benefits through public outreach initiatives; leading by example in obtaining LEIs for the central bank and other public sector bodies, especially issuers of public debt; and considering the potential for LEI use before introducing new identifiers (**recommendation 1c**).

Other identified obstacles to further LEI adoption and implementation relate to the LEI content, processes and business model.

First, the usability of relationship data has been considered insufficient by many public sector users. [1] The steps taken to increase coverage, especially among parent entities, would contribute to addressing this issue. The LEI ROC and GLEIF could facilitate reporting by the parent entity, introduce flags acknowledging the completeness of relationship data at entity and group level,

---

[1] Some of the barriers highlighted in section 5 suggest that, to improve relationship data, several avenues may need to be pursued, e. g. making it easier for the parent entity to provide consent, or include the collection of confidential information; increase LEI coverage among parent entities; record relationships under other definitions than accounting consolidation; and include relationship with natural persons.

determine criteria in consultation with relevant bodies (such as the OECD and BIS) to identify corporate groups that should be a priority target (e. g. large multinational enterprises), and promote voluntary adoption campaigns or possible new regulations that would cover these groups.

It was also noted that the addition of relationship data (beyond accounting consolidation, funds/pooled investment vehicles and branches) would make the LEI more useful. For instance, information on beneficial owners would support AML/CFT and the compilation of foreign direct investment statistics based on the Ultimate Investing Country. Information on directors would also support AML/CFT and digital signatures that would make the link between the signature and the entity that is represented. Industry sector information would support transaction monitoring, and facilitate the exchange of information on the holders and issuers of securities in the IMF Coordinated Portfolio Investment Survey. However, some stakeholders caution that issuance and renewals would be more complex if more information is added in the GLEIS. A solution could be in some cases that data on entities be published with LEIs by third parties, which would allow the data to be retrieved more easily, without the need to have all data elements included in the GLEIS database and verified by LOUs. Such links to other sources outside the GLEIS may be considered as a possibility when adding confidential data such as some relationship data. [1]

- The LEI ROC and GLEIF should enhance the scope and usability of Level 2 (relationship) data by:
  ○ considering cost-effective and reliable ways to add relationship data that would increase the value of the LEI (e. g. confidential relationships subject to access rights and appropriate controls; beneficial owners; other definition of parents); and (**recommendation 4d. i**)
  ○ expanding the coverage of such data, for instance by conducting

---

[1] The FSB had already noted in 2012 that the GLEIS "must also provide appropriate protection of data covered by confidentiality and privacy restrictions governing some potentially important reference data in some countries, particularly regarding information on corporate relationships and ownership structures". See http://www. fsb. org/2012/06/fsb-report-global-legal-entity-identifier-for-financial-markets. One of the objectives of the LEI ROC is to ensure that "confidential data should be safeguarded and with due regard for any applicable data protection legislation" [LEI ROC Charter Art. 2 (a) (1) (iii)].

targeted LEI adoption campaigns for large multinational firms and by facilitating relationship reporting by parents of their group entities (**recommendation 4d. ii**).

Another issue relates to data quality. While only about 20% of authorities noted quality was an issue (see section 5), responses from the public noted that quality is better than many other sources, but can still be improved in a number of areas: for instance the legal address given is frequently identical to the headquarters address, and there is not a common understanding of the field to use to determine the jurisdiction of an entity. The proportion of lapsed LEIs was also raised as a source of concern for the quality of LEI data, as information may become out of date. Industry participants also encouraged regulators to more frequently mandate LEI renewals. The LEI ROC could continue monitoring, as part of its inventory of LEI related rules, the inclusion of explicit requirements to keep LEI reference data up-to-date and work on processes encouraging renewals.

- The LEI ROC and GLEIF should consider data quality process enhancements to increase the reliability of the LEI data so as to improve its usability by market participants and regulators, including processes to encourage and monitor updates of LEI reference data (**recommendation 4b**).

Another key issue is the current business model, which does not fully align the benefits and costs of LEI use for participants. Some academic literature has noted that "bottom line return are the most powerful reason for adoption" without regulatory compulsion and also compare with the adoption of GS1 bar codes:[1] "Individual firms have a strong private incentive to adopt and use these standards because without them they cannot participate in global supply as either a supplier or customer. Regulatory compulsion is not needed to make the system work. LEI must offer similar benefits to wholesale financial market participants". [2]

- The LEI ROC and GLEIF should consider enhancements to the LEI

---

[1]   See https: //www. gs1. org/standards/barcodes.

[2]   Ka Kei Chan and Alistair Milne, The Global Legal Entity Identifier System: How Can It Deliver?
Journal of Risk and Financial Management, 7 March 2019, https: //www. mdpi. com/1911-8074/12/1/39/htm.

business model to lower the cost and administrative burden for entities acquiring and maintaining an LEI, for instance adjusting funding approaches to align the benefits and costs for users more closely, and exploring ways to foster complementarity between the issuance and maintenance of the LEI and other processes involving similar tasks (e. g. issuance of domestic identifiers and digital certificates, financial institutions' customer due diligence) (**recommendation 4a**).

Finally, there would be scope to minimise potential duplication between activities performed by the GLEIS and similar processes performed by market participants, for instance by allowing banks to perform verification of customer information on LEI records (something they already do to comply with regulatory requirements), or through greater integration with business registries (who already require notification of name and address changes, for example). This would enhance, rather than replace, the current business model, as for instance LOUs could outsource some verifications to banks, and some LOUs are already business registries. In addition, it is likely that different variations of the business model would coexist depending on the country and type of entities.

Annex 1: Abbreviations for financial authorities in FSB jurisdictions cited in this report

Australia

ASIC   Australian Securities and Investments Commission

European Union

EBA   European Banking Authority
ECB   European Central Bank
EIOPA   European Insurance and Occupational Pensions Authority
ESMA   European Securities and Markets Authority
SRB   Single Resolution Board

Hong Kong

HKMA   Hong Kong Monetary Authority
SFC   Securities and Futures Commission

India

RBI   Reserve Bank of India

Japan

JFSA   Japan Financial Services Agency

Korea

FSC   Financial Services Commission

Singapore

MAS   Monetary Authority of Singapore

United States

CFTC	Commodity Futures Trading Commission
FDIC	Federal Deposit Insurance Corporation
FRB	Federal Reserve Board
FSOC	Financial Stability Oversight Council
OFR	Office of Financial Research
SEC	Securities and Exchange Commission

Annex 2: Non-LEI identifiers used by jurisdictions

Jurisdictions use a variety of identifiers other than the LEI. Some jurisdictions (Brazil, France, Italy, Switzerland, Turkey, and Spain) appear to have a main domestic identifier covering all or most legal entities, which are largely used for multiple purposes. Other jurisdictions have a plurality of identifiers, with no clear "main" identifier (India, Saudi Arabia, and the US).

These identifiers are generally not linked to the LEI, though there are some exceptions. For example, identifiers of lenders and borrowers of the ECB's recently established granular database on credit (AnaCredit) are mapped to the LEI in the context of its Register of Institutions and Affiliates Database (RIAD). EIOPA's code is linked at an entity level in the EIOPA's reference database. In the US, the OCC has mapped its Charter ID, the FDIC's Certificate Number, and the Federal Reserve's RSSD Number to the respective financial institutions' LEI. Mapping with the LEI allows to access richer datasets. [1] The identifier of the entity in the business registry in which the entity was formed, where applicable, is part of the mandatory data elements in the GLEIS. However, the interpretation of the qualifier "where applicable" seems to have led to diverging practices by LOUs, in the process of being addressed by GLEIF. The incomplete mapping with domestic identifiers resulting from this divergence was seen as an important obstacle by a number of FSB members, and some have developed their own mapping outside the GLEIS (e. g. Brazil). Other identifiers in Brazil, Germany, Hong Kong, Spain, Switzerland and the US are mapped to the LEI.

A variety of identifiers, both proprietary and others, are used for entities incorporated or established in foreign jurisdictions. Some of the most common such identifiers are the BIC and international bank account number (IBAN) for banks and accounts, respectively. European authorities mention the

---

[1] For instance, the SEC staff publishes Investment Adviser Information Reports that contain information about investment advisers who are registered with the SEC or who are filing reports as Exempt Reporting Advisers with the SEC, and the LEI is included in the file if the adviser has one.

LEI, Le（a national identifier issued to foreign entities）, financial regulator proprietary codes, and financial institution proprietary client codes. For trade repository data and EMIR data the LEI and Market Identifier Code（MIC）are used. For EMIR reporting, some market participants had requested that the BIC be accepted during a transition period, but analysis showed that the proportion of trades reported with a BIC was minor or negligible, and a substantial number of such trades originated from jurisdictions where the LEI was already implemented. The generalisation of the LEI requirements for derivatives reporting in November 2017 in the EU led to replacing 9,362 BICs, national codes and client codes（out of some 130,000 entities）. In Russia, there are the LEI, legal name, and tax IDs. In the US, the CFTC allows, if necessary to comply with foreign law, reporting of a privacy law identifier（PLI）, a proprietary client code created by the reporting counterparty. The FDIC uses the entities' legal names and home country national identifiers. In Mexico and Saudi Arabia, foreign entities are identified by copies of the articles of incorporation or business registration certificate.

Many identifiers could be eliminated if the LEI was more widely adopted across jurisdictions and agencies within jurisdictions. Some identifiers already in use are being replaced or complemented by the LEI.

Table A2：Identifiers replaced by, to be replaced by, or mapped to the LEI

Jurisdiction	Identifier replaced/planned to be replaced by the LEI	Identifier mapped to the LEI	Comments
Brazil		National Registry of Legal Entities（CNJP）, a unique ID number assigned by the national tax authority	Brazilian entities with an LEI must include it into the CNJP.

France	BIC		The LEI has fully replaced the BIC code for the identification of investment firms taking part in the execution of a transaction within MiFIR regulation.
France	CIB		In November 2018, banks were consulted on the project to identify with an LEI to report the ACPR instead of CIB. Implementation is foreseen end 2020.
France	SIREN		In October 2018, insurers were consulted on the project to identify with an LEI to report the ACPR instead of SIREN. Implementation is foreseen end 2020.
Germany		Creditor ID and Borrower ID of the Central Credit Register	Mapping done by the Bundesbank.
Germany		RIAD code	Mapping done by the Bundesbank.
Hong Kong	HKTR member code		For OTC derivatives trade reporting, when the first phase of mandatory use of LEI commenced (1 April 2019), the HKMA and SFC removed the HKTR members codes (which currently has the same priority as LEIs) from the waterfall of identifiers in the Supplementary Reporting Instructions (SRI).
Hong Kong		HKTR member code	TR Member has to provide all its third party codes (if any) when registers with the HKTR and is responsible to review and update their identifiers regularly. HKTR will map all these third party identifiers to the LEI under the HKTR system accordingly.
Spain		All identifiers in RIAD (NIF, REN, BIC, RIAD)	NIF is the legal unique Spanish identifier provided in Spain by the Tax Office. REN is the official code provided by Banco de España to financial institutions.

Switzerland		UID	An automatic mapping of the UID number to the LEI occurs if a Swiss enterprise applies for an LEI from the Swiss LOU operated by the Federal Statistical Office (who also operates the UID registry). LOUs can also achieve a mapping by including the UID in the reference data when issuing an LEI.
United States	CFTC Interim Compliant Identifier (CICI)		As the CFTC swap data reporting rules became effective prior to the establishment of the GLEIS, swap counterparties were initially required to be identified using a CICI. Once the GLEIS was developed, the CFTC mandated thatswap counterparties be identified instead with the LEI.
United States		The OCC's Charter ID, the FDIC's Certificate Number, andthe Federal Reserve's RSSD Number	The OCC has mapped these identifiers to the respective financial institutions' LEI (when the LEI has been provided on the Bank/BHC Call Report).

Annex 3: Strategies for LEI implementation per jurisdiction

Jurisdiction	Adopted at national, supranational or authority level	Developed how?	Motivation/Objective	Description
		Strategy features		
Australia	National	Dialogue and consultation between authorities and financial institutions and local Registration Agents	Facilitate the aggregation of transaction data at the entity level for measuring and monitoring trading and clearing activity and large exposures	Adoption of LEI is promoted by inclusion as a required identifier for OTC trade reporting (with AVIDs or BICs as alternatives) and as requested field for reporting by regulated entities under market integrity rules (securities markets), clearing rules and prudential standard for reporting of large exposures
Brazil	National	Dialogue between authorities	Information for tax and other domestic authorities	Legal entities with an LEI must include it in the national registry
Canada	National	Dialogue between authorities	Facilitate the aggregation of transaction data at the entity level for measuring and monitoring trading activityand interconnections between entities	LEI requirements for OTC derivatives, exchange-traded derivatives and securities markets

Jurisdiction	Adopted at national, supranational or authority level	Strategy features		Description
		Developed how?	Motivation/Objective	
China	Authority (Shanghai Head Office of People's Bank of China and some market infrastructure including the China Foreign Exchange Trade System/National Interbank Lending Center, the Shanghai Clearing House and the China Central Depository & Clearing Co. Ltd.)	Dialogue and consultation between authorities and financial institutions	Guarding against macro systemic financial risks, strengthening the identification of foreign institutions to participate in Chinese market	Foreign institutions in the Bond Market Access Record System (BMARS), China Interbank Bond Market (CIBM) and in the interbank market financial derivatives CCP clearing report would (starting in 2020) need to provide an LEI, if available
EU (**EBA**)	Supranational	EU decision making process	Quality of reporting, better data analysis, facilitating risk analysis	Promote LEI use
EU (**ECB**)	Supranational	EU decision making process	Better data analysis	Require entries into RIAD be identified with an LEI
EU (**EIOPA**)	Supranational	EU decision making process	Effective supervisionthrough data quality	Promote LEI use

Jurisdiction	Adopted at national, supranational or authority level	Strategy features		Description
		Developed how?	Motivation/Objective	
EU (ESMA)	Supranational	Stakeholder dialogue + EU decision making process	Consistent approach across all sectoral legislations under ESMA's mandates	Mandatory (i. e. required also if the entity does not already have an LEI) for financial and non-financial counterparties to OTC derivatives contract, investment firms trading in financial instruments, trading platforms, credit rating agencies, central securities depositories and settlement internalisers. Reporting by the above must (i. e. required also if the entity does not already have an LEI) include an LEI for: clients of investment firms; CCPs; intermediaries and counterparties of the reporting entities; entities for which a credit rating have been issued; issuers of financial instruments; participants in the CSD system and settlement banks
Hong Kong	National	Stakeholder dialogue	Follow international trend, benefits for financial sector as a whole	Phased-in approach to mandating LEI use in OTC derivatives trade reporting, starting April 2019

Jurisdiction	Adopted at national, supranational or authority level	Developed how?	Strategy features	
			Motivation/Objective	Description
India	National (interagency)	Consultation (Inter Regulatory Technical Group)	Helps to achieve financial stability objectives, better risk management (in particular across jurisdictions)	Phased-in approach to mandating use of LEIs for OTC derivatives trading, for entities with large credit exposures, and for non-derivative markets. Entities that do not obtain an LEI as schedules are restricted from bank credit
Japan	Authority (JFSA)	Stakeholder consultation	Facilitates aggregation of trading volumes, enhancement of cross-border transactions	JFSA to communicate benefits of LEI to Financial Instruments Business Operators and encourage the use of the LEI
Korea	Authority (FSC)	Stakeholder consultation	Compliance with G20 call, improve management of systemic risk	Request the use of LEI in periodic reporting of OTC derivatives contracts. Will soon require the use of the LEI as a unique identifier for financial institutions in trade repository and gradually phased in
Mexico	National	National financial authorities (in Financial Stability Council)	Improvement in the identification of risks for both, financial entities and authorities.	Require LEIs for all the parties and counterparties operating in financial markets, and gradually incorporate regulation to require use of the LEI as identifier for reporting to Banco de México financial market operations

Strategy features				
Jurisdiction	Adopted at national, supranational or authority level	Developed how?	Motivation/Objective	Description
Saudi Arabia	National	National financial authorities.	n/a	Phased requirements to obtain an LEI, first by financial institutions, next certain financial transactions
Singapore	Authority (MAS)	Public consultation	Enables authorities to better view and analyse potential systemic risk (in particular as regards business across multiple legal entities)	Require by regulation reporting entities and (where available) counterparties to report the LEI in reporting of derivatives contracts
Switzerland	National	Legislative procedure with stakeholder involvement (authorities and industry)	Improvement of the financial data quality facilitates assessment of systemic risks, contributes to reinforce financial stability	Participate on LEI ROC; update legislation to allow Federal Statistical Office to become an LOU; include LEI in OTC derivatives and securities transactions reporting
Turkey	Authority	National financial authorities	Compliance with other countries practices to improve data quality	Requiring the use of the LEI as a unique identifier in OTC derivatives trade reporting

Jurisdiction	Strategy features			
	Adopted at national, supranational or authority level	Developed how?	Motivation/Objective	Description
United Kingdom	Authority	EU decision making process, stakeholder consultation	Consistent, efficient and effective supervisory practices to ensure high quality, reliable and comparable data, bridging data silos and better monitoring systemic risk	Support for LEI requirements in EU requirements e. g. CRR, Solvency II and MiFID II/MiFIR and EMIR; incorporation of LEI in regulatory reporting and other collected datasets wherever possible
United States	Authority (OFR, OCC, FRB, CFTC, SEC)	Stakeholder involvement	Lowering regulatory compliance costs and improving data quality	Encourage the use of the LEI in new US and global financial regulation (OFR); mandate that all entities that are counterparties to swap transactions be identified with an LEI (CFTC); require all participants of security-based swaps to use the LEI for reporting (SEC); investment advisers report an LEI if they have one (SEC); require registered investment companies to obtain and report an LEI (SEC); including recommendations about the use of LEI in regulation in the FSOC Annual Report of Congress

Jurisdictions with no strategy in place yet: Argentina, Indonesia, Russia, South Africa.

Annex 4a: Percentage of OTC derivatives trades where the reporting entity or counterparty is identified with an LEI

Jurisdiction	Open transactions (stock)		New transactions (flow)		Open transactions (stock)		New transactions (flow)	
	Percentage of all OTC derivative trades where the reporting entity is identified with a current LEI				Percentage of all OTC derivative trades where the counterparty of the reporting entity is identified with a current LEI			
	By transaction count	By gross notional outstanding	By transaction count	By gross notional outstanding	By transaction count	By gross notional outstanding	By transaction count	By gross notional outstanding
AU	100	100	100	100	90	Not available	87	87
CA	96	97	98	96	94	98	86	98
Euro area	99	96	100	100	90	99	97	99
FR	100	100	100	100	79	100	74	100
DE	99	100	100	100	93	100	99	100
HK	100	100	100	100	92	98	89	97
IN	100	100	100	100	89	98	96	97
IT	99	99	100	100	97	NA	100	100
JP	100	100	100	100	67	94	63	94
MX	100	100	100	100	3.8	6	4	47
NL	100	100	100	100	100	100	100	100
RU	NA	NA	100	100	NA	NA	100	100
SG	100	100	100	100	75	86	77	90

Jurisdiction	Percentage of all OTC derivative trades where the reporting entity is identified with a current LEI				Percentage of all OTC derivative trades where the counterparty of the reporting entity is identified with a current LEI			
	Open transactions (stock)		New transactions (flow)		Open transactions (stock)		New transactions (flow)	
	By transaction count	By gross notional outstanding	By transaction count	By gross notional outstanding	By transaction count	By gross notional outstanding	By transaction count	By gross notional outstanding
ES	99	100	100	100	90	99	93	100
UK	100	100	100	100	93	99	96	99
US	100	100	96	100	98	100	92	100
TR	100	100	100	100	89	89	86	86

Source: Responses to FSB peer review questionnaire. Data unavailable for Argentina, Brazil, China, Indonesia, Korea, Saudi Arabia, South Africa and Switzerland. For Russia, data on open transactions is not available but is estimated by its authorities to be between 90%-100%.

Annex 4b: LEI coverage for securities issuers in FSB jurisdictions (end-September 2018)*

	Non-financial corporations LEI coverage in % of			Financial institutions** LEI coverage in % of			General government LEI coverage in % of			Total economy** LEI coverage in % of		
	issuers	instruments	outstanding amounts	issuers	instruments	outstanding amounts	issuers	instruments	outstanding amounts	issuers	instruments	outstanding amounts
AR	6%	4%	75%	22%	24%	75%	55%	87%	99%	9%	10%	90%
AU	9%	3%	39%	25%	73%	90%	43%	96%	100%	13%	23%	71%
BR	0%	1%	25%	8%	54%	42%	10%	99%	100%	0%	24%	50%
CA	6%	5%	84%	16%	57%	90%	6%	24%	97%	7%	25%	89%
CH	3%	3%	91%	18%	90%	96%	6%	23%	65%	5%	42%	91%
CN	1%	2%	5%	6%	27%	68%	2%	24%	42%	2%	15%	36%
DE	14%	14%	99%	47%	99%	99%	94%	66%	100%	19%	97%	99%
ES	18%	8%	93%	61%	92%	100%	100%	100%	100%	27%	29%	98%
EU	17%	12%	94%	48%	98%	97%	38%	78%	100%	22%	88%	97%
FR	8%	8%	99%	21%	86%	99%	62%	95%	100%	10%	33%	99%
HK	9%	8%	43%	53%	84%	91%	100%	100%	100%	22%	50%	63%
ID	7%	4%	30%	18%	71%	85%	100%	100%	100%	10%	20%	62%
IN	5%	14%	85%	7%	45%	81%	5%	5%	3%	5%	22%	58%
IT	45%	50%	93%	69%	93%	97%	12%	28%	100%	47%	69%	98%
JP	7%	14%	56%	44%	88%	87%	2%	12%	92%	9%	46%	77%
KR	1%	3%	53%	2%	90%	81%	4%	13%	96%	1%	48%	70%
MX	9%	10%	54%	26%	65%	59%	25%	95%	100%	13%	35%	61%
NL	26%	32%	100%	83%	100%	100%	89%	95%	100%	56%	97%	100%
RU	1%	4%	66%	32%	46%	91%	4%	58%	93%	4%	11%	75%
SA	6%	1%	60%	62%	68%	97%	100%	100%	100%	21%	8%	78%
SG	12%	3%	65%	44%	82%	92%	100%	100%	100%	18%	28%	80%
TR	8%	3%	65%	34%	5%	92%	67%	100%	100%	14%	7%	88%
UK	25%	4%	91%	57%	99%	94%	42%	85%	95%	34%	84%	94%
US	6%	4%	92%	21%	40%	61%	13%	43%	95%	10%	24%	83%
ZA	2%	4%	48%	10%	46%	69%	13%	82%	99%	3%	24%	64%
FSB total***	9%	6%	75%	26%	80%	76%	15%	44%	89%	12%	58%	79%
Rest of the world****	3%	4%	49%	29%	53%	76%	61%	22%	86%	7%	30%	64%
World total	8%	6%	73%	27%	78%	76%	17%	38%	89%	11%	55%	78%

Notes:

* LEI coverage statistics are calculated on the basis of micro data from the ESCB's Centralised Securities Database (CSDB). The CSDB is a multi-source security-by-security database that automatically combines security and issuer information from multiple data sources and derives a "golden copy" for each security and issuer. It is jointly operated by the ECB and 27 ESCB national central banks under a clearly defined data quality management framework. It should be noted that the data for the non-EU FSB member jurisdictions cannot be checked with the same depth as for the EU countries and that there may possibly be some coverage gaps for the non-EU FSB jurisdictions. Thus, the LEI coverage statistics for the non-EU FSB members should be treated as approximate estimates and interpreted with these caveats in mind.

** Data cover all subsectors except for money market funds and non-money market investment funds (i.e. SNA sectors S.123 and S.124).

*** The FSB total includes all EU member states as part of the EU aggregate.

**** Rest of the world refers to jurisdictions which are not members of the FSB (non-FSB EU member states are covered in the FSB total as part of the EU aggregate).

Annex 4c: Reasons given by entities for not providing information on their direct and ultimate parents

% of issued and lapsed LEIs (except last line)	AR	AU	BR	CA	CH	CN	DE	ES	FR	GB	HK	ID	IN	IT	JP	KR	MX	NL	RU	SA	SG	TR	US	ZA	EU	allFSB	ROW
Ultimate parent																											
Ultimate parent reported	18	12	14	10	9	22	6	4	7	6	14	27	10	4	5	23	22	3	14	22	19	26	6	16	6	6	6
of which lapsed	1	8	30	11	8	12	9	11	13	38	13	14	0	7	2	10	8	10	8	11	11	7	10	22	14	13	14
Ultimate parent not reported and exception given	62	76	70	64	86	59	84	91	81	92	78	66	78	83	90	69	66	84	53	55	67	69	58	56	86	80	87
of which: Consent not obtained or other obstacles	12	32	23	15	8	18	2	1	6	4	18	14	3	2	2	12	12	1	6	11	19	5	22	7	4	7	14
Natural persons	11	8	7	12	19	7	7	1	27	11	15	54	54	39	1	26	7	0	26	13	14	33	6	10	21	19	25
Non-consolidating parent	8	16	7	17	14	14	8	84	32	37	19	14	10	11	6	16	29	78	5	21	13	14	14	11	32	28	23
of which funds	2	7	1	6	5	1	0	3	8	1	6	1	0	0	1	9	2	0	0	1	3	1	4	3	2	3	3
No known person controlling the entity (e.g diversified shareholding)	17	14	27	12	40	8	64	3	9	1	11	11	5	27	81	10	11	1	11	6	10	7	9	11	25	22	18
of which funds	0	3	22	2	3	0	5	0	1	1	2	1	0	0	0	0	0	0	0	0	1	0	2	3	2	2	2
Parent has no LEI	14	6	6	7	5	12	2	2	7	3	13	20	5	3	1	6	7	3	6	5	11	9	7	19	4	5	8
Direct parent																											
Direct parent reported	16	11	12	9	7	17	5	3	8	5	12	20	9	4	3	19	17	3	18	19	16	29	5	13	5	6	5
of which lapsed	1	1	1	1	0	2	0	0	1	0	1	2	0	0	0	2	1	0	1	2	1	2	0	1	0	0	0
Direct parent not reported and exception given	65	77	72	64	87	64	85	91	81	93	80	73	79	82	92	73	70	85	50	57	70	66	60	59	86	81	88
of which: Consent not obtained or other obstacles	13	32	23	15	8	19	2	1	8	4	18	14	3	2	3	13	15	1	6	12	21	5	22	8	4	7	14
Natural person	10	8	8	12	20	6	7	7	26	10	15	7	54	39	1	26	6	0	18	13	13	30	6	10	21	18	24
Non-consolidating parent	10	17	8	17	16	16	9	84	32	38	20	17	11	11	6	19	30	79	6	21	14	12	15	12	32	28	24
of which funds	2	6	1	6	5	1	0	3	8	1	6	0	0	0	1	9	2	0	0	1	3	1	4	2	2	3	3
No known person controlling the entity (e.g diversified shareholding)	16	14	27	12	37	8	64	3	9	37	10	11	5	27	81	10	11	1	8	6	10	6	9	10	25	22	18
of which funds	0	3	22	2	6	0	5	0	1	1	2	1	0	0	1	0	0	0	0	0	1	0	2	2	2	2	2
Parent has no LEI	15	6	8	7	6	15	2	2	7	4	15	23	6	3	1	6	8	3	12	5	13	14	8	19	4	5	8
No parent reported and no exception given	9	11	15	27	5	15	10	5	11	2	6	5	0	14	5	7	12	10	33	15	12	5	35	11	8	12	6
Cases where no accounting consolidation parents should be reported																											
Sole proprietors	10	1	0	0	1	4	0	1	0	0	2	2	12	0	0	0	0	2	0	6	1	0	0	12	1	1	1
Branches	1	0	0	0	0	0	0	0	0	0	0	0	0	0	0	0	0	0	0	2	0	0	0	5	0	0	0
Total number of issued and lapsed LEIs*	511	12175	1663	28872	14409	1668	114019	94646	67914	133677	5031	649	19924	98926	8084	1054	3299	97622	1266	381	4716	1598	179668	1239	914554	1200761	126835

Source: *GLEIF*, files "reporting exceptions v1.1", LEI-CDF v2.1 Concatenated file, RR-CDF v1.1 as of 3 January 2019, available at https://www.gleif.org/en/lei-data/gleif-concatenated-file/download-the-concatenated-file# calculation FSB. Calculations only take into accounts LEIs with an "issued", "lapsed" or "pending transfer" status (as well as records with a "pending archival status" in the absence of a more recent record). It may happen that several exceptions are reported for the same relationship. ROW: rest of the world.

Annex 4d: LEI coverage in the customer base of a sample of GFMA and ISDA members

Respondent based in North America	% of European clients with LEIs	% of North American clients with LEIs	% of APAC (excluding Japan) clients with LEIs	% of Japan clients with LEIs
Low	10	3	5	1
High	100	99	100	100
Average	58	52	42	33
Mode	Not applicable	Not applicable	Not applicable	Not applicable
Median	70	65	20	19

Respondent based in Japan	% of European clients with LEIs	% of North American clients with LEIs	% of APAC (excluding Japan) clients with LEIs	% of Japan clients with LEIs
Low	8	4	1	5
High	100	100	100	100
Average	87	81	59	59
Mode	100	100	Not applicable	82
Median	100	100	90	67

Note: The survey was conducted by ISDA and GFMA in March and April 2019 and the results are based on 21 responses (mostly from the sell side). No responses were received from Europe, while one response from an institution in the APAC region (other than Japan) was excluded as it was considered as potentially not representative. The main business line where LEI implementation was completed is derivatives (around 80%, where the LEI is mandated). One-third implemented the LEI for derivatives even when not mandated, with another quarter of respondents in the process of doing so. LEI implementation was also well advanced for client onboarding (around 40% of the sample) but very low for trade finance, interbank payments and securities trading, where two-thirds of respondents had not even started planning implementation.

Annex 5: Summary of public feedback and roundtable with market participants

The FSB invited feedback from the public on the areas covered by the peer review. Over 20 written responses were received. Respondents were overwhelmingly supportive of the LEI and the FSB peer review. Many suggested steps to improve adoption and applying new use cases, with most calling for regulatory mandates (including for LEI renewals). The main points raised in the written public feedback are summarised below, together with the highlights of the roundtable organised in London on 10 December 2018, where the peer review team met with over 50 stakeholders, including representatives of banks, credit unions, securities dealers, investment advisers, stock exchanges, data vendors, the payment industry, participants in the GLEIS, issuers of other types of identifiers or digital certificates, and regulators.

LEI implementation: coverage achieved, progress made and lessons learnt from implementation strategies

The LEI has so far primarily been implemented through regulations, notably to support the reporting of financial transactions and risk aggregation. In general, awareness is growing but driven largely by regulatory mandates; consequently, written responses suggested less awareness in jurisdictions (and sectors) not subject to regulatory mandates for obtaining and maintaining LEIs. In some instances, respondents highlighted confusion among participants over whether they needed an LEI.

Roundtable participants considered that LEI uptake among derivative market participants, and to a lesser extent for securities markets, has been a considerable achievement. Large financial institutions consider the LEI as very beneficial for their own processes, such as making sure that the entity they are dealing with has been adequately identified and has up-to-date contractual documentation, and managing limits applying to that entity. However, small banks with local customers see less benefits in the LEI.

Regulatory mandates were seen by a majority as a necessary and preferred approach, at least until a tipping point of adoption is reached. Otherwise institutions do not have the incentive to rework their processes, especially given the increased benefits that accrue with joint adoption by all participants. One participant noted however that it was unlikely that all countries would mandate the LEI, and that other approaches relying on incentives would therefore be necessary.

The main implementation difficulties were:

Differences in the timing and scope of requirements across jurisdictions: Requirements to have an LEI for derivatives applied in a similar timeframe in the US and the EU, which was very effective for LEI adoption in these major markets. However those regulations required market participants from other jurisdictions to have an LEI, although those jurisdictions did not always mandate the LEI for derivatives. This is even more so for some requirements beyond the derivatives space, which tend to be more jurisdiction-specific, such as EU requirements for securities issuers to have an LEI. The issue is compounded when regulated entities in the country that mandates the LEI do not have a contractual relationship with the foreign entities expected to have an LEI: for instance, any broker can list a security on a German stock exchange, without the consent of the issuer. The burden fell on the industry to educate and convince these participants to have an LEI. The difficulties of convincing entities in Asia, due to the lesser scope of LEI requirements in some Asian jurisdictions, was mentioned several times. Differences in the timing of requirements also put financial institutions in first-mover countries at a disadvantage. A number of industry participants therefore recommended that, within an agreed scope, such as derivatives and listed securities, regulatory requirements have an LEI apply globally to all entities.

Difficulties in convincing small entities to get an LEI: Some participants wondered whether it made sense to require the LEI in all cases, especially for small entities that trade infrequently. The cost of acquiring an LEI may be perceived as disproportionate for very small accounts and these entities do not see any use of the LEI. However, a majority of participants considered that it was preferable to cover all entities, as all would ultimately benefit from operational efficiencies, for instance if the LEI supports the straight-through processing of cross-border payments and reduces false positive in sanction screening, which delay payments. Small entities may also be the first impacted in case of a financial crisis, and the LEI helps to assess the impact of a shock, or to ensure that the collateral posted by a customer can be appropriately traced. Some regulators noted that small transactions may be relevant from a conduct perspective, and a large number of small risks can together be systemic. In addition, one regulator observed that the millions of records collected would not be manageable without the LEI.

Operational issues: delays in the publication of LEIs, or the update in status, can cause issues and delay transactions.

Recommendations from participants to increase LEI adoption included:

- mandating the use of the LEI (discussed above);
- pursuing joint education efforts by regulators and industry where the take-up is not high, such as through webinars, seminars and forums by industry associations. There was a sense that the GLEIF and LOUs have been helpful in the past, as was an industry FAQ made available in multiple languages, but that lawmakers and business registries should be part of the outreach. In this regard FSB country peer reviews also had a positive impact, as had thematic papers by policy makers, such as the consultation by the Bank of England on payments;
- using the LEI for as many uses as possible, including for tax purposes;
- incorporating additional data in the GLEIS: some participants suggested adding data elements that do not change at every trade and currently burden trade reporting, for instance whether an entity is a US person, or adding the industry sector of entities, to support AML/CFT. A solution could be that data on entities be published with LEIs by third parties, which would allow the data to be retrieved more easily, without the need to have all data elements included in the GLEIS data base and verified by LOUs;
- reducing costs and the duplication of processes; especially with other identifiers (for instance embedding issuance at the local business

registry), and ideally replacing other identifiers with the LEI. Banks could play a role in issuance and maintenance, although one participant underlined this should not replace the responsibility of the entity to update its data, and another cautioned that we should not go back to situations where a bank could request an LEI for a customer without the customer's authorisation, which led to several identifiers being requested for the same entity;

- addressing the issue of lapsed LEIs. The absence of updates on lapsed LEIs is an issue. For instance, if the name of an entity is not updated, this may result in a new LEI being issued. Several participants highlighted the need for regulators to clearly mandate renewals; and

- cooperation between the public and private sector on new areas, for instance in payments and KYC, where some suggested the adoption of new regulatory requirements, after consultation with industry groups such as the Wolfsberg Group.

Benefits and challenges to market participants from LEI adoption

In addition to regulatory objectives, the LEI is intended to support improved internal processes and bring other benefits to market participants. In written contributions, identified uses included client/counterparty identification, data aggregation and analysis, systemic risk identification, efficient supply chain management, government-to-business relationships, payments and AML/CFT compliance.

Roundtable participants illustrated the following benefits of the LEI:

- it avoids the costs of manually reconciling data on entities, which is complicatedby variations in the use of names, the translation or transliteration of different languages and character sets;

- its use in ISDA documentation facilitates updates;

- its use in settlement instructions avoids ambiguity on entity identification; and

- it allows leveraging of other data points on the same entity within complex institutions.

Potential future uses:

The LEI was introduced in XBRL taxonomy, which will help standardise how entities are referred to in areas such as regulatory reporting, registration in business registries, financial disclosures, tax reporting, and compliance. XBRL is used in some 70 countries, with 142 mandates covering 20 million companies. Adding the LEI to the taxonomy will encourage XBRL users to consider the LEI when there is a need to identify entities. Roundtable participants noted one could imagine that financial statements identify with an LEI the entity issuing the statements as well as the related entities referred to in the statements and that the electronic signature of the auditors that certified the statements, and the regulators that received them, also include the LEI.

Participants noted the LEI is starting to be included in digital certificates, which are a key feature for secure websites and for electronic transactions more generally. Digital certificates generally refer to names of entities, which means that the certificate needs to be changed when the name of the entity changes, or in case of mergers. The LEI would avoid this issue, and would allow connecting reliably all certificates used by an entity with reliable data on the identity of the entity. Embedding the LEI in digital signatures would facilitate the management of contracts.

The identification by accounting firms of the entities their customers are related to would benefit greatly from the LEI, as these processes currently rely on vendors' data from multiple source and a large amount of manual work.

Challenges

The main obstacles cited in written contributions were the lack of regulatory mandates impacting coverage and renewals, different requirements across jurisdictions, costs, and data quality issues. Some of these challenges were discussed during the roundtable:

Levels of coverage vary widely and remain very low in some regions: A large international bank noted that LEI coverage reached 69% for its European customers, 29% for its US customers, and 4% for customers in the Asia-Pacific region. While some LEI benefits materialise even with partial coverage, a large coverage justifies additional investment in processes. In addition, as long as the

LEI cannot be used for all entities, other identifiers need to be maintained.

Quality is better than many other sources, but can still be improved in a number of areas: for instance the legal address given is frequently identical to the headquarters address, and a there is not a common understanding of the field to use to determine the jurisdiction of an entity. Furthermore, the business registry number is still frequently absent.

The high level of lapsed LEIs is an obstacle to some uses, such as KYC requirements. Some participants wondered whether a longer time period between renewals would be acceptable if the data does not change. However, this would not inform users as to whether the data is still up-to-date. Other avenues may help reach higher renewal rates: for instance in Spain, where many LEIs are managed by the local business registry, LEI renewals, which are above 90%, are perceived to be part of the annual process by which entities submit their financial statements to the registry.

Adoption strategies

In the written contributions received, the majority of respondents called for increased use of regulatory mandates. Other proposals include lowering costs to acquiring and renewing LEIs, linking the LEI to other identifiers (such as ISIN), and increasing awareness of the existence and benefits of the LEI.

Roundtable participants discussed how examples from other areas could inspire LEI adoption, and other ways to foster adoption:

- Digital certificates were made compulsory in some jurisdictions, for instance Italy mandated them for the communication of all companies with the government, and this supported additional uses in the private sector.
- Bar codes were required by large retailers, as this helped those retailers to manage more efficiently their sales and inventories. This market requirement forced companies that wanted to sell through them to tag their goods with such codes.

Participants suggested that getting all data vendors to include the LEI in their feeds on entities would support adoption.

The perspective of entities acquiring and maintaining their LEIs:

Addressing costs, the user experience and other challenges in order to promote wider LEI adoption

Some industry participants consider the LEI too costly and registration too cumbersome, which may impact the expansion of the LEI and also explain difficulties in achieving the yearly confirmation of LEI reference data by legal entities.

The main costs identified in written contributions were for acquiring an LEI and for accommodating them in internal systems. A few responses made the point that costs are borne entirely by the entity acquiring the LEI but the benefits are widespread (for both the public and private sector). One suggested the goal should be a system with no costs to the entities acquiring an LEI. Some respondents noted instances where mandates covered LEI acquisition, but not renewal, and suspected that given the cost many entities that are not required to renew will let their LEIs lapse. One respondent noted that costs have been falling for renewal and another argued costs are low; in contrast, fund organisations cited the high cost of managers having to acquire LEIs for their funds.

Participants discussed potential ways to address these challenges.

A number of other parties perform similar tasks as LOUs, such as: banks in their customer due diligence; issuers of digital certificates; tax authorities; and business registries. There would be scope for removing some of these duplications, for instance:

- by accepting that LOUs rely on banks to perform the verification of the LEI record: banks already perform such verifications, generally with a frequency of one, two or three years, and go even beyond the information required in the GLEIS. Banks would not replace LOUs, as they would be unlikely to want to manage the LEI record, respond to challenges, etc. ; or
- through a greater integration with business registries. One LOU which is also a business registry notifies the contact person of entities when records in the business registry change, so as to be able to modify as well the LEI record. Participants noted that business registries could not entirely replace LOUs: not all entities are in business registries, some business

registries do not have sufficient quality, or do not have appetite for the activity.

Competition brings LEI costs down, but may also impact quality: it is important that GLEIF quality monitoring covers not only the formal quality of LEI records, but also the correspondence with public sector groups. The cost recovery principle in the GLEIS avoids excessive prices not justified by costs, and is also seen by LOUs as a recognition that they are not expected to operate at a loss.

Exploring the use of LEI in payments and KYC

Several market participants and public sector groups have noted the potential benefits of using the LEI in correspondent banking. This includes use of the LEI in payment messages (e. g. SWIFT) to facilitate the unambiguous identification of the originator/beneficiary of payments and a more reliable screening of payment messages; and supporting customer due diligence processes. The current screening of text strings is unreliable. The LEI appears as an appropriate medium to exchange information on entities between financial institutions. The LEI could for instance be used in high risk jurisdictions to address the decline in correspondent banking, especially if additional information could be conveyed with the payment message, such as whether a transaction has an Office of Foreign Assets Control (US) license.

A change request is under way to include the LEI in ISO 20022. The migration of correspondent banking messages to ISO 20022 would be the opportunity to use the LEI in payment messages, which would be easier than using the LEI option in current formats, given the lack of space. Four years of coexistence are scheduled from November 2021, but the bulk of the payment traffic is expected to migrate early. Until all are able to process LEIs, messages will have to include both the LEI and the name and address.

In the UK, the LEI will be made compulsory for payments between financial institutions. The same benefits of avoiding manual checks, facilitating reconciliations, and increasing efficiency would also manifest themselves in retail payments, but the challenge is here the larger number of entities. A participant also noted that the LEI would support the processing of credit card payments, especially for the identification of web merchants.

Roundtable participants discussed that more information may be needed to support due diligence in payments, such as the industry sector, beneficial ownership, whether the entity is regulated and by whom. The cost of such information could be reduced if for instance regulators published lists of the entities they regulate with an LEI. This could apply to other data, such as financial statements signed by auditors, etc.

Using the GLEIS as a utility that banks could rely upon to verify an address is more challenging. Local regulation such as in the UK requires the constituting documents of the company before the banks can open a relationship. Relying on the LEI would require a change in regulations.

Annex 6: Questionnaire responses by SSBs and IOs

Responses were received from the Basel Committee on Banking Supervision (BCBS), the Bank for International Settlements (BIS), the Committee on the Global Financial System (CGFS), the Committee on Payments and Market Infrastructures (CPMI), the International Association of Insurance Supervisors (IAIS), the International Accounting Standards Board (IASB), the International Monetary Fund (IMF), the Organisation for Economic Cooperation and Development (OECD), the World Bank and the International Organization of Securities Commissions (IOSCO).

SSBs and international organisations (IOs) reported that the LEI was used in policy documents relating to enhanced transparency of information on financial markets, especially for OTC derivatives reporting, data aggregation and risk reporting by banks, customer identification, especially in the context of international payments (correspondent banking) and credit reporting. Thanks to the recently added information on parent entities, the GLEIS is also seen as facilitating the understanding and dissemination of information on group structures, thereby supporting insurance supervision, and a better understanding of cross-border flows of capital, goods and services.

The LEI is already used in data collection to support the information on counterparties of G-SIBs, on central clearing interdependencies, and collections on the group structures of insurance groups by the IAIS to support the development of the Insurance Capital Standard. It is also used in a pilot project by the OECD on 100 multinational enterprises.

Additional uses of the LEI are contemplated to support the IMF Coordinated Portfolio Investment Survey (especially facilitate the retrieval of information on the sector of entities holding and issuing securities), the collection of Foreign Direct Investment (FDI) statistics and statistics to improve the understanding of trade depending on the characteristics of enterprises.

The value of the LEI is to identify entities in a non-ambiguous way, especially in a cross border context, make information on the immediate and ultimate parent company of entities more accessible, especially given the non-proprietary nature of LEI data. The LEI also starts providing mapping to other identifiers, although this is limited to date to the BIC and national business registry numbers, and more recently to ISIN.

The main limitation is the insufficient coverage of the LEI. While coverage was reported to be close to 100% for borrowers of large corporate loans in the EU, the coverage is insufficient in other regions, especially Asia. The LEI was provided for 73% of the legal entities included on the scope of the insurance groups participating in the IAIS data collection, but only one third of the insurance groups were covering almost all their entities. In the banking sector, G-SIBs report LEIs to the BIS for their top entities, but only a few firms report the LEI for their counterparties. In several projects targeting non-financial companies, low LEI coverage is an obstacle to LEI uses.

Other limitations include insufficient mapping with other identifiers, especially those by data vendors, which remain necessary to access additional information on entities. The need for additional, proprietary, information also reduces the benefits of the open nature of LEI data. The information on group structures is also seen as insufficient, either because reporting is incomplete, in part due to the lack of LEI for the ultimate parent, or because the definition of parents do not match all needs (for instance, lack of information on publicly available beneficial owners, including individuals). Finally, in areas where the LEI is more developed (such as derivatives), other obstacles prevent a full use of the LEI.

1. Use of the LEI in policy work of standard setting bodies

The BCBS refers to the LEI in two policy documents described in the LEI ROC Progress report of April 2018:

- *Principles for effective risk data aggregation and risk reporting* (2013); and
- the *General guide to account opening*, which is set out in Annex IV of *Sound management of risks related to money laundering and financing of terrorism* (2017).

BCBS explains that LEI could facilitate **customer identification** and **data aggregation**, and therefore help improve banks' risk management and risk assessment.

CPMI and IOSCO also confirmed that the list of policy uses in the LEI ROC progress report is comprehensive, with mentions of the LEI in:

- the *CPMI-IOSCO Technical guidance on harmonisation of the UTI* (February 2017);
- the *CPMI-IOSCO Technical guidance on harmonisation of critical OTC derivatives data elements (other than UTI and UPI)* (April 2018);
- the *CPMI report, Correspondent banking* (July 2016); and
- the FSB-CPMI recommendations from the *Report to the G20 on actions taken to assess and address the decline in correspondent banking* (November 2015).

The LEI supports the objective of CPMI to **promote financial stability through enhanced transparency of information on financial markets and of IOSCO to address systemic risks**. For instance, the CPMI-IOSCO report on OTC derivatives data reporting and aggregation requirements (2012) recommended "the expeditious development and implementation of a standard LEI capable of achieving the data aggregation purposes discussed in the report". [1]

The World Bank refers also to the LEI in two publications on correspondent banking, in connection with CPMI recommendations and the FSB action plan. [2] In the second one, the International Finance Corporation notes that many stakeholders recognise that harnessing emerging technology can enhance financial institutions' risk management capabilities. There is a shift toward a customer-centric infrastructure that takes advantage of multiple disruptive technologies in

---

[1] See https://www.bis.org/cpmi/publ/d100.htm.

[2] World Bank Group, *Withdrawal from correspondent banking where, why, and what to do about it*, November 2015 http://documents.worldbank.org/curated/en/113021467990964789/pdf/101098-revised-PUBLIC-CBR-Report-November-2015.pdf; World Bank Group, *De-Risking and Other Challenges in the Emerging Market Financial Sector, Findings from IFC's Survey on Correspondent Banking*, September 2017 http://documents.worldbank.org/curated/en/895821510730571841/pdf/121275-WP-IFC-2017-Survey-on-Correspondent-Banking-in-EMs-PUBLIC.pdf.

the areas of enhanced identity verification. This includes biometric technology and LEIs. Central banks have proposed a number of specific changes to **global payments systems to improve safety and lower barriers**, including standards for unique institution identifiers: Proper identification of respondents and their customers in a transaction is essential for correspondent banks to manage risk and ensure regulatory requirements are properly applied. The application of an efficient global standard to identify specific legal entities, such as LEIs [for which there is already an International Organization for Standardization (ISO) standard].

The World Bank also looked at the use of the LEI in **credit reporting**. Some credit reporting service providers (CRSPs), including credit registries in Germany and Spain, use LEIs to identify firms. However, only a tiny percentage of CRSPs globally use LEIs in credit reporting. More extensive use of LEIs will make firm identification easier and more accurate, generating benefits for small and medium enterprises (SMEs), credit issuers and regulators at both the national and international levels. [1] The World Bank also observes that the LEI could prove helpful in linking databases not only at the domestic level but also and especially for the cross-border dimension, as it provides a mechanism to identify and match the data subjects in each database. [2] The World Bank included a question on the LEI in its Doing business, Getting Credit, Credit Registry Questionnaire, 2018 [3] and looked at the LEI in its report on *Implementing a Unique Business Identifier in Government*, *Guidance Note for Practitioners and Nine Country Case Studies.* [4]

The Irving Fisher Committee on Central Bank Statistics (IFC) hosted by the

---

[1] World Bank Group, Improving access to finance for SMEs, Opportunities through Credit Reporting, Secured Lending and Insolvency Practices, May2018, http://documents.worldbank.org/curated/en/316871533711048308/pdf/129283-WP-PUBLIC-improving-access-to-finance-for-SMEs.pdf.

[2] World Bank Group, the role of credit reporting in supporting financial sector regulation and supervision, Jan. 2016 http://pubdocs.worldbank.org/en/954571479312890728/CR-2016-role-credit-reporting-in-supporting-financial-regulation.pdf.

[3] See http://www.doingbusiness.org/content/dam/doingBusiness/media/Methodology/Survey-Instruments/DB18/DB18-Credit-Public-questionnaire-en.pdf.

[4] See http://documents.worldbank.org/curated/en/471531468196759403/pdf/103570-REVISED-Implementing-a-unique-business-identifier-in-government.pdf.

BIS mentions the LEI on the IFC Bulletin on Trade Repositories data. [1] The report discusses the potential usefulness of the LEI to manage trade repository data. Central banks agree that in many instances counterparties cannot be identified with the LEI thus limiting policy interest within their institutions.

The IAIS underlined, in the context of their data collections, that the **LEI is seen as a facilitator to understand evolutions in group structures over time**.

The IASB responded that IFRS Standards are principles-based and do not include the level of detail that would encompass the LEI. IFRS Standards are primarily applied by listed companies for their consolidated financial statements, and account standards do not require detailed information about subsidiary companies in such financial statements. Such requirements may be stipulated by company law or Listing Rules at a national or regional level. The CGFS had no activity to report related to the LEI.

2. Use of LEI in data collection or research projects

A. Current uses of the LEI

The LEI is being used in a number of research projects in BIS Monetary and Economic Department, mostly to track firms' activities in capital markets.

The LEI was also used:

- By the FSB-CPMI-IOSCO Study Group on Central Clearing Interdependencies.
- In IAIS annual data collections conducted since 2014 to support the development of the Insurance Capital Standard whose adoption as part of the Common Framework for Internationally Active Insurance Groups is forecasted to happen in late 2019. The quantitative component of these data collection-known as Field Testing-requests volunteer insurance groups to provide their group-level LEI if available as well as to identify the legal entities included in the scope of their data transmission by their LEI.
- In a pilot OECD project, the ADIMA, [2] which compiles publicly available statistics on the scale and scope of the international activities of

---

[1] See https: //www. bis. org/ifc/publ/ifc_report_cb_trade_rep_deriv_data. pdf.

[2] See the OECD Analytical Database on Individual Multinationals and their Affiliates (ADIMA).

MNEs, thus providing a unique 'whole of the MNE' view. ADIMA attempts to meet these goals through the development of three distinct (but related) outputs for 100 of the largest MNEs by sales: a series of economic indicators at both the level of the MNE and the individual countries in which it operates; a register of MNE parent-affiliate structures; and a Monitoring tool that aims to provide a timely flow of information on MNEs restructurings to aid the work of national compilers. the LEI is an integral data source for ADIMA, both in identifying relationships between parents and affiliates as well as assigning the LEI identifier (alongside ISIN, national business identifiers, websites, and other innovative identifiers) to improve identification of MNE entities within and linkage with existing national and international (typically confidential) databases.

The BCBS has not used the LEI in data collections. All the data collected through the BCBS Quantitative Impact Study (QIS) process are anonymised, so using the LEI is not necessary.

B. Potential future uses

- The implementation of the LEI by jurisdictions participating in the IMF CPIS would support the centralised exchange of data on a from-whom-to-whom basis. The Statistics Department of the IMF plans setting up a pilot CPIS database of issuers' sectors that would permit reporters to break down their portfolio assets by (non-resident) issuer sector and eventually provide users with from whom to whom CPIS positions by economy and sector of holder and issuer. It is expected that some reporters will use the LEI. [1]

- IAIS intends to include the LEI in any future data collections as long as they encompass granular information on group structures.

- The OECD observes that the LEI could potentially support the collection and compilation of statistics, particularly international investment and trade statistics.

---

[1] See https://www.imf.org/external/pubs/ft/bop/2018/pdf/18-08.pdf.

The OECD has been examining these potential uses of the LEI. For international investment statistics, the relationship information could be useful for improving the completeness of the statistics and the geographic attribution. Foreign Direct Investment (FDI) statistics are compiled on an immediate investor basis (i. e. the one with a direct influence/linkage to the investment enterprise). The Level 2 data in the GLEIS could be used to identify direct investment relationships not currently captured in the statistics as well as clarifying the country of the immediate investor. In addition, the information on the ultimate investor would be helpful for the supplemental presentation of FDI statistics by ultimate investing country. The complexity of ownership structures within MNEs often impedes the correct interpretation of public FDI statistics as it obscures the ultimate sources and destinations of FDI. The OECD 4th Benchmark Definition[1] recommended that countries compile inward investment positions according to the Ultimate Investing Country (UIC) to identify the country of the investor that actually controls the investments in their country. This is done by proceeding up the direct investor's ownership chain, until an entity that is not controlled by another entity is reached, i. e. the ultimate beneficial owner (UBO) of the investment; the LEI information could help with the attribution to ultimate investing countries.

It should be noted that the definitions used in FDI statistics are not completely aligned with the current Level 2 data, as these are based on accounting consolidation terms only and, thus, do not include individuals and minority interests. Therefore, the integration of information on Beneficial Owners would be a useful tool for compiling FDI statistics by UIC. Nevertheless, this relationship information would be useful to address some of interpretation challenges of FDI statistics as well as facilitating data sharing between National Statistical Institutes and International Organisations.

---

[1] The OECD's *Benchmark Definition of Foreign Direct Investment*, 4th *edition* (BD4) was published in 2008. It provides the most complete and detailed guidance on the coverage, collection, compilation, and dissemination of FDI statistics. In addition to providing guidance on the collection of aggregate FDI statistics that is aligned with the IMF's *Balance of Payments and international Investment Positions Manual*, 6th *edition* (BPM6) but also offers guidance on compilation of supplemental FDI series that enhance the usefulness and relevance of FDI statistics.

Foreign Affiliate Statistics (FATS), also called the Activities of Multinational Enterprise (AMNE) statistics, are another statistical domain that could benefit from the relationship data from the LEI. As for FDI statistics, the information could be used to improve the coverage and geographic attribution of the statistics, but, unlike FDI statistics, the accounting consolidation concepts used in the LEI are much more closely aligned with the concepts and definitions used in FATS.

As discussed further below, both FDI statistics and FATS would benefit from improved coverage of non-financial entities in the LEI.

Trade statistics disaggregated by ownership (Foreign MNE/Domestic MNE/ non-MNE) are a related statistical domain that benefit from the above-mentioned improvement in ownership relationships articulated through the LEI. This data is part of a larger statistical domain, Trade by Enterprise Characteristics,[①] which relies on data linkage between national customs data and national business statistics (often the centralised statistical business register). There is therefore considerable interest at the OECD on any partnerships between GLEIF and national policy and statistics departments to link LEI and customs data.

C. Value of the LEI for data collections and research projects

In a BIS project, the LEI was used as an identifier of entities borrowing in capital markets through corporate loans. For each entity the BIS identified as well the **immediate and ultimate parent company**, and their corresponding LEIs. Then BIS aggregated loans at the entity level, and on a consolidated basis. BIS managed to construct institution-parent relationships.

In the IAIS Field Testing, the LEIs are collected to enable cross checking of data collected through this exercise with other data sources, in a **non-ambiguous** way. The IAIS also noted that adding the LEI request for entities included in the scope of the groups did not add any specific costs while the availability of this information may prove useful to understand the changes in group perimeters over years as a side effect of mergers and acquisitions.

For the IMF, if available within CPIS participating economies, the LEI

---

① See http: //www. oecd. org/sdd/its/trade-by-enterprise-characteristics. htm.

could be an important component to efficiently identify the sector to which a security's holder belongs, following internationally accepted standards. For this project, the envisaged **links between ISIN/LEI standard identifiers and national identifiers** will be beneficial.

For the OECD ADIMA project, the LEI is a key data source given the **open data** aspect. The data are useful for comparison and sharing purposes. The accessibility/open data serves an important function in compiling data on MNEs, the primary focus of OECD ADIMA.

D. Limitations of the LEI

The main limitations reported:

i. Insufficient coverage of the LEI

The BIS reported that, in the context of a methodological paper exploring how to construct bank-firm exposures through large corporate loans, the main conclusion is that the LEI is not available for all companies; in particular, few companies in Asia have an LEI. Thus as of today it cannot be used as a global identifier, which means that the benefits of the LEI were low in this project, and resulted in the LEI not being used in other projects. In contrast, the common identifiers generated by commercial data providers (Thomson Reuters permanent ID, or Bloomberg FIGI), are useful. [1]

At the time of the BIS research project on bank-firm exposures through large corporate loans, the LEI was available only for half of the entities borrowing in markets, so in practice it was not useful. However, the coverage among EU firms was good, and in many countries as high as 100% and the BIS thinks the LEI is already useful to track developments in the EU, but the BIS focus is generally more global. Separately, BIS explored the availability of LEIs for the top 10,000 companies in market capitalisation and found similar conclusions, and the same regional imbalances in availability. BIS did not find sectoral differences.

There is also incomplete coverage among central banks that are counterparties to the BIS.

---

[1]   Serena Garralda, J. M. *Cross-country bank-firm exposures: What can we learn from public data?*

For the last IAIS data collection, an LEI was provided for around 73% of the legal entities included on the scope of the groups participating in this data collection. A third of the participating groups were able to provide the LEI for all or almost all the legal entities in their groups while 40% didn't provided any LEI. The remaining groups were in an intermediate position where LEI was only available for a subset of entities included in the consolidation scope.

For the IMF Coordinated Portfolio Investment Survey, the challenges for the use of LEI reside with reporters since there is no obligation for them to use it in the pilot. A generalised absence of LEIs could prove to be a challenge in the creation of a highly operational centralised database.

The LEI will not provide adequate coverage for OECD ADIMA. The absence of a regulatory requirement on non-financial firms per se reduces the likelihood of the LEI covering the ADIMA parent-affiliate universe as these firms register for an LEI when involved in financial transactions. Another is the related challenge of articulating relationships within the LEI between affiliates of the same Parent and between affiliates and their Parent (when the relationship has not been identified/when the Parent does not possess an LEI). Despite these coverage gaps, the LEI focus on data accessibility is highly valuable for the project.

Similarly, for FDI statistics, the OECD has a research project to examine the complex ownership structures of MNEs and to consolidate the FDI positions and present them by the ultimate investing country. Part of this project is to examine these structures and understand the purposes they serve for the companies. The relationship information could be useful for this project in the future if the coverage improves, but could not be used as of now.

ii. Insufficient mapping with other identifiers

The authors of the aforementioned BIS research paper for the IFC have accessed the LEIs through Thomson Reuters. This creates important restrictions to data sharing, publication, and distribution. BIS could not conduct their analyses with the LEIs provided by the GLEIF, since GLEIF did not include links between the LEI and other publicly available common identifiers for non-financial companies; in particular, links with Thomson Reuters permanent ID (which is open source) would have been useful. These mappings have been constructed by Thomson Reuters, but are only accessible through their system. The BIS noted that although the GLEIF has a Certification of LEI mapping service, the BIC-LEI mappings are the only available as open source.

The OECD also noted that mapping the LEI to other identifiers (e. g. Thomson Reuters Permid) to facilitate identification and linkage with other databases is important to OECD ADIMA. Therefore, this has been integrated in ADIMA.

iii. Insufficient information on group structures

Should the use of the LEI be further considered for future data collection purposes, the BCBS noted that more information on group structure (e. g. information on subsidiary entities) would be needed in order to support risk assessment of banking groups.

The OECD also observes the definitions used in FDI statistics are not completely aligned with the current Level 2 data in the GLEIS, as these are based on accounting consolidation terms only and, thus, do not include individuals and minority interests. Therefore, the integration of information on Beneficial Owners would be a useful tool for compiling FDI statistics by Ultimate Investing Country.

iv. LEI still too recent to have meaningful data series

The BCBS-CPMI-IOSCO-FSB Derivatives Assessment Team tried to use LEI data to understand the composition of the OTC derivatives market over time. [1] Unfortunately this was impossible as the relatively recent LEI adoption made a time series impossible to build (along with other challenges).

v. Other

For the BIS Banking Department, the LEI could support easier recognition of trading entities at trade entry and confirmation's reconciliation. The BIS Banking Department includes LEI information in its own risk systems and

---

[1] The Derivatives Assessment Team published in November 2018 an evaluation report on effects of reforms on *Incentives to centrally clear over-the-counter (OTC) derivatives*. See http://www. fsb. org/ 2018/11/fsb-and-standard-setting-bodies-publish-final-report-on-effects-of-reforms-on-incentives-to-centrally-clear-over-the-counter-derivatives/.

acknowledges the advantages it brings, for instance to manage the basic identification of entities. However, at present, the BIS Banking Department has an impression that the use of LEI has been very limited; for instance, LEI does not appear in SWIFT confirmations, whereas this is technically feasible.

The World Bank Treasury also uses the LEI as it is recorded for MarkitWire trades and in MarkitWire counterparty manager system.